C 1547 +

Readings: A New Biblical Commentary

General Editor
John Jarick

R E V E L A T I O N

REVELATION

Jonathan Knight

Sheffield Academic Press

Published by Sheffield Academic Press Ltd
Mansion House
19 Kingfield Road
Sheffield S11 9AS
England

Printed on acid-free paper in Great Britain
by Bookcraft Ltd
Midsomer Norton, Bath

British Library Cataloguing in Publication Data

A catalogue record for this book is available
from the British Library

ISBN   1-85075-962-6
1-85075-967-7 pbk

Contents

Preface

My interest in Revelation was stimulated as an undergraduate when I was introduced to Jewish and Christian apocalyptic literature by Dr (now Professor) Christopher Rowland. Revelation continues to fascinate me because, of all the New Testament literature, this text lends itself most especially to eisegesis and thus potentially to misinterpretation. The continual question remains of what we are to make of this strange and surprising Apocalypse with which the canon of Scripture comes to its conclusion. There is no single answer to this question, but it will be helpful to ask in brief compass what the Apocalypse meant to its original readers and why it was written. These are the questions that led me to write the present volume.

Biblical citations in this book are taken from the New Revised Standard Version (Oxford: Oxford University Press, 1989). I cite the non-canonical literature from the two-volumed series edited by J.H. Charlesworth, *The Old Testament Pseudepigrapha* (London: Darton, Longman & Todd, 1983–85).

I dedicate this book to John Sweet and Geoffrey Styler, both of whom helped me very much to understand what little I have of the complex world of the New Testament.

Abbreviations

AV	Authorized Version
GAP	Guides to the Apocrypha and Pseudepigrapha
JSPSup	*Journal for the Study of the Pseudepigrapha*, Supplement Series
JTS	*Journal of Theological Studies*
NEB	New English Bible
NICNT	New International Commentary on the New Testament
NRSV	New Revised Standard Version
NTT	New Testament Theology
SBT	Studies in Biblical Theology
WUNT	Wissenschaftliche Untersuchungen zum Neuen Testament

Introduction

The book of Revelation has inspired a variety of reactions across the centuries.[1] Originally included in the canon because of its supposed authorship by John the Apostle, it has attracted many readers but repelled many others. Revelation's vivid imagery means it has probably suffered from more of a 'caricaturing' than any other New Testament document. It is often supposed to have come from a time of intense persecution in the church. It has been treated in a quite literal way by interpreters who have claimed its eschatology as a literal prediction of the end of human history. Other interpreters have rejected it for just this reason, that its symbolism is so bizarre they have felt unable to engage with it at all. The literary genre of Revelation, that of the apocalypse, has been in no small measure responsible for this polarized reaction. The general recognition that an apocalypse addresses a crisis situation and invokes a supernatural remedy has either struck or failed to strike a sympathetic chord with later readers. For this reason it is fair to say that no New Testament document—not even those which like James were much undervalued by the Reformers—has provoked such a diverse reaction among its subsequent readership.

This book is written in the recognition that scholarship on the book of Revelation, as indeed on apocalyptic literature more generally, has progressed considerably over the last decade and that the time has come for a reading of Revelation which takes these new developments into account. It is now, for instance, questioned whether there was a persecution of the Christians by Domitian towards the end of the first century CE. A book by Thompson asks whether it is appropriate to refer the New Testament Apocalypse to a 'crisis situation' at all.[2] Bauckham has done sterling work on the text's interpretation in a collection of essays and a book on its theology.[3] Clearly, the contents and purpose of

---

1. Besides the literature mentioned in this Introduction, I draw my readers' attention to three works which I have found helpful in the preparation of this volume. These are R.H. Mounce, *The Book of Revelation* (NICNT; Grand Rapids: Eerdmans, rev. edn, 1998); C.C. Rowland, *Revelation* (London: Epworth Press, 1993); and A.J.P. Garrow, *Revelation* (London: Routledge, 1997). I am aware that both Rowland and S. Smalley are currently writing commentaries on Revelation but regrettably I have not had the opportunity to consult the work of either scholar.

2. L.L. Thompson, *The Book of Revelation: Apocalypse and Empire* (Oxford: Oxford University Press, 1990).

3. R.J. Bauckham, *The Climax of Prophecy: Studies on the Book of Revelation* (Edinburgh: T. & T. Clark, 1993); *The Theology of the Book of Revelation* (NTT; Cambridge: Cambridge University Press, 1993).

the Apocalypse will benefit from further review given this continuing research. This is what has led me to offer my own short reading of Revelation.

Those who know my work will recognize that I bring my own research interests to this project. My particular interest is in the history of early Christian doctrine. Two areas that fascinate me about the Apocalypse are its eschatology and Christology. It is often supposed that the eschatology of the book of Revelation is substantially different from that of other New Testament literature. The truth is that Revelation has major points of contact with wider Christian eschatology, not least in its hope for the Messiah's earthly reign (ch. 20) and the recreation of heaven and earth (ch. 21). These are important themes for Paul and the other New Testament writers.[4] The origins of Christology have aroused interest in recent years. One contentious question is whether Jewish angelology contributed to the development of beliefs about Jesus. Some scholars think it was merely a peripheral source, but a growing number of studies has shown that it exercised an extensive influence on Christology. The New Testament Apocalypse enshrines what I shall call an 'angelomorphic Christology'.[5] By this I mean that its Christology uses imagery derived from angelology in a way which recognizes that Jesus comes from the human world and that his position in heaven cannot be reduced to that of an angel. The angelological affinities of Revelation's Christology are particularly obvious in 1.12-16 where the author draws on a complex of traditions to depict Christ as a divine being in language that stems from the Jewish theophanic and angelophanic traditions.[6] The eschatology and Christology of the Apocalypse deserve careful

---

4. See, e.g., Paul in Rom. 8.18-25; and cf. Mt. 19.28 ('at the renewal of all things').

5. I have borrowed this term from R.N. Longenecker, *The Christology of Early Jewish Christianity* (SBT, 17; London: SCM Press, 1970), pp. 26-32. A recent study of this issue is L.T. Stuckenbruck, *Angel Veneration and Christology: A Study in Early Judaism and in the Christology of the Apocalypse of John* (WUNT, 70; Tübingen: Mohr Siebeck, 1995). See also C.H.T. Fletcher-Louis, *Luke–Acts: Angels, Christology and Soteriology* (WUNT, 94; Tübingen: Mohr Siebeck, 1997). Fletcher-Louis defines the adjective 'angelomorphic' in the following way: 'We propose the use of the term angelomorphic wherever there are signs that an individual or community possess specifically angelic characteristics or status, though for whom identity cannot be reduced to that of an angel. In this case we understand the word angel to be defined by the constellation of characteristics and motifs which commonly occur across a broad spread of Jewish texts from the second Temple and early rabbinic periods' (pp. 14-15).

6. See C.C. Rowland, 'The Vision of the Risen Christ in Rev. i,13ff.: The Debt of an Early Christology to an Aspect of Jewish Angelology', *JTS* 31 (1980), pp. 1-11. Rowland shows that the crucial feature of Rev. 1 is the way the author depicts the heavenly Christ as a divine being when other apocalypses use the same language to describe an angelophany.

examination to see the extent of their affinities to other literature. These issues will receive special attention in my reading of the text.

A word is in order about the style and format this book will adopt. I shall base my reading on the English text of the Apocalypse provided by the New Revised Standard Version (NRSV). I rarely refer to the Greek and, when I do, I do so only in transliterated form.[7] My aim is to offer a reading of the Apocalypse that tries to make sense of the text and the different sections into which it falls. It is difficult to do this without considering structural issues. These are by no means as clear cut as might at first sight appear. This observation determines my method of working in this book. I have taken the decision to read the Apocalypse in its entirety before commenting on the structure of the text and on what might be said about its meaning on the basis of a structural reading. Although I recognize that some readers may find this an unsatisfactory method, I think that Revelation is a difficult book whose contents need careful exposition. I shall therefore explain the meaning of the material, with its intertextuality and complex allusions, before considering how the material coheres within itself. This is not intended to marginalize a structuralist approach but to make things easy for my reader who may find Revelation an obscure text.

The Literary Genre of Revelation

An important preliminary question is the work's literary genre. Genre is a significant topic in New Testament studies. In the case of the Apocalypse there are crucial reasons why readers should consider this matter carefully. The fact that Revelation *looks* quite different from the other New Testament writings has often led to the assumption that its *theology* must be different too. This assumption is far from correct. The real difference between Revelation and the other New Testament texts is one of genre and not for the most part of ideas. Revelation is an 'apocalypse'. It is the *only* New Testament apocalypse. The genre 'apocalypse' features in the Hebrew Bible in the book of Daniel (second century BCE). It was well known in post-biblical Judaism. The genre has a number of distinctive features which I shall consider in a moment.

Related to this question is the question of to what extent the choice of genre determines the selection and presentation of material in Revelation. Given that most apocalypses contain warnings of cataclysm and disaster, these are exactly what we should expect to find in Revelation irrespective of its actual 'setting in life'. We do indeed find them there. One should thus beware of extrapolating from the work's selection of themes, which reflects a literary tradition, to a situation of 'acute crisis'

---

7. In places in this book, I cite the Qumran scrolls. I have used the translation of G. Vermes, *The Complete Dead Sea Scrolls in English* (London: Allen Lane, The Penguin Press, 1997).

that is judged to lie behind it. There may be no direct connection between the imagery of an apocalypse and the situation that it addresses. Interpreters must not *assume* that crisis language reflects a crisis situation in the absence of convincing evidence for that crisis.

The nature of the genre 'apocalypse' is much discussed in scholarly literature. A research project, edited by J.J. Collins in 1979, proposed the following definition. An apocalypse is 'a genre of revelatory literature with a narrative framework, in which a revelation is mediated by an otherworldly being to a human recipient, disclosing a transcendent reality which is both temporal, insofar as it envisages eschatological salvation, and spatial, insofar as it involves another, supernatural world'.[8] Collins and his team support this definition from a comprehensive review of all the Jewish, Christian, Gnostic, Classical and Persian apocalypses. It lets them construct a paradigm that notes the different modes of revelation in the extant apocalypses and the variety of subjects that features in them. This subject matter includes eschatology, especially eschatological upheaval and the question of punishment or salvation, but also other topics such as cosmogony, angelology, historical review and theodicy.

The merit of the Collins study is that it assembles all the apocalypses of late antiquity, whether or not they form individual texts, under a single banner and constructs a morphology on the basis of this evidence. The Collins team show that the following features are essential to the genre. In the first place, an apocalypse purports to be a revelation or disclosure of esoteric information. In this sense it reveals information not otherwise accessible to the human intellect. The nature of the revealed material varies across the literature, but the conviction of presenting revelation is a constant theme of the apocalypses. It is of course a different question, and a much less certain one, of how far the contents of an apocalypse actually derive from revelatory experience. Clearly, the author's own imagination and creative ability have played a major part in the compilation of many if not most texts (not least in the case of Revelation). This point must not be neglected in any reading of the apocalypses. But the *claim* to present revealed material is an essential feature of the genre once this uncertainty is acknowledged.

The revealed material is set, secondly, in the context of an encounter with a supernatural mediator. The manner of revelation again varies across the apocalypses. Some texts locate the seer on earth where he is

---

8. 'Apocalypse: Morphology of a Genre', *Semeia* 14 (1979), p. 9. Collins reviews this definition in his later article, 'Genre, Ideology and Social Movements in Jewish Apocalypticism', in J.J. Collins and J.H. Charlesworth (eds.), *Mysteries and Revelations: Apocalyptic Studies since the Uppsala Colloquium* (JSPSup, 9; Sheffield: Sheffield Academic Press, 1991), pp. 11-32. He proposes some minor modifications but without revoking the overall thesis. The revelatory element in the apocalypses is explored also by C.C. Rowland, *The Open Heaven* (London: SPCK, 1982), pp. 70-72.

greeted by an angel. Others describe an other-worldly journey in which the mediator acts as guide. Revelation interestingly does both.[9] The mediator's activity is an integral part of the claim that heavenly mysteries are disclosed in the apocalypse. His appearance reinforces the assertion that the contents are learned through revelation and not through human reason or enquiry.

Thirdly, an apocalypse gives its revelation a narrative framework. The seer reports what he hears and sees. No apocalypse outside Gnosticism contains an unbroken monologue by the heavenly mediator. The narrative often draws attention to the revealed nature of the material by describing the exceptional circumstances under which it was received. Very often it describes the seer's helpless response to the revelation—in a trance, a dream or some other mode of reception. Such perception of the supernatural has an extensive background in Hebrew prophetic literature. The book of Daniel set a precedent for later apocalypses when it describes the seer's helpless response to the communication of revelation (e.g. 8.18; 10.7-8). The notion that the seer is the passive recipient of revelation perpetuates the belief that his is no ordinary experience. The origin of this response lies deep in human psychology, as Otto has shown.[10]

Concerning the contents of an apocalypse, the Collins team note the following features. An apocalypse includes protology, theogony, primordial events, historical review, eschatological crisis, eschatological judgment and eschatological salvation (e.g. resurrection, afterlife). Their analysis places a heavy emphasis on the eschatological content of the apocalypses. They show that the 'temporal axis' extends from protology to eschatology and that the dominant interest of the authors falls on the hope for supernatural intervention through which they expect a decisive change to be secured for those judged worthy to receive it.

This explanation of the place of eschatology in the apocalypses (and in the broader apocalyptic mentality) has not gone unquestioned in research. Beside the Collins analysis must be set the work of Stone who draws attention to what he calls the 'lists of revealed things in apocalyptic literature'.[11] These lists detail the various items that catch the apocalyptist's interest. They indicate that any explanation of the apocalyptic interest in Judaism must be broader than eschatology alone. A

9. See 1.12-16; 4.1; 10.1. In the first of these references the mediator is Christ and not an angel.

10. In his book, *The Idea of the Holy: An Inquiry into the Non-Rational Factor in the Idea of the Divine and its Relation to the Rational* (ET; repr.; Oxford: Oxford University Press, 1981).

11. M.E. Stone, 'Lists of Revealed Things in the Apocalyptic Literature', in F.M. Cross, W.E. Lemke and P.D. Miller (eds.), *Magnalia Dei: The Mighty Acts of God* (Garden City, NY: Doubleday, 1976), pp. 414-52.

typical list of revealed material is found in *2 Baruch*, itself a very typical apocalypse:

> For he showed him [Moses] many warnings together with the ways of the Law and the end of time, as also to you; and then further, also the likeness of Zion with its measurements which was to be made after the likeness of the present sanctuary. But he also showed him, at that time, the measures of fire, the depths of the abyss, the weight of the winds, the number of the raindrops, the suppression of wrath, the abundance of long-suffering, the truth of judgment, the root of wisdom, the richness of understanding, the fountain of knowledge, the height of the air, the greatness of Paradise, the end of the periods, the beginning of the day of judgment, the number of offerings, the worlds which have not yet come, the mouth of hell, the standing place of vengeance, the place of faith, the region of hope, the picture of the coming punishment, the multitude of the angels which cannot be counted, the powers of the flame, the splendor of lightnings, the voice of the thunders, the orders of the archangels, the treasuries of light, the changes of the times, and the inquiries into the Law (*2 Bar.* 59.4-11).[12]

This material, from the late first century CE, shows that the apocalyptic writers' interest ranged very widely. Many of the items in this list have an eschatological reference. But with items such as 'the weight of the winds, the number of the raindrops', this is not so obvious, even when it is acknowledged that eschatology supplies the context in which they are discussed. The precise function of these lists in the apocalypses remains uncertain. They quite conceivably *legitimate the investigation of these areas* for the Jewish intellect and imagination. It is certain that we must take account of this broader material in commenting on the apocalypse genre. Non-eschatological material is in fact more obvious in the non-biblical apocalypses, for both Daniel and Revelation are heavily dominated by eschatology.

The revealed material in the apocalypses almost invariably has a soteriological purpose. It is included to help readers make necessary changes in their situation as the author's perspective is imparted to them. On the spatial axis, the apocalypse discloses a heavenly view of reality that enables readers to alter their perspective through the disclosure of what is by definition an authoritative understanding. We can see this in Revelation where the shifting imagery encourages the readers to believe that discipleship to Jesus means the rejection of all forms of accommodation with Asian urban life. Readers are called to be unambiguous about their Christian profession in the midst of a pagan culture and to consider how their religion translates into their attitude towards their social environment. To this ethical appeal are linked John's constant warnings of judgment. These predict the loss of eschatological benefits for those who fail to do what he requires. Judgment is the converse of salvation in the

---

12. Translation by A.F.J. Klijn from *The Old Testament Pseudepigrapha*, I (London: Darton, Longman & Todd, 1983), edited by J.H. Charlesworth.

apocalypses. The literature generally adopts a dualistic outlook. It offers eschatological salvation and judgment as the *only* options that will be revealed in the future.

Revelation as an Apocalypse

Revelation clearly belongs to the apocalypse genre. It has a narrative setting (ch. 1) and embodies the claim to present revealed information (see 1.10-11). Its subject matter is the secrets of the heavenly world. These permit an authoritative view of the readers' situation. Although there is no doubt that Revelation is an apocalypse, we must mention some areas where this (Christian) text is different from the Jewish apocalypses.

Chapters 2 and 3 include a series of letters sent by the heavenly Christ to seven representative churches in Asia Minor. This material shows that Revelation also embodies the form of the letter. John thirdly calls his work 'prophecy' (1.3). 'Prophecy' was a familiar entity in early Christianity, formally distinct from apocalyptic and practised by a number of figures.[13] 'John' the author of Revelation was evidently a well-known Christian prophet. A particular feature of his prophetic consciousness is his use, both deliberate and unconscious, of Hebrew Bible passages that supply the raw material for the rebirth of imagery that takes place in his text.[14] Revelation offers no mere repetition of these biblical themes, but a brilliant meditation on them by which new meanings are skilfully presented.

It is chs. 4-22 of Revelation that most obviously conform to the apocalypse genre. The link between John's self-understanding as a Christian prophet, his mediation of the letters to the churches and his writing of an apocalypse is the belief that he has been commissioned by the heavenly Christ to write in this way (1.19). It remains an open and no doubt an insoluble question of what relation existed between John's personal (and perhaps to some extent quite private) experience of revelation and the text that he dispatched from Patmos to Asia. The seer's own creativity clearly played a part in the construction of this material. The inclusion of the letters, which have no parallel in the Jewish apocalypses, arguably indicates that Revelation has a genuine revelatory basis even when this authorial creativity is acknowledged. But we would be hard pressed to comment with authority on this matter beyond noting that as a possibility.

Another difference from the Jewish apocalypses is the absence of

13. See the studies of it by D.E. Aune, *Prophecy in Early Christianity and the Ancient Mediterranean World* (Grand Rapids: Eerdmans, 1983); and D. Hill, *New Testament Prophecy* (London: Marshall, Morgan & Scott, 1979).

14. This aspect is brilliantly explored by A.M. Farrer in his *A Rebirth of Images* (Westminster: Dacre Press, 1949).

pseudonymity in the book of Revelation. Most if not all the Jewish apocalypses are pseudonymous.[15] The author of Revelation boldly departs from this convention and issues his Apocalypse under his own name (1.9). John was followed in this by the author of the *Shepherd of Hermas*, but interestingly not by the second-century author of the *Ascension of Isaiah* who retains the pseudonymous form. The lack of pseudonymity in the New Testament Apocalypse is prompted by John's conviction that he is a prophet on a par with the prophets of old (cf. 22.6), and probably also by the belief that the final events of history have been inaugurated. This gives his work an eschatological authority (cf. 1 Cor. 10.11). The lack of pseudonymity is an important (and sometimes neglected) link with the Hebrew prophetic tradition from which many scholars think that Jewish apocalyptic at least in part originated.

Bauckham notes a further difference from the Jewish apocalypses in the extent of Revelation's visual imagery.[16] Other apocalypses include dialogue between the seer and the mediator. This is strikingly absent from the New Testament Apocalypse which also lacks long passages of narrative prophecy (contrast, for instance, Dan. 11.2–12.4). Instead, readers are encouraged to reflect on the meaning of the visual symbols that are presented before them in riotous colours. The teasing of the readers' response which this symbolism represents is a significant feature of the author's rhetorical strategy. The symbols gain their force when they impact on the readers' perception of reality. John does not simply tell his readers what to think. He lets their imagination do the thinking by offering them a rich assortment of material to work on.

A fourth difference from the Jewish apocalypses is eschatology. Here, we are moving from form to content. The progress of thought in Revelation (however rough a guide this is) moves towards the Messiah's expected return from heaven and his rule on earth (chs. 19–20) under the influence of the Christian eschatological tradition. The goal of Revelation's eschatology is the recreation of heaven and earth (chs. 21–22). This understanding of eschatology contrasts with a work like *4 Ezra* where the Messiah is mentioned in one of the visions (ch. 7) but is not otherwise central to the work.[17] Although eschatology is a familiar feature of the Jewish apocalypses, the point should be repeated that the *specific content* of Revelation's eschatology has more in common with the New Testament writings which are not apocalypses than with the other Jewish apocalypses.

This issue must be probed, both in general and in particular, because

15. See the discussion of pseudonymity by D.S. Russell in *The Method and Message of Jewish Apocalyptic* (London: SCM Press, 1964), pp. 127-39.

16. *Theology*, pp. 9-10.

17. The evidence of *4 Ezra* is examined by M.E. Stone, 'The Question of the Messiah in 4 Ezra', in J. Neusner *et al.* (eds.), *Judaisms and their Messiahs* (Cambridge: Cambridge University Press, 1987), pp. 209-25.

it is sometimes suggested that there was a brand of eschatology in post-biblical Judaism which can be called an 'apocalyptic eschatology'. This view is advocated by no less an authority than Philipp Vielhauer in the Hennecke-Schneemelcher translation of the *New Testament Apocrypha*.[18] Vielhauer sees the special features of 'apocalyptic eschatology' as a contrast between the present and the new age; the belief that the new age will break in through divine intervention; and that it will concern the future of humanity rather than narrowly the destiny of Israel.

Although this definition mirrors certain themes of the apocalypses, it also draws a distinction between the eschatology of the apocalypses and that of other Jewish literature which cannot be sustained with precision from an examination of the primary sources. Rowland observes that many of these allegedly 'apocalyptic' elements are found also in rabbinic eschatology (see for instance the *Shemoneh Esreh*, Benediction 14).[19] We must certainly observe that, especially in the non-biblical apocalypses, eschatology is not always the dominant theme of the literature and that the 'apocalyptic' element of these writings consists more in the disclosure of heavenly secrets in a broad sense than narrowly in the revelation of what will happen in the future. As Rowland says, it would be unwise to 'separate out a strand of eschatological expectation which is coherent enough to be distinguished as an *apocalyptic sectarian ideology*'.[20] The eschatology of the apocalypses has parallels beyond its immediate genre. The 'apocalyptic' element of such writings lies in the *disclosure* of the eschatological future and not in the *nature* of the eschatology which is disclosed in that way.

This observation has important implications for the interpretation of Revelation. There are parallels between the eschatology of Revelation and that of Daniel in the sense that, in both apocalypses, a better future is expected through the intervention of a heavenly mediator (see Dan. 12.1-4; Rev. 19.11-16). But we must be clear that Revelation's genre as an apocalypse is certified more by the fact that it purports to present heavenly revelation (ch. 1) than by the transcendental nature of its future hope alone. To say that Revelation has an 'apocalyptic eschatology' in this sense is potentially to mask the contact which its eschatology has with the other New Testament literature, as I have observed.

To summarize this matter, Revelation is rightly classed as an apocalypse when viewed against the Collins morphology of the genre. One must, however, see Revelation's eschatology in proper perspective.

18. *New Testament Apocrypha* (ET; 2 vols.; London: SCM Press, 1963-64), II, pp. 608-42.
19. *Open Heaven*, pp. 29-37. Benediction 14 reads: 'And to Jerusalem, thy city, return in mercy, and dwell therein as thou hast spoken; rebuild it soon in our days as an everlasting building, and speedily set up therein the throne of David. Blessed art thou, O Lord, who rebuildest Jerusalem.'
20. *Open Heaven*, pp. 36-37 (italics added).

Interpreters must also note some key differences from the Jewish apocalypses. These include John's conviction of being a Christian prophet; his inclusion of the letters to the seven churches; the content of his eschatology; and the extent of his visual symbolism.

The Date of Revelation

There has been a debate in scholarship as to whether Revelation should be dated in the reign of Domitian, in the last decade of the first century CE, or whether it was written rather earlier than this just after the reign of Nero (69 CE). This problem can best be approached by working, so to speak, backwards through the available evidence.

The earliest documented use of Revelation comes from the reign of Hadrian, probably between 125 and 135 CE, with Papias of Hierapolis. Andreas of Caesarea, who wrote in the sixth century, says that Papias knew the Apocalypse.[21] In the first third of the second century, the author of the *Ascension of Isaiah* produced his own apocalypse which holds a number of themes in common with Revelation. This raises the question of whether knowledge of Revelation may have helped to shape that author's form of material.[22] We cannot answer this question with certainty, but Papias's use of Revelation makes a knowledge of the Apocalypse by the author of the *Ascension of Isaiah* a possibility. Both Justin Martyr (c. 150 CE) and Irenaeus (c. 185 CE) knew Revelation too.

This evidence shows that Revelation was in Christian use within a century of the resurrection of Jesus. The evidence of Papias places its origin almost certainly in the first century CE. A first-century origin is supported also by Irenaeus who says that the Apocalypse was seen at the end of the reign of Domitian (*ob.* 96 CE; *Adv. Haer.* 5.30.3). Eusebius adds to this the report that John was banished to Patmos by Domitian (*Hist. Eccl.* 3.18.1). This collective information has been responsible for the dominant theory that Revelation was written in the last decade of the first century, in the years preceding the death of Domitian.

This 'consensus theory' has been challenged by scholars who argue on internal grounds that Revelation was written in the 60s and not the 90s of the first century. This view is argued forcefully by Robinson. Robinson bases his case on Rev. 17.9-11 which says that, of the seven horns (i.e. emperors), five have fallen, one is reigning and the last has

21. See A.Y. Collins, *Crisis and Catharsis: The Power of the Apocalypse* (Philadelphia: Westminster Press, 1984), p. 25. There is an important discussion of Papias also in M. Hengel, *The Johannine Question* (London: SCM Press, 1989), pp. 16-23.

22. On the *Ascension of Isaiah* see J.M. Knight, *The Ascension of Isaiah* (GAP, 2; Sheffield: Sheffield Academic Press, 1995); and the same author's *Disciples of the Beloved One: Studies in the Christology, Social Setting and Theological Context of the Ascension of Isaiah* (JSPSup, 18; Sheffield: Sheffield Academic Press, 1996).

yet to come.[23] Robinson thinks that the first emperor is Augustus. He includes the so-called 'soldier emperors' (Galba, Otho and Vitellius) in the list. This leads him to suggest that the Apocalypse was written in the reign of Galba (68–69 CE) and before the accession of Otho (69 CE). Against this interpretation, however, it must be objected that the number seven has a symbolic significance in the Apocalypse and that it is far from certain John offers a historically precise review in 17.9-11. That information can be read in more than one way. 17.9-11 yields a date in the reign of Domitian if the list begins with Caligula, on the grounds that he was the emperor who first offended Jewish scruples; and the reigns of Galba, Otho and Vitellius are omitted as too short to be considered significant. The list would then consist of Caligula, Claudius, Nero, Vespasian and Titus. Domitian would be the reigning emperor. On this hypothesis, the author wrote before the accession of Nerva (96 CE), so that 17.9-11 can also be made to support the consensus theory.

The question is whether the internal evidence of the Apocalypse, which is quite ambiguous, should be allowed to outweigh the externally attested date for Revelation at the end of the first century CE. Despite the frequent references to martyrdom in the Apocalypse, there is little concrete evidence that this was a feature of the author's recent experience (see below on 2.13). We would expect more to be made of the Neronian Persecution (64 CE) had the Apocalypse been written in close proximity to that event. Nor might John so readily have disclosed his own identity then. Moreover, the material which addresses social attitudes in the readers' communities finds a natural setting at the end of the first century, as I shall argue in this book. Given the uncertainty surrounding 17.9-11, it does not seem appropriate to set aside the external evidence, even when the question of Irenaeus's critical awareness is treated with some caution. The view adopted here is that Revelation was written in the last decade of the first century CE at some point before the murder of Domitian in 96 CE.

The Author

The Apocalypse entered the New Testament canon through its presumed connection with the Johannine writings. The text says that its author was 'John' (1.9). John was a common name in early Christian circles. Justin Martyr says that the author of Revelation was 'John, one of the apostles of Christ' (*Dial.* 81.4). Papias makes much of John the Elder who was a venerable Christian leader in Ephesus (see Eusebius, *Hist. Eccl.* 3.39.4). In the third century the belief in common authorship with the Fourth Gospel began to be rejected, not least because of the support

---

23. J.A.T. Robinson, *Redating the New Testament* (London: SPCK, 1976), pp. 221-53.

that Revelation offers for millenarianism which was coming to be judged unsound at that time. Dionysius of Alexandria, who is reported by Eusebius in his *Hist. Eccl.* 7.25, is an early representative of the argument that John the Evangelist was not the author of the Apocalypse. The majority of recent scholars agree with this assessment even though it is often conceded that the author of the Apocalypse may have had a loose connection of some kind with the Johannine 'school' in Ephesus.

The reasons for denying common authorship of the Gospel and Apocalypse are compelling. They rest on matters of style and content. The language of the two texts is quite different, as is their conceptual world, not least the expression of eschatology in the two writings. Although there are certain similarities between them, these are never so great as to *demand* a theory of common authorship. The differences militate against it. It is not difficult to see that the identification of common authorship brought a real benefit in the second century. It enabled mainstream Christians to claim apostolic authority for Revelation's eschatology, including its millenarianism (20.4), which was used against the Gnostic denial of belief in the bodily resurrection. Modern criticism has identified too many differences between the Apocalypse and the Gospel for this identification of common authorship to be retained convincingly.[24] We must look elsewhere than John the Evangelist to find the author of the Apocalypse.

Some scholars think the Apocalypse is pseudonymous and that an unknown Christian prophet attributed his work to John the Apostle.[25] This theory, too, is unconvincing. The fact that the Apocalypse does not establish its author's identity as *this* John strongly suggests that the author did not make that connection. The situation is quite different, say, from the Pastorals and 2 Peter which all make great efforts to present their authors as front-rank apostles. The theory of pseudonymous authorship in fact detracts from the prophetic impact of the Apocalypse. The work gains its force from the assertion that a contemporary prophet has been commissioned by Christ to write to the churches in this way. To assign that prophecy to a figure from the past (even from the recent past) is tantamount to the denial that prophecy was a living force at the time of writing. This ignores the spirit of the Apocalypse which gives every sign of having been written in a living prophetic tradition. We should not suppress this conviction by positing pseudonymous authorship.

The author's identity thus remains obscure but we can surmise that he was a well-known prophet on the Asian Christian scene who had

---

24. The case is summarized by W.G. Kümmel in his *Introduction to the New Testament* (ET; London: SCM Press, rev. edn, 1973), pp. 330-31.
25. See Collins, *Crisis*, p. 27, for an explanation of this view.

gone to Patmos for a purpose which also remains obscure.[26] Eusebius reports that John had been 'condemned' (i.e. banished) to Patmos 'because of his testimony to the word of God' (*Hist. Eccl.* 3.18.1). It is surprising how many scholars have been willing to treat this as a historically reliable statement. Eusebius reports a number of other events, such as the story of the grandsons of Jude being hauled before Domitian,[27] which makes one wonder whether he really had the ability to distinguish between history and legend in the discussion of first-century Christianity. The Apocalypse itself gives no indication that John was on Patmos as the result of banishment. We would expect the text to make it clear had a formal exclusion order been issued against its author. Nor indeed was Patmos the dark and depressing place it is sometimes made out to be. There are no records that it was used as a prison settlement. The seer possibly went there as a form of retreat. Such seclusion may have resulted in the oracles presented in the Apocalypse. Alternatively, if John was a wandering prophet, as his awareness of responsibility for a number of churches suggests, he may have gone to Patmos in the normal exercise of his ministry. The reason for John's presence on Patmos should be held an open question and Eusebius's report treated with caution in the absence of corroborating evidence for the theory that John had been banished to the island.

The Question of a Domitianic Persecution

It is also commonly thought that Revelation was written during a Roman persecution of the Christians in the later years of Domitian's reign. But, again, scholars have assumed much too uncritically that there was such a persecution on the basis of the evidence of Eusebius.[28] Eusebius states that many people fell victim to Domitian's appalling cruelty and were executed, banished and fined in the later part of his reign (*Hist. Eccl.* 3.17-20). This may be true, but the internal evidence of Revelation hardly supports the view that the Apocalypse was addressed to a situation dominated by martyrdom. The only martyr mentioned by name is the Antipas of Rev. 2.13, and it is far from certain how this person died. The other references to martyrdom in Revelation are essentially symbolic and they must be judged in the wider context of the imagery

26. The author's status as a Christian prophet is explored by Collins in her *Crisis*, pp. 37-46. Another valuable study is E. Schüssler Fiorenza's *The Book of Revelation: Justice and Judgment* (Philadelphia: Fortress Press, 1985), pp. 133-56. Collins however criticizes Schüssler Fiorenza's suggestion that Revelation presupposes a *circle* of prophets active with John.

27. The story derives from Hegesippus and is reported by Eusebius in his *Hist. Eccl.* 3.19.1-20.7. On this report see R.J. Bauckham, *Jude and the Relatives of Jesus in the Early Church* (Edinburgh: T. & T. Clark, 1990), pp. 94-106.

28. This cautionary remark is made by Thompson in his *Book of Revelation*, pp. 15-17.

that the Apocalypse constructs. The threat of widespread martyrdom is significantly unconfirmed by the letters to the seven churches which, if anything, indicate that the Apocalypse was addressed to a situation dominated by complacency and not by conflict.

The most recent research—the book by Thompson—draws a very different conclusion about the behaviour of Domitian. Thompson begins by asking why so many ancient sources adopt a pessimistic attitude towards Domitian.[29] Suetonius says for instance that from an early age Domitian 'exercised all the tyranny of his high position so lawlessly, that it was even then apparent what sort of a man he was going to be' (*Dom.* 1.3). Tacitus mentions his unbridled passions (*Hist.* 4.68); Pliny describes the imperial household as the place where 'that fearful monster built his defences with untold terrors, where lurking in his den he licked up the blood of his murdered relatives or emerged to plot the massacre and destruction of his most distinguished subjects' (*Pan.* 48.3). Thompson argues that this harsh portrait of Domitian comes from writers concerned to eulogize the reign of Trajan. He draws attention to their promulgation of Trajan's reign as a 'new era' that had adopted a change in tone from its predecessor.[30] These writers praise Trajan as a new-style libertarian. Pliny's *Panegyricus* is typical of this approach when it declaims that 'the sufferings of the past are over: let us then have done with the words which belong to them' (2.12). Thompson concludes that 'the opposing of Trajan and Domitian in binary set serves overtly in Trajan's ideology of a new age as well as covertly in his praise. Newness requires a beginning and therefore a break with the past; such a break is contrasted rhetorically through binary contrast.'[31] The bad press that Domitian receives in later literature was due, so it seems, as much to the demands of a new age as to his own undoubted weaknesses and foibles.

Evidence from Domitian's own time shows that his reign was not unsuccessful. Domitian is reported as having taken the lead in the Senate before his full accession in recommending that the wrongs of the past be forgotten. He acted in support of the army (see Tacitus, *Hist.* 4.44-46). He was zealous in propagating the cult of Titus and completed the temple that had been begun for Vespasian.[32] The well-known story of incest between Domitian and Julia which was often used against him was perhaps a legendary distortion of what Scott calls the 'normal affection between uncle and niece'.[33] This evidence, although somewhat patchy, does not support the picture of Domitian as a reckless tyrant that emerges in sources from the reign of Trajan. It must be set alongside

29. *Book of Revelation*, pp. 95-115.
30. *Book of Revelation*, pp. 111-15.
31. *Book of Revelation*, p. 115.
32. See K. Scott, *The Imperial Cult under the Flavians* (New York: Arno Press, repr., 1975), pp. 62-63.
33. *Imperial Cult*, p. 76.

that other evidence to yield a more balanced portrait of Domitian.

It is also often said that Domitian demanded to be called *dominus et deus noster* ('our Lord and God') during his lifetime and that this demand is reflected in Revelation (e.g. 13.5-6). This belief is on the face of it confirmed by the ancient sources. Suetonius says that Domitian sent out letters under this title and that 'the custom arose of addressing him in no other way even in writing or in conversation' (*Dom.* 13.2). Pliny complains about the number of statues that the emperor had erected in his honour (*Pan.* 52.3; cf. Dio Cassius 67.8.1). Scott is typical of many scholars when he concludes that 'what Domitian did was to permit and encourage to an excessive degree homage which had been shown— generally with more restraint—to his predecessors'.[34]

Yet this issue is not so clear cut as Scott's verdict suggests. Thompson observes that, if Domitian had demanded this title of *himself*, we should expect to find this mentioned in writings which come from his own time; specifically, in the writings of Statius and Quintillian.[35] The title, however, never features there. These authors use *Caesar, dux* and *parens* of Domitian, but never *dominus* or *deus*. The imperial coinage of the period lacks the relevant titles.[36] Statius even says that, when Domitian was acclaimed *dominus* at one of his Saturnalia, he forbade the use of that title (*Silv.* 1.6.81-84). This evidence by no means encourages the conclusion that Domitian thought about himself as *dominus et deus*, despite what is said in the later sources.

This means that another explanation is needed for the frequent use of *dominus* as an epithet for Domitian in Martial. Where Scott argues that Domitian's megalomania developed as his reign progressed, Thompson examines the power structures of the imperial court to explain this accolade.[37] Martial wanted to gain entrance into the emperor's circle. Thompson thinks that he adopted this mode of address to curry favour with Domitian. Martial significantly uses such language of Trajan too (*Epi.* 10.72). That Martial never gained his social promotion suggests his ambitions were recognized for the flattery they were.

This brings us back to the question of whether Domitian persecuted the Christians towards the end of his reign. The evidence that he persecuted *Christians* at this time is scanty indeed. Revelation 2.13 mentions only one martyr known to the author of the Apocalypse. The theory of a Domitianic persecution comes from Eusebius who wrote many decades later. There is some evidence that *Jews* suffered repressive measures at this time. Dio Cassius says that Domitian killed Flavius Clemens and

---

34. *Imperial Cult*, p. 89.
35. *Book of Revelation*, p. 105.
36. See the unpublished work of Viscusi which is mentioned by Thompson in his *Book of Revelation*, p. 105.
37. *Book of Revelation*, p. 106.

others and banished his wife, Flavia Domitilla, to Pandateria on the charge of atheism (67.14.2). But there is nothing to indicate that these Jews were Christians. The charge of atheism probably stems from the refusal of these people to acknowledge the Roman pantheon. It is not necessary to assume christological resilience to explain the report of Dio Cassius.

The total silence about a Domitianic persecution in Christian sources before Eusebius is a significant thing. Irenaeus says nothing about it, although he says that the Apocalypse was composed at the end of Domitian's reign (*Adv. Haer.* 5.30.3). The evidence of the *Ascension of Isaiah* is important as well. This apocalypse was written in Syria some 20 or 30 years after Revelation and after Pliny had put numbers of Christians to death in Bithynia.[38] In this context the author of the *Ascension* specifically mentions the Neronian Persecution (4.3). It is hard to believe this person would have failed to mention a (much more recent) Domitianic persecution had this in fact occurred. The silence of the *Ascension of Isaiah* is important evidence that there was no formal persecution of Christians at the end of the first century. This makes it unlikely that Revelation was written to deal with the outbreak of persecution under Domitian. We must look elsewhere to discover why the Apocalypse was written.

The Social Setting of the Apocalypse

Account must here be taken of Thompson's sketch of Asian society in the late first century CE, and of the place of the Christians within it.[39] Asia during the reign of Domitian was quite a prosperous place to live.[40] The Jews of Asia were perhaps the most socially and culturally integrated of those outside Palestine (although in general they remained faithful to their religious traditions). The Asian Christians (as throughout the empire) came from different economic backgrounds. Their leaders were relatively prosperous people with sufficient resources to let them travel, own large houses and act as patrons of the Christian congregations. These wealthier Christians took their full part in civic life. We know from the sources (especially Pliny, *Ep.* 10.96-97) that imperial officials did not go on the offensive to persecute Christians. Such trials as there were (at least by the second century) came from individual initiatives in which information was laid by private citizens. 'Atheism', by which was meant the refusal to honour the state pantheon, was the principal cause of offence in such investigations. This stemmed from the belief that the corporate well-being was threatened by the alienation of

38. See Knight, *Ascension of Isaiah*, pp. 21-23, 38-43.
39. *Book of Revelation*, pp. 116-32.
40. *Book of Revelation*, pp. 133-45.

the gods who felt themselves spurned by the refusal of worship from stubborn members of the population.

The issue of how the church should relate to the world is crucial for Revelation. This had been a matter for Christian reflection from at least the Pauline letters onwards. John's perspective in the Apocalypse is more critical of Christians who are open to cultural assimilation than is either Paul or the author of Acts.[41] John complains that more than one church was tempted to eat food sacrificed to idols and to practise fornication (2.14, 20). I shall argue in this book that the primary meaning of 'fornication' in this context is metaphorical: John inveighs against Christians who had assimilated the pagan ethos and not specifically against sexual misbehaviour in the narrow sense. Thompson cites Theissen's research in explication of these references.[42] Theissen shows that people in late antiquity had the opportunity to eat meat in a cultic setting at both public (festivals and funerals) and private occasions (guild meetings and banquets). These occasions were representative of social connections and they indicated the status that an individual enjoyed in society. They almost invariably had religious connotations in the customary invocations that were offered to the gods. Theissen argues that this issue would have affected Christians of different status in different ways. Wealthier Christians with civic responsibility would have eaten meat sacrificed to idols more often than poorer Christians who had no such respectable connections. Wealthier Christians might even have found it necessary to host these occasions themselves. They would certainly have found it difficult to abstain from meat-eating if they wanted to retain their civic position.

The question of whether it was permissible to eat meat sacrificed to idols had divided the Corinthian church 40 years earlier. Paul argued then that the practice was legitimate provided that the 'weaker brother' was not offended by it (1 Cor. 8.1-13). The implication of his statement is that only in cases where *different strata* of the church met together were Christians to abstain from this practice, as if less well-placed Christians (who met this problem much less often) were more likely to be offended by it.

Thompson's reading of the Apocalypse concludes that John was a rigorist who objected to Christians accommodating to this and other social demands of urban life in the late first century.[43] There is a variety

41. Cf. Thompson, *Book of Revelation*, p. 174: 'Christian leaders who espouse participation in the life of the empire as harmless and as irrelevant to Christian existence are made homologous to evil, mythic forces such as Babylon, the Great Whore. The peace and prosperity of Roman society is, from his point of view, not to be entered into by faithful Christians.'
42. *Book of Revelation*, p. 122; citing G. Theissen, *The Social Setting of Pauline Christianity: Essays on Corinth* (ET; Edinburgh: T. & T. Clark, 1982), pp. 132-36.
43. *Book of Revelation*, pp. 123, 174.

of evidence in the Apocalypse to support this interpretation. John tells the churches at Pergamum and Thyatira to rid themselves of false teaching advocated by leaders who permitted the eating of meat sacrificed to idols (2.14-15, 20). Thompson compares these 'opponents' to the liberal wing of the Corinthian church and contrasts John's attitude with the partial support that Paul had offered for such behaviour. Thompson thinks these 'opponents' of John belonged to the wealthier stratum of the church who had greater social opportunities. 'In contrast to most Christians in Asia', he writes, John 'views urban society and the empire as antithetical to Christian existence and in league with Satan.'[44] This is why Christians who advocate compromise with pagan culture are polemicized in the Apocalypse and why Jews who succeed socially are called the 'synagogue of Satan' (2.9).

John's criticism extends to the economic besides the social order.[45] Buying and selling require the mark of the beast (13.16-17). This explains the extended description of the goods that can no longer be sold when Babylon falls (18.11-13). This catastrophe causes the merchants (18.15) and the shipmasters and seafarers (18.17) to regret the city's demise. The description of the fall of Babylon is a symbolic rejection of Rome's attraction for those who benefited from supplying her with goods. That probably included some of John's Asian readers, so that the criticism has a cutting edge for those who perceive its meaning.

Only the letters to Sardis and Laodicea fail to mention specific adversaries. Both are set in ironic terms: the Christians at Sardis are called 'dead' (3.1) and the Laodiceans 'poor', among other things (3.17). Sardis and Laodicea were important centres of Judaism, yet Thompson notes John does not mention opposition from Judaism there.[46] Jewish opposition is, however, mentioned in Smyrna and Philadelphia where the Jewish presence was much less concentrated. From this information, Thompson infers a link between his readers' assimilation to their urban environment and the absence of conflict with Judaism, and the opposite situation where Jews persecuted Christians who maintained high social boundaries. The references to conflict in the letters depend on whether or not the churches were following John's teaching to keep themselves 'separate' from wider society in a way that Paul had not required of his readers.

Thompson argues this is why the Apocalypse was written. John *encourages* his readers to see themselves in conflict with society as part of his distinctive vision of the world that he communicates to the churches. The Apocalypse *creates* the notion of conflict through its choice of genre, where conflict and world-negation are prominent

---

44. *Book of Revelation*, p. 174.
45. *Book of Revelation*, p. 175.
46. *Book of Revelation*, pp. 124-25.

themes, and also through the language and imagery as the different visions unfold. Thompson thereby turns on its head the long-established view that the Apocalypse is 'crisis literature'. There is indeed a crisis in Revelation—but the crisis lies in the author's rhetoric and not in the nature of the situation addressed. The author wants his readers to *perceive* a crisis, and thus to take a responsible course of action, when in fact the lives of at least the wealthier members of the churches may have been strikingly free of apprehension. By reworking apocalyptic traditions, John calls his churches to action and threatens the security of their existence. He does this from the conviction that they had become too comfortable in their world and needed decisive action to return to their calling as a priestly people.

Thompson's research shows that any reading of the Apocalypse must carefully consider the letters to the churches. The letters set the matrix in which the text must be read. They introduce the situations (no doubt typical rather than exhaustive) from which the symbolism gains its meaning. The letters also introduce us to the seer's special language (e.g. 'conquering', 'crown of life'). This language recommends the separatist pattern of behaviour by portraying the non-Christian social world in demonic terms through the use of binary contrasts. Thompson compares this literary strategy with Berger's category of 'deviant knowledge' (knowledge that signifies a different perspective from the prevailing norm).[47] The ancient world knew a variety of 'deviants'. They included magicians and diviners who were believed to disturb the public mind through private teaching. Thompson argues that it is helpful to portray the seer of Revelation in a similar light.[48] John introduces subversive themes in his Apocalypse, like the Nero mythology (ch. 13) and the secret names (e.g. 2.17; 3.12). These emphasize the need for Christians to maintain a distance from the dominant world. Here, the status of 'apocalyptic' as 'revealed knowledge' comes into full play. John's 'revealed knowledge' opposes itself to the 'public knowledge' of the Asian social world. It offers an alternative order accentuated by the apocalyptic claim that it is based on a *higher* form of wisdom derived from revelation.

A not-insignificant feature of this subversion is John's peculiar Greek. This draws attention to the fact that the normative canons of discourse, and by extension the nature of reality, are being challenged. This would have had a considerable rhetorical effect since the Apocalypse was first *declaimed* to the churches (1.3). Better-educated Christians, who had much to gain from social accommodation, would have been struck by the barbarous Greek and prompted to reflect on why it is used. This might lead them to reflect on the imagery and to consider the difference

---

47. P. Berger, *A Rumor of Angels* (Garden City, NY: Anchor Press, 1970), p. 6.
48. *Book of Revelation*, pp. 186-97.

between the seer's constructed world-view and the world-view to which they had grown accustomed. The effect of John's language and imagery is to foreground the need for different behaviour in the Apocalypse. This challenge doubtless proved uncomfortable for those who had gained much from the way things were.

The effect of Thompson's research is to divert scholarly attention from its preoccupation with the theme of Christian conflict with Rome towards internal issues in the Christian congregations: specifically, towards the possibility that John was engaged in a cognitive struggle with his churches and advocated a different outlook from the one that many people accepted. We know that John's was not the only voice heard on this issue in the Asian Christian communities. In 2.20, he tells the Thyatiran Christians: 'You tolerate that woman Jezebel, who calls herself a prophet and is teaching my servants to practise fornication and to eat food sacrificed to idols.' 'Jezebel', so it seems, is John's unflattering title for an otherwise unknown prophetess who was teaching people more or less what Paul had taught the Corinthians about the eating of meat. Revelation must be seen within the context of a debate about this issue in which John's position may have been the minority one. John uses forceful imagery to undergird his exhortation. His polarized images offer an 'explanation' to the minority of why the majority behave as they do. This is because, so he claims, they have been misled by Satan (2.9) and are not true followers of Christ. The logic of John's argument is that only those who do what the Apocalypse commands are obeying the revealed commands of Christ. Apocalyptic wisdom is thus used internally in the Christian congregations to combat what other Christian prophets are saying.

The Nature of This Book

At the start of this book I want to acknowledge what I have learned from Thompson's approach and explain the theory on which this reading of the Apocalypse will rest. I have been convinced by the paucity of evidence for a Domitianic persecution that this putative event does not explain the writing of the Apocalypse. I shall therefore explore an approach in which the 'persecution theory' is set aside and the 'crisis theory' in consequence reshaped. I shall read Revelation on the assumption that John is *telling* his readers about a crisis and try to explain how this theory explains the sequence of visions assembled in the text.

My reading yields the conclusion that the primary purpose of the text is to 'raise awareness of difficulty' in a culture where the Asian churches were divided over their attitude towards the existing order. I have briefly introduced this approach and shall develop it in the course of the book. I want to note that it is an important observation for the study of early Christianity. Revelation shows the variety of responses adopted by

Christians at a time when the return of Jesus was proving more sub-stantially delayed than had at first been envisaged. Many Christians evidently followed Paul's lead towards social integration. John deemed this impermissible, perhaps because he was worried about what this might mean for the survival of his churches and their distinctive witness in the world. He told the churches not to adopt pagan practices. In the form found in the Apocalypse, this is tantamount to the call to be a sectarian countercommunity in the midst of an unbelieving world.[49]

It is difficult to say how far John's recommended sense of distance from the world was sustained as time wore on, but clearly this could not have gone on for ever in unmodified form. The Apocalypse advocates a position whose logical conclusion is absolute sectarianism.[50] This is a position that Paul at least rejects. Unfortunately, we have no way of telling what happened in John's churches beyond observing that Ignatius is aware of continuing problems at Ephesus and Smyrna some 15 years later.[51] Christianity certainly survived in these cities, but one wonders how far this was through the impact of the Apocalypse.[52] This radical text requires careful handling in any discussion of the place of the church in the world that might be undertaken today.

49. Such a position is well explained by P. Berger, *The Sacred Canopy* (Garden City, NY: Anchor Press, 1969), p. 164: 'The sect, in its classical sociology-of-religion conception, serves as the model for organizing a cognitive minority *against* a hostile or at least non-believing milieu.'

50. In the history of post-biblical Judaism, the most extreme model of 'absolute sectarianism' is that of the Qumran community who retreated to the Dead Sea in protest at what they took to be the religious and ethical laxity of the rest of contemporary Judaism.

51. E.g. Ignatius, *Eph.* 5.2, 'Let no one deceive himself: if anyone is not within the altar, he lacks the bread of God'; *Eph.* 9.1, 'I know that some have passed by on their way from there with evil teaching, whom you did not allow to sow among you'; *Smyrn.* 8.2, 'It is not permissible apart from the bishop either to baptize or to cele-brate the love-feast; but whatever he approves is also pleasing to God, that everything you do may be sure and valid' (Schoedel's translation). Although the situation Ignatius addresses should not be confused with that of the Apocalypse, the Ignatian letters do show that division continued to characterize the Christian communities in these cities.

52. Cf. the following provocative comment from W. Bauer, *Orthodoxy and Heresy in Earliest Christianity* (ET; London: SCM Press, 1972), pp. 77-78: 'There is also room for doubt as to whether the apocalypticist, with his extremely confused religious outlook that peculiarly mixes Jewish, Christian, and mythological elements and ends in chiliasm, can be regarded in any sense as an intellectual and spiritual leader of an important band of Christians in western Asia Minor.'

Revelation 1

Chapter 1 introduces the Apocalypse as the record of the revelation that God gave to Jesus and that was revealed to John by an angel. The chapter is a patchwork of traditions that include a number of set formulae (1.4-8), the report of a vision of the heavenly Christ (1.9-16) and the words of Christ himself (1.17-20). It has been composed from more than one source but the present arrangement of material is far from accidental. The function of ch. 1 is to authenticate everything that is said in the rest of the Apocalypse by specifying the revealed nature of the material. This claim for the divine origin of the revealed knowledge emphasizes its superiority to the public and social knowledge which John's readers possessed as urban Asians in the late first century. It encourages them to pay careful attention to what follows on the grounds that the revelation has been disclosed by Christ himself.

There is some ambiguity about how the revelation was received. John refers initially to an angel (1.1) but in the later part of the chapter he describes a vision of the heavenly Christ who commissions him to write to the churches (1.9-20). Not too much should be read into this inconsistency. The Apocalypse contains a cycle of material. John does not say that the whole text was dictated by Christ. However, 1.9-11 does indicate that one exceptional experience of revelation stands behind the work. There are no grounds for identifying the angel of 1.1 with the 'one like the Son of Man' of 1.13. The angel is merely the messenger of Christ. As I said in the Introduction, we must constantly remember the creative exchange that takes place between the seer's experience of revelation, which came to him from without, and his own meditation on that experience where his mind was fully engaged. The most important feature of this chapter is the statement that the revelation come directly from Christ himself. In John's view, this gives his text divine authority.

The opening section (1.1-3) introduces the text as an 'apocalypse' (lit. 'the revelation of Jesus Christ'). 'Apocalypse' is a term which we have seen that modern scholarship uses to denote a literary genre. It is not clear that John was conscious of writing *an apocalypse* with the literary self-consciousness that assails the modern mind, but he does write in a particular way that has parallels (with the differences noted) with other Jewish and Christian literature. The 'apocalyptic' aspect of Revelation lies in its disclosure of an authoritative perspective on human reality through which the seer tells his readers to consider their behaviour. This insistence on divine revelation authenticates the truth of the message. That is what John means by calling his work 'the revelation of Jesus Christ'.

In the logic of the chain of mediation, the description of John as a 'servant' (lit. 'slave', 1.1) means he is a servant of Jesus Christ. This term mirrors the style of other New Testament writers including Paul (e.g. Phil. 1.1) and the pseudonymous author of 2 Pet. 1.1. Its origins lie in Hebrew prophecy where several prophets call themselves 'servants' of Yahweh (quite apart from the figure of that name who appears in Second Isaiah). Although the term projects a humble form, considerable prestige must have attended the claim to be a 'servant' of Jesus where the speaker is a well-known prophet and heavenly mysteries are disclosed. One might be inclined to see here a thinly veiled claim to authority that goes beyond the self-understanding of the wider Christian body as 'servants' of Jesus (for which see, e.g., Eph. 6.6). 'Prophets' enjoyed a status second only to the apostles in the primitive church (see 1 Cor. 12.28). John appeals to this view and deliberately imitates the style of the Hebrew prophets.

The phrase 'the revelation of Jesus Christ' (1.1) can be taken in two different ways. It can mean either 'the revelation granted by Jesus' ('subjective genitive') or the 'revelation that concerns Jesus' ('objective genitive'). The former sense is preferable because of John's reference to the chain of mediation and because the mysteries disclosed in the Apocalypse are not exclusively christological ones. The second sense should not be completely excluded, however, because the Apocalypse has much to say about the wrath of the Lamb and the kingdom of Christ as the different visions unfold. The ambiguity of the Greek is happily preserved in the NRSV translation.

What is meant by this concept of 'revelation' is explained as the Apocalypse unfolds. In 1.2, John is said to 'testify' to the word of God and the 'testimony' of Jesus Christ. This phrase is a hendiadys (it expresses the same thought in two different ways). 'The word of God' recalls the prophetic expression 'the word of the Lord' (e.g. Isa. 1.10). The 'testimony of Jesus' can again be taken in two different ways as subjective or objective genitive. The ambiguity is deliberate. It makes Jesus both the agent and the content of the revelation.

The Greek phrase 'testified' (1.2) is related to the English term 'martyr'. The 'martyr' complex of words is used in the New Testament in two distinct ways. Its primary meaning is 'witness' in a legal sense. This is found in many references in John's Gospel (e.g. Jn 1.7) and in other writings too (e.g. Acts 22.15). At the heart of the word lies the question of truth. The ultimate testimony to the truth is given by the second sense of 'martyr'. This denotes the willingness to die for what one believes to be true. Several New Testament passages use the word in this more technical sense. Among these we must mention Acts 22.20 ('your witness Stephen'), Rev. 2.13 ('Antipas my witness') and also

Rev. 1.5 ('Jesus Christ, the faithful witness'). This double sense of 'martyr' is an important feature of Revelation. The prominence of the 'martyr' theme in the Apocalypse is perhaps to be explained by the observation that the author has a connection with the Johannine school for whom the concept of 'witness' is an important one. It is not obvious that martyrdom was a recent and significant feature of the readers' experience. There is little concrete evidence for such martyrdom in the Apocalypse (and no external corroboration). The frequent references to martyrdom have a mainly symbolic significance. They highlight the sense of absolute commitment that John requires of his churches.

1.3 pronounces a blessing on those who 'read aloud' the Apocalypse and calls the work 'prophecy'. In the author's symbolic style there are seven such blessings in all (see 14.13; 16.15; 19.9; 20.6; 22.7; 22.14). This verse explains how the Apocalypse was originally delivered to its recipients. This was through oral declamation, doubtless in the context of a meeting for worship. The author invokes his blessing on his readers to compensate for the fact that he cannot bless them in person. His blessing contains a thinly veiled ethical exhortation (cf. Dan. 12.12-13). As in the tradition of the sayings of Jesus, the notion of 'hearing the word' means not just hearing but action too. The action John envisages is described in the letters to the churches. It involves maintaining high social boundaries by Christians in their urban environment. It is implied, but not said explicitly, that those Christians who fail to hear (i.e. to act on) what is said will be liable to judgment. This is suggested also by the uncompromising dualism that runs throughout the Apocalypse, which supplies the rhetorical basis for the visions and exhortations presented there.

The concluding phrase of 1.3 gives an urgency to this appeal by reiterating the thought of 1.1 that 'the time is near'. Early Christian eschatology was founded on the hope for the return of Jesus from heaven but it was not known when this would happen. No first-century text abandons the hope for his return, so far as we can tell, but there is evidence that some Christians were beginning to find this kind of eschatology difficult to sustain towards the end of the first century. *1 Clement* 23, *2 Clement* 11 and 2 Pet. 3.4 all show some Roman Christians wavering in their belief, but the texts significantly indicate that the church leaders rebuked them for their doubts. There was no doubt a spectrum of opinion about the reliability of the hope for the return of Jesus when Revelation was written. This uncertainty explains the different views about social accommodation that are revealed in the Apocalypse. Looking back on the Apocalypse from our vantage point at the beginning of the twenty-first century, we can say that the dissolution of its imminent eschatological framework was the most important change that early Christianity had to make. This is not yet reflected in the Apocalypse but it was a problem that occupied Christian theologians for several centuries after the Apocalypse was written.

The Salutation

In 1.4 the seven Asian churches are mentioned for the first time. Asia was a Roman province that roughly corresponds with modern-day Turkey. It covered the territory of the ancient kingdom of Pergamum which the Romans had annexed in 133 BCE. There were more than seven Christian churches in Asia. It has been suggested (by Bauer, *Ortho-doxy and Heresy*, pp. 77-94) that John's reference to *only* seven churches reveals substantial apostasy there, but the number 'seven' more likely has representative and not exclusive significance. John addresses 'typical' churches and 'typical' situations, the latter heavily defined by symbolism. This means we should not necessarily expect to find a literal description of church life in any of the letters, still less a full-scale portrait of the churches addressed. There are substantial dangers in 'allegorizing' this material, however tempting it is to do so. The symbolism is not the form of the content but the actual content of the letters.

The author wishes his readers 'grace...and peace' (1.4). This formula represents a Christian adaptation of the secular letter-form. It has parallels in other New Testament literature (e.g. 1 Cor. 1.3). The concept of 'grace' is the ground of all New Testament theology. It denotes God's unmerited action in the provision of salvation (cf. 7.10). Revelation 1.4 shows that 'grace' is by no means exclusively a Pauline concept. As used throughout the New Testament, it carries the eschatological connotation that those who have received grace from God will be spared punishment at the last assize provided that they remain faithful to their calling. 'Peace' is also an eschatological term. Paul presents it as the result of justification in Rom. 5.1.

Grace and peace come to the Christians from God, not initially from John. The title used for God in 1.4, 'him who is and who was and who is to come', acknowledges God's eternal existence which is not affected by the passage of time. The author makes a swipe at the increasing number of Roman deities which stands in the spirit of Hebrew literature (e.g. Isa. 46.1; Ps. 115.6). The notion of God as 'him who is' looks back to the revelation of the divine name in Exod. 3.14 ('I AM') which the LXX translates as 'I am who I am'. This allusion to the biblical 'I AM' asserts that God not only is (at the time of writing) but was (in the period of the biblical Israel) and always will be (up to and including the time of the eschatological climax). John's development of the name of God foregrounds his belief in future divine intervention. God's status as 'he who is to come' is authenticated by his status as the One who was and is.

Readers would have expected grace and peace to flow from God (and from Jesus Christ, 1.5) but it is surprising to find them sent also from 'the seven spirits who are before his throne' (1.4). This passage has a trinitarian air but it certainly does not use the language of later trinitarian orthodoxy. That the 'seven spirits' are the rough equivalent of 'the Spirit' in 22.17 seems likely. Two sources have been proposed to explain this phrase in the Apocalypse. These are the seven archangels of Jewish literature (e.g. Tob. 12.15) and the seven eyes of God that are mentioned by Zech. 4.10. Commentators are divided on which of these sources influenced the Apocalypse, but the former is perhaps the more likely. The question of why the author does not mention '*the* Spirit' here, as he does later in the Apocalypse, is difficult to answer. Perhaps John deliberately employs an archaism to remind readers of their Jewish heritage with its ethical standards. The number 'seven' is an important aspect of John's apocalyptic symbolism. It must, however, be said that the Spirit is striking by his absence in John's vision of the heavenly court (Rev. 4–5) where if anywhere he might have been included. The conclusion seems inevitable that it lies beyond the author's purpose to offer a developed trinitarianism within the context of the revealed mysteries. This passage indirectly confirms that Jewish angelology was a source for the Christian understanding of the Spirit.

The heavenly Jesus also sends grace and peace to the churches (1.5). Jesus is called 'Christ', the 'faithful witness', the 'firstborn of the dead' and 'the ruler of the kings of the earth'. This cluster of titles shows the author's tendency to pile up nouns for rhetorical effect which is found, for example, in 10.11 and other references. This cluster incorporates an important difference from the description of the eternal God. Jesus is *not* said to have an eternal existence. The reference to his resurrection ('firstborn of the dead') recalls the early christological conviction that Jesus was shown to be a divine being through his death (cf. Phil. 2.6-11). 'Pre-existence' thinking was beginning to appear in late first-century Christology (see, e.g., Col. 1.15-20; Jn 1.1-18) but John uses what is again perhaps an archaic usage to recall his readers to their first convictions. Jesus is here called a 'witness' in the technical sense of someone who was faithful to the point of death. He is in this sense the archetypal New Testament witness (cf. 1 Tim. 6.13). The portrait of the faithful Jesus is used later in the Apocalypse to commend perseverance to the Christians (2.10). The notion that Jesus is the *faithful* witness mirrors Johannine language (cf. Jn 8.26).

The phrase 'firstborn of the dead' picks up the idea of 'witness' and indicates that Jesus' death was not the end but the beginning of a new order of existence (cf. Acts 26.23; 1 Cor. 15.20; Col. 1.18). The crucial point is not that Jesus was the *first* to rise from the dead, as if priority in time is the crucial thing, but that he was the first to rise from the *dead*. The resurrection of Jesus in this sense signifies the onset of the eschatological order. Implicit in the designation '*first*-born' is the notion of rank or superiority that attaches to the first-born male in Jewish society. Jesus is universally presented in early Christian literature as a divine being. He is distinguished as such from Christians who are seen as 'children of God' (only) by adoption through their incorporation into Christ (see Rom. 8.23).

That Jesus is 'the ruler of kings on earth' is a significant designation in view of the situation that the Apocalypse addresses. The language deliberately controverts the *status quo*. It calls on Christians to challenge the standards of the present order through the reminder that Jesus is the Lord whose reign on earth will soon begin (cf. 20.4). This triumphalism goes against the readers' perception of reality where to be a Christian was to be a member of a minority religion that was often misunderstood in the ancient world (see, e.g., 1 Cor. 1.23; Gal. 3.13).

Doxology and Introduction

Following this salutation, the author turns to formulaic material. 1.5b-6 is a doxology that describes Jesus in a further series of affirmations. John says that Jesus loves the readers and has freed them from their sins by his blood. He has made them a kingdom of priests to serve his God and Father. That the death of Jesus secures freedom from sin is also a Pauline concept (cf. Rom. 3.21-6). The statement that this redemption was achieved by the shedding of blood is alienating to modern readers but it finds a natural background in the Hebrew sacrificial ritual (cf. Lev. 9). It is an important New Testament concept that cannot be set aside without loss or damage (see Mt. 26.28; Jn 6.53-54; Acts 20.28; Rom. 3.25; Eph. 2.13; and esp. Heb. 9.12). Implicit in this concept is a reference to the Israelite Exodus from Egypt when the blood of the lamb was sprinkled on Jewish doorposts to ward off the angel of death. This saved those inside the house (see Exod. 12.13). John does not say *how* the blood of Christ frees people from their sins; but he does presuppose that sin brings punishment and that this has been averted through the death of Jesus.

John continues by saying that Jesus has made the readers a 'kingdom' and 'priests to his God and Father' (1.6). The kingdom in question is the counterpart of the biblical Israel. Where other New Testament passages expect the full emergence of God's kingdom in the future (e.g. Mk 9.1), John says that Christians *already are* the kingdom of God (cf. 1 Pet. 2.9). The primary reference is to Exod. 19.6 where Yahweh tells Moses that Israel is a 'priestly kingdom'. John presents the Christians as the true Israel who continue the history of the Hebrew people. Their status as a kingdom means that they must adopt the ethical standards that the Hebrew Bible enjoins on its readers. This is implied especially by their description as 'priests' of God. The imagery of 1.6 is not detrimental to the hope that a decisive change is impending, but the language is striking nonetheless.

There is a problem of consistency in Revelation for, where 6.9 locates the souls of the martyrs beneath the heavenly altar and implies there is a temple in heaven, 21.22 denies that there is a temple in the new Jerusalem when the city descends from heaven. This is because God and the Lamb have taken the place of the temple in the closing vision of the Apocalypse. It would be pedantic—and in fact misleading—to press this discrepancy because constant reworking of imagery is a feature of John's symbolism. 1.6 identifies the primary duty of these Christian priests as the service of God in a context where liturgical and ethical, but significantly not sacrificial, activity is implied.

1.7 is an explicit prediction of the return of Jesus from heaven. The form of words probably had a considerable history before the writing of the Apocalypse. They let us see one of the ways in which first-century Christianity expressed its eschatological hope. John promises that Jesus will come with the clouds, that every eye will see him, including those who had pierced him, and that on his account all the tribes of the earth will wail. The notion that Jesus will 'come with the clouds' draws on Dan. 7.13 where the man-like figure of that prophet's vision is said to come 'on the clouds of heaven' towards the Ancient of Days. This allusion to Daniel is introduced without the 'Son of Man' title that features in the Gospels' use of that passage (see Mk 13.26 and par.). Revelation 1.7 nevertheless shares with the Gospels the reversal of the direction of movement that Daniel 7 describes. In Dan. 7.13 the man-like figure proceeds towards the Ancient of Days in heaven. The Christian sources take this passage to signify the return of Jesus from heaven to earth in what had become a familiar exegetical tradition before the Gospels were written. Paul expresses this view in 1 Thess. 4.17 where he anticipates that those who are alive will be 'caught up in the clouds' to meet the Lord in the air; apparently to escort him back in triumph to earth where his reign will begin. Daniel 7 was an important proof text for early Christianity because it describes the promotion of a second authoritative figure in the heavenly court. Christianity universally proclaimed the heavenly Jesus as divine and drew on earlier passages to provide authority for its expressions of belief about Jesus.

John continues that 'every eye' will see the returning Messiah, including those who had pierced him. The source for this statement is Zech. 12.10 ('they look on the one whom they have pierced') which Jn 19.37 applies to the crucifixion of Jesus. John the Apocalyptist maintains a sense of contrast (with appropriate continuity) between the Jesus who died and the Lord who will return from heaven for judgment. John expects the Lordship of Jesus to be universally demonstrated at this time. John says further that 'all the tribes of the earth will wail because of him'. He is thinking not so much of the tribes of Israel, who are mentioned by name in 7.5-8, as of the wider tribes of humankind, several of which are mentioned in the Pentateuch (e.g. Gen. 36.29). Revelation 1.7 makes the returning Jesus the judge of all human beings. This is a major theme of the Apocalypse on which the author bases his dualistic world-view. The final 'So it is to be. Amen' is John's vigorous assent to this eschatology.

1.8 is a divine pronouncement in the first-person form. God says that he is the Alpha and the Omega. This is amplified by the repeated statement that God 'is and was and is to come' (cf. 1.4) and fixes this belief (with its implications of judgment) in the readers' minds. Speculation about letters and numbers is an important feature of Jewish literature where both have a designated value (cf. 13.18). The statement that God is the first and the last letter of the Greek alphabet demonstrates his transcendence of creation. The phrase possibly alludes to a mystical name of God that John does not wish to put into writing (cf. 3.12; 14.1), but it is impossible for us to speculate on this matter at our distance from the unwritten traditions of first-century Christianity.

The Commission by Christ

In 1.9-11 John explains why he writes the Apocalypse. He tells the readers he was on Patmos when he witnessed a vision of the heavenly Christ who told him to write to the churches. John calls himself 'your brother' (1.9). This noun reflects Jewish religious custom (cf. Jer. 22.18); the Essenes at Qumran apparently regarded each other as 'brothers' (see Josephus, *War* 2.122). The Christians developed a specific understanding of the term through Paul's assertion (Rom. 8.15-16, 23) that they are children of God by adoption. None of this disguises the fact that John believes he is an authoritative figure for the readers (cf. the use of 'servant' in 1.1). He refers this authority to his commission by Christ in the tradition of apocalyptic revelation.

John continues that he shares with the readers 'the persecution and the kingdom and the patient endurance' (1.9). In the Introduction I mentioned the lack of any convincing evidence for a Domitianic persecution of the Christians at the end of the first century CE. This lack of evidence has implications for exegeting the references to 'persecution' here and elsewhere in the Apocalypse. If there was neither a persecution of the Christians nor a general political crisis towards the end of Domitian's reign, the term 'persecution' must carry a symbolic sense. 'Persecution' is used in other Christian literature in an eschatological context as a description of what must happen before the end (see, e.g., Mt. 13.21). This material almost certainly explains its usage in the Apocalypse. 'Persecution' as John uses the term is a description of life before the end. It encourages the readers' perception of a crisis and a view of society at variance with what some if not many of them were entertaining. 'The kingdom' is what the Christians already are (1.6). 'Patient endurance' is the seer's rhetorical reminder of what the Christian life should be like. For John, it means high social boundaries and no compromise.

Patmos lies in the Aegean, in the Sporades group south-west of Samos. John does not say he has been banished there. The report that he had is found only in late Christian sources, notably Eusebius (see the Introduction). The reason that John gives for his presence on Patmos echoes the thought of 1.2. It is 'because of the word of God and the testimony of Jesus'. This ambiguous phrase might mean a number of things. It most obviously implies that John had gone to Patmos in the exercise of his prophetic ministry—perhaps to receive apocalyptic revelation. The one feature of 1.9 that might suggest an act of repression is the noun 'persecution'. We have seen that this bears a symbolic meaning. The tradition that John had been banished to Patmos must itself be banished from the exegesis of the Apocalypse as unsupported by external and internal evidence.

John proceeds to describe his reception of the vision (1.10-11). He says he was 'in the Spirit on the Lord's day' (1.10). Revelation 4.1 is quite restrained about its seer's psychology of inspiration. It leaves many of the details unexplained. John says only that he saw a door open in heaven (4.1). The spiritual origins of this experience lie in a passage such as Ezek. 11.1. We can gain further knowledge of early Christian apocalyptic practices from ch. 6 of the *Ascension of Isaiah*. This text contains a fascinating description of the preparations for heavenly ascension which reveals that it involved a trance-like state and an 'out-of-the-body' journey in which the seer thought that he journeyed towards the divine presence while his body remained inert on the ground. There is further evidence for this kind of experience in the Jewish text called *Hekhaloth Rabbati*. When John says he was 'in the Spirit', he means that he entered a trance. This is evidenced by the reference to the open door in 4.1.

John says that this trance occurred 'on the Lord's Day' (1.10). This reference to 'the Lord's Day' has provoked a variety of interpretations. It most obviously designates Sunday, the day when Jesus rose from the tomb. There is evidence for a weekly meeting of Christians in a passage from Pliny in the early second century (*Ep.* 10.96). Revelation 1.10 implies that this took place on a Sunday in distinction from the Jewish Sabbath because of the impact made by the resurrection of Jesus.

It is difficult to decide whether the experience described in v. 10b ('I heard behind me a loud voice like a trumpet') denotes a frequent or an exceptional experience of revelation, but perhaps the latter is more likely (cf. 2 Cor. 12). The succeeding verses make it clear that the voice belongs to the heavenly Christ. Christ directly addresses the seer. He instructs John to send a message to 'the seven churches' which are mentioned by name in 1.11. We have seen that this list is representative and almost certainly neither exhaustive nor exclusive. John turns on hearing the voice and sees 'seven golden lampstands' (1.12; cf. Zech. 4.2). These are symbols of the seven churches (see 1.20). Their light has not been snuffed out but it is obvious from the letters that the author thinks that it burns quite dimly in places. The fact that John's heavenly ascension is not mentioned until 4.1 suggests that he experiences this vision on earth.

John sees Christ 'in the midst of the lampstands' (1.13). The passage is worth citing in full because it offers a remarkable visual description of Christ which derives from Jewish literature:

> In the midst of the lampstands I saw one like the Son of Man, clothed with a long robe and with a golden sash across his chest. His head and his hair were white as white wool, white as snow; his eyes were like a flame of fire, his feet were like burnished bronze, refined as in a furnace, and his voice was like the sound of many waters. In his right hand he held seven stars, and from his mouth came a sharp, two-edged sword, and his face was like the sun shining with full force (1.13-16).

This description recalls a medley of Jewish literature. The phrase 'one like the Son of Man' derives from Dan. 7.13. The long robe recalls the dress of the Jewish High Priest (Exod. 28.4) and both the linen-clothed man of Ezek. 9.2 and the deity of Dan. 7.9. The white colour of Christ's hair and head reflects the description of the Ancient of Days in Dan. 7.9. The most important source for this passage, however, is the angelophany of Dan. 10.5-6:

> I looked up and saw a man clothed in linen, with a belt of gold from Uphaz around his waist. His body was like beryl, his face like lightning, his eyes like flaming torches, his arms and legs like the gleam of burnished bronze, and the sound of his words like the roar of a multitude.

Several features of this angelophany have contributed to the description of the heavenly Christ in Revelation 1. They include the flaming eyes, the bronze colour of the feet and the description of the mediator's face and voice. The effect of this usage is to present Christ in language forged out by Jewish angelology (which had itself been resourced by the theophany) but in a context where Christ is introduced as a divine being (so 5.12). This is good evidence that Jewish angelology helped the rise of Christology.

The reference to the seven stars (1.16) is less easy to explain from within Jewish tradition. The stars, like the lampstands, are identified with the seven churches in 1.20. Stars are associated with angels in Jewish literature (e.g. Dan. 12.3). John may be thinking of a heavenly counterpart of the churches in a way that is suggested by *Asc. Isa.* 3.15 ('and the descent of the angel of the church which is in the heavens, whom he will summon in the last days'). The thought in any event is that the seven churches are protected by their heavenly patron and that in this sense he owns them. The two-edged sword symbolizes the words that Christ speaks (cf. Eph. 6.17; Heb. 4.12-3; cf. Isa. 49.2).

The seer's prostration (1.17) is a traditional response to the appearance of a heavenly visitor (cf. Dan. 8.17, 10.15; Mt. 28.9). It implies the offering of respect but also the experience of awe and wonderment that undergirds the numinous experience (on which see Otto, *The Idea of the Holy*). There is a tradition in Revelation and other apocalyptic literature in which a seer who witnesses an angel falls at his feet but is rebuked for doing so (see Rev. 19.10; 22.8-9). Clearly, the apocalyptic tradition was sensitive to the need not to present an angel as a divine rival; *a fortiori* in an apocalypse where angelophanic traditions are used to describe Christ as a divine being who receives worship.

The chapter closes with Christ's command to John to write what he sees (1.19). John's vision is given a specifically eschatological content ('what is, and what is to take place after this'). 1.20 identifies the seven stars as the angels of the churches and the lampstands as the churches themselves.

Revelation 2 and 3

Chapters 2 and 3 belong together. Here we find the letters to the churches which Christ dictates to the seer. The inclusion of these letters distinguishes Revelation from the other Jewish and Christian apocalypses. We have seen that they are central to the text inasmuch as they set the terms in which the seer's special language should be understood. For all their symbolism, the letters give a comprehensible picture of why John thinks that the churches need criticism. It emerges from reading them that this is because of the problem of social accommodation by which high boundaries were being removed by some in the Christian communities.

Ephesus

The first letter is addressed to the angel of the church at Ephesus (2.1). Ephesus was a major city of Asia Minor (but not the capital). It formed the centre of the Artemis-Diana cult in that region (cf. Acts 19.23-41). Ephesus had a strong Jewish community with syncretistic tendencies. There were temples there to Claudius, Hadrian and Severus. The city was a major commercial centre for the province of Asia. Ephesus had been evangelized by Paul (see Acts 18.19–20.1). It served as a base for Paul's missionary endeavours in the surrounding territory. It was the home of the Johannine school and the reported city of John the Elder (according to Papias). We have seen that the Apocalypse displays certain affinities with Johannine language (e.g. the 'witness' theme). If the author was in contact with Johannine Christianity, it would have been natural for him to write to Ephesus. This might explain why Ephesus heads the list of churches addressed.

Christ tells the Ephesians that he knows their works, their toil and patient endurance (2.2). This partly repeats the language of 1.9 and emphasizes the conflict motif at the beginning of the letters. John does this to create a sense of crisis among his readers. The implication of 2.2 is that Christians in Ephesus have achieved a reasonable success in resisting accommodation with pagan culture. No doubt this reflects the prominence of the Artemis cult there which would have polarized the need for Christian 'separateness'. There is, most importantly, no suggestion that the Ephesian Christians have suffered persecution of any kind. The problems mentioned here are internal to the church, but the code in which the letter is written is not initially easy to decipher.

'Works' in Jewish literature are deeds of righteousness associated with the hope for eschatological reward (cf. Jas 2.18-26). 'Toil' is associated with specifically Christian work in the New Testament (see, e.g., 1 Thess. 2.9). 'Patient endurance' denotes the refusal to compromise. 1.9 makes this critical to Christian discipleship.

The second half of 2.2 reveals a dispute about authority in the Ephesian church. The author says that Christians there have tested people who claimed to be 'apostles' and found them to be false. The term 'apostle' in early Christian literature denotes a circle wider than the Twelve (Paul, for instance, was an apostle). It includes all who were commissioned by Jesus for missionary work. Those mentioned by 2.2 were presumably recognized as apostles in the Ephesian church. That they are *false* apostles is the author's evaluation of them that reflects his view of their teaching. From the information presented in the letters we can surmise that they taught accommodation with urban society was permissible, as Paul had done; but this information is not disclosed (for rhetorical effect) until 2.14. The as-yet-unexplained designation of them as 'false apostles' encourages readers to reflect on what it is that makes them false. We shall see that all the different terms for opponents in the letters denote a homogeneous complex of false teaching which the author wholeheartedly resists.

The situation John describes in Ephesus can be illumined with reference to other literature. When Ignatius wrote to the Ephesians some 15 years later he makes a similar comment, observing that 'some have passed by on their way from there with evil teaching, whom you did not allow to sow among you, stopping your ears that you might not receive what was sown by them' (*Eph*. 9.1). This confirms that Ephesus was known as a place where teachers of different persuasions promulgated their message. The earlier part of Ignatius's letter, especially his statement about 'running together with the purpose of the bishop' (4.1), indicates that disputes about authority continued to be a problem in Ephesus after Revelation was written. In *Eph*. 5.1-3, Ignatius adds the information that some people refused to come to worship, as if rival Christian factions existed in the city. The evidence of the Johannine Epistles is also significant if they have a connection with Ephesus. Secessionists who have gone out from the community are mentioned in 1 Jn 2.19, while 2 John 7 states that many 'deceivers' have 'gone out into the world'. Whatever this statement means—and opinions have varied on this issue—it shows that these people were no longer regarded, and doubtless no longer regarded themselves, as in fellowship with the elder and his community, so that it is right to detect a split within the Johannine community on the basis of this evidence.

None of this material provides an unambiguous picture of church life in Ephesus but it does help to piece together the situation mentioned allusively by Rev. 2.2. In particular, it shows that party factions were a familiar feature of Christianity in Ephesus. Revelation suggests that these occurred over ethical rather than doctrinal questions; 2.2 shows that part of the problem lay in the attitude of different Christians towards the existing order. The 'false apostles' had presumably told the Ephesians roughly what Paul said in his letter to the Corinthians: that an idol has no existence (1 Cor. 8.4) and that Christians can participate in banquets with a clear conscience. The author of Revelation, for whom 'separate-ness' is a profound concern, criticizes the Christians at Pergamum for doing this (2.14). The church at Ephesus evidently knew both shades of opinion. They were probably encouraged by different teachers. We can doubtless conclude from Ignatius that the Apocalypse did not still the Ephesian situation once for all. But the evidence for it is scanty, and our reconstruction remains tentative for that reason.

These 'false apostles' have been identified with a number of different groups: with Judaizers, with the Nicolaitans of 2.6 (although that refer-ence is also obscure) and with other anonymous figures who claimed authority at Ephesus. The Nicolaitan hypothesis has much to commend it but does not of itself explain the nature of the false teaching until we link it with the more precise information imparted in the letter to Pergamum (2.14-15). We can, however, say that the author's claim to recent and personal commission by Christ is striking rhetorically. It con-trasts the teachers' claim to apostolic commission with his own apoca-lyptic mandate to resist what they were saying. The author's suggestion that the Ephesians were doing well (2.2-3) but were not above criticism (2.4) shows that a timely reminder is needed.

In this context Ephesus is criticized for losing its first love (2.4). What this means is not said explicitly, but the comment probably refers to the wider problem of reducing high social boundaries. 'Not growing weary' (2.3) has the same meaning. For this reason Christ tells the Ephesians to repent and he threatens the church with judgment (2.5). The threat to 'remove your lampstand from its place' is a strong one. It hints at the eschatological vulnerability of the unrepentant church.

The letter to Ephesus ends with the first occurrence of what will be a repeated phrase in the Apocalypse: 'Let anyone who has an ear listen to what the Spirit is saying to the churches' (2.7a). 'Hearing' denotes action. Action is what John wants. The saying provides a rhetorical con-tinuity with the sayings of Jesus who spoke in a similar way (e.g. Mt. 11.15). The author himself adds 'what the Spirit is saying to the churches' to confirm that he speaks with divine authority. The plural 'churches' shows that the warning is intended for a circle wider than Ephesus alone. The required action will be given a specific focus by 2.14, 20.

The concluding promise (2.7b) is that 'everyone who conquers' will eat from the tree of life in the paradise of God. This promise looks back to the story of the Garden of Eden where the tree of life is in the Garden

(Gen. 2.9). The end of this story states that a flaming sword bars access to the tree lest people eat of it and live for ever (Gen. 3.22-24). John uses this idea in a symbolic way to assert that the eschatological age will yield paradisial benefits that have been inaccessible since primaeval times (see Rev. 21-22). His striking promise draws attention to the term, 'to conquer',which is used here for the first time in the Apocalypse. 'Conquering' means persevering in the author's recommended pattern of behaviour and securing the rewards that will be revealed at the return of Jesus from heaven.

Smyrna

The letter to the church at Smyrna follows (2.8-11). Smyrna is the modern Izmir in Turkey. It lies at the mouth of the river Izmir at the foot of Mt Pagros. Smyrna had a prominent Jewish community. It was the home of Bishop Polycarp who was martyred there in the middle of the second century CE. Ignatius wrote letters to the Smyrnaeans and to Polycarp. The church at Smyrna was probably founded by Paul on his third missionary journey (see Acts 19.26). The *Life of Polycarp* 2 says that Paul visited Smyrna on his way to Ephesus. Christ's message is again addressed to the angel of the Smyrnaean church (2.8) in the logic of the chain of mediation (cf. 1.1).

Smyrna receives much praise from the seer. John says that the Christians there are afflicted but have remained faithful. 2.9 states in rhetorical terms that they appear poor but are rich. This does not mean that the Smyrnaean Christians come (only) from the poorer classes but it probably means that they experienced *relative* deprivation which was related to their unwillingness to engage in the full social life of the city. Ignatius's letter to Smyrna confirms that the church was made up of different social classes, including at least one well-placed person and perhaps not too many slaves. This contrast between poverty and riches recalls the contrast between the riches and poverty of Jesus which Paul makes in 2 Cor. 8.9, which the Smyrnaeans conceivably knew. They are reminded that they are following the authentic path of Christian discipleship even though the circumstances of their lives seem difficult.

The second half of 2.9 alludes to opposition in Smyrna from 'those who say they are Jews and are not' and who in the author's opinion constitute a 'synagogue of Satan'. John says that these false Jews have slandered the Smyrnaean Christians. The statement that Christian poverty at Smyrna was exacerbated by Jewish opposition is confirmed by the *Martyrdom of Polycarp* which says that the Jews joined the pagans in calling for the bishop's death (12.2). The precise nature of the allusion in 2.9 should be treated with caution given the symbolic nature of Revelation's language and the fact that Jewish opposition to Christianity was commonly found throughout the empire; but we have no cause to doubt that it flourished in Smyrna. It is, of course, possible that these 'false Jews' are Christians who refuse to do what John says, like the 'false apostles' of 2.2 (cf. 3.9).

The author deals with this problem by denying the religious authenticity of those who behave in this way. The issue of what makes a true Jew comes down to behaviour, as the letters indicate. 'The Jews' (whoever they are) become a 'synagogue of Satan' when they engage in practices such as social relations with the outside community of which the author disapproves. The language shows the polarized view of the world that John impresses on his readers. Those who will not desist from such practices—even if they are Christians—pledge their support for Satan and deny their new religion.

2.10 alludes to impending suffering at Smyrna. John says that the devil is about to throw some of the church into prison and that they will have affliction for ten days. Those who are faithful until death will be given the crown of life. Suffering is a familiar feature of the Christian eschatological tradition. The Synoptic eschatological discourse anticipates a variety of suffering (see, e.g., Mt. 24.21). Such material doubtless featured in the eschatological instruction which all Christian converts received. John warns his readers about suffering because in his view they are not suffering enough. A church that is doing well must be warned not to slip. The figure of 'ten' days has symbolic significance (cf. Dan. 1.12-15). It is a feature of apocalyptic literature that the dimensions of an impending crisis are defined to delimit it and provide assurance that readers can survive it. John creates awareness of a crisis to encourage a committed response from his readers.

This warning about suffering is addressed to 'some' in the church. 'Some' is a rhetorical qualification. It challenges people to ask whether *they* are prepared to experience hardship because of their beliefs. Conflict is the inevitable result of Christian authenticity in John's view. Only in those cities where Christians are heavily criticized is a reference to conflict not found. This signifies that Christians in those cities are not living authentically. John promises the 'faithful'—the faithful in conflict—the 'crown of life'. The crown is a garland of leaves awarded to the victor in athletic contests. Here it denotes the promise of resurrection for those who die as martyrs. The phrase reflects the belief that martyrdom leads to vindication which is mentioned by Paul and Ignatius (Phil. 1.23; Ignatius, *Rom.* 4.3). This is one of the ways in which ancient Judaism and Christianity conceived of the eschatological life of the faithful.

The letter to Smyrna closes with the promise that the person who 'conquers' will not be hurt by the 'second death'. This 'second death' is mentioned later in the Apocalypse in 20.14 and 21.8. It signifies the ultimate punishment of those who are excluded from the kingdom of Christ. John does not promise that readers will be spared the first—that is, normal human—death. The 'second death' is an essentially dualist conception that distinguishes the followers from the adversaries of Jesus in terms of their eschatological destiny. Here, it has rhetorical significance. People fall into one of these two camps depending on their reaction to what John says. John underscores this warning with his statement about the person with the ear to hear (which is a further warning in itself).

Pergamum

2.12 introduces the letter to the church in Pergamum. Pergamum was the capital city of Asia, situated above the Caicus valley. The city had a notable library and was a centre of pagan religion. A temple was dedicated there to Augustus and Rome by the Provincial Synod in 29 BCE (cf. Tacitus, *Ann.* 4.37). There were also temples in honour of Zeus Soter, Athena Nikephoros and other pagan divinities.

John describes Pergamum as the place where Satan has 'his throne' (2.13). The introductory phrase, 'I know where you are living', contrasts with the 'I know your works' which introduces most of the other letters. It implies that life for the Christians was exceptionally difficult in Pergamum, no doubt because of the city's importance as the imperial capital with its variety of pagan cults. This must have made social accommodation all the more tempting. The 'throne of Satan' probably denotes the Roman seat of government but some commentators have taken it more specifically with reference to the pagan cults and even to particular pagan cults (such as that of Zeus Soter). The crucial point is that the throne is said to be Satan's. The trappings of the Roman world are portrayed in demonic terms.

Revelation 2.13 contains the only named and documented instance of martyrdom in the Apocalypse. The author mentions Antipas, 'my witness, my faithful one'. Nothing more is said about this person, including when and how he died. It is significant that even in Pergamum, which is the absolute blackspot in the churches addressed, the author can point to only one martyr. This confirms that Christianity had not been made the target of official repression in Asia and that the theory of persecution does not adequately explain the writing of the Apocalypse. Revelation 2.13 concludes with another reference to Pergamum as the place 'where Satan lives' to emphasize the particular difficulties felt by Christians in that city, but again without mentioning specific instances of martyrdom.

The author nevertheless makes some criticism of the Christians in Pergamum. He says that some people 'hold to the teaching of Balaam' (2.14). Balaam, as John notes, was a false prophet whom the Moabite king Balak persuaded to curse the Israelites when they invaded his territory (see Num. 22). Numbers 31.16 says that it was on Balaam's advice that the people of Israel played the harlot with the daughters of Moab.

Balaam for John symbolizes those who recommend compromise with urban standards. John makes this point initially by allusion; but the allusion is swiftly interpreted to answer the questions raised by the earlier letters. John says plainly that the followers of Balaam teach people to 'eat food sacrificed to idols' and to 'practice fornication' (2.14). The first phrase is explicit and gives the meaning of the second. 'Fornication' in the Hebrew Bible denotes religious apostasy; specifically, the service of pagan deities (see, e.g., Jer. 2.20; Ezek. 16.15). This is what it means in the Apocalypse, in conjunction with the reference to 'eating food sacrificed to idols'. 2.14 confirms that the temptation to compromise with pagan standards in this way attracted the churches addressed. 'Some'— but not all—the Christians in Pergamum had advocated greater compromise than John allowed. 2.14 is with 2.20 the clearest evidence we have for the actual setting of the Apocalypse. The letters disclose the real situation, in word and symbol, before the Apocalypse proper begins.

John again mentions the 'teaching of the Nicolaitans' (2.15; cf. 2.6). It would be wrong to look for different kinds of opponents in the letters in the absence of a clear textual indication that we should be doing this. The different titles for opponents are stylistic variations and portray John's opponents in terms that the readers recognize as notorious. Like the biblical allusions in Jude and 2 Peter, they are introduced for rhetorical effect. They designate the *character* of the sin and not the precise identity of those who commit it. Second- and third-century commentators took the Nicolaitans as the followers of Nicolaus, the Antiochene deacon mentioned in Acts 6.5, but this identification is not certain and in any event it does not reveal anything about their specific practices. Irenaeus (*Adv. Haer.* 1.26.3) connects the Nicolaitans with Cerinthus whom he presents as an opponent of John at Ephesus. Tertullian mentions another group of the same name (*Praesc. Her.* 33); Eusebius (*Hist. Eccl.* 3.29.1) says that the group was short-lived. This last statement casts general doubt on the reliability of all patristic reports about the Nicolaitans. John does not tell us anything about them, but his comment about eating food sacrificed to idols and fornication (2.14) no doubt reveals all. The 'Nicolaitans', like the Balaamites, are people who promulgate ethical teaching with which John disagrees and which he tells his readers to resist.

This reference to the Nicolaitans is followed by the command to repent and the warning of judgment if this is ignored (2.16). If the church does not repent, Christ says that he will 'come to them soon' and 'make war against them' with the 'sword of his mouth'. This language calls on readers to consider their behaviour and to make appropriate changes. It is unnecessary to engage in detailed discussion of whether the author thinks that judgment will take place at the return of Jesus or on some special occasion beforehand. Either conclusion is possible. Neither is excluded but the former is more likely. The language reflects the apocalyptic distinction between the decision for judgment that has already been taken in heaven and its exercise on earth at some future point.

The (by now familiar) saying about the person with the ears to hear (2.17a) is followed by the statement that those who 'conquer' will receive 'some of the hidden manna' and a white stone with a new name written on it 'that no one knows except the one who receives it' (2.17b). Manna was the miraculous food that sustained the Israelites in the wilderness. *2 Baruch* 24.8 expects that manna will descend from heaven in the messianic age. This expectation explains the present allusion which has an eschatological orientation. Manna is mentioned in John 6 in a context with eucharistic overtones. It is difficult to exclude these from this passage, given the complex nature of Revelation's symbolism, but it is fair to say that a eucharistic allusion is not made prominent here. The emphasis falls on the 'hiddenness' of the manna and not on its relation to early Christian worship. That implies its heavenly origin and eschatological significance.

The reference to the 'white stone' has prompted several interpretations. Among the most plausible are the stones cast into an urn by ancient jurors (cf. Ovid, *Met.* 15.41); the stone that gave free admission to a royal assembly; and the stone that *b. Yom.* 8 says fell with the manna from heaven. Charles, however, may be right to suggest that the stone has a predominantly mystical significance and alludes to the new name that will be given to victorious people in the eschatological age to link them with an angel (*Critical and Exegetical Commentary*, I, pp. 66-67). The 'white' colour picks up the description of Christ in 1.14 and symbolizes the purity of those of whom the author approves (cf. 3.4; 4.4). We are here on the threshold of the mystical traditions of primitive Christianity which for the most part we cannot penetrate.

Thyatira

Thyatira is perhaps the least important of the cities addressed but it receives the longest letter. The city lay some 40 miles south-east of Pergamum. It was a trading centre with numerous guilds of craftsmen. It became a centre of Montanism in the late second century CE (see Epiphanius, *Haer.* 51.33).

Christ says that he 'knows' the Thyatirans' works (2.19). This reflects his position as a heavenly being from whom nothing is hidden. 2.19 praises these Christians for the fact that their 'last works' have exceeded their former ones. Their love, faith, service and patient endeavour are mentioned in this context. This introduction stands in marked contrast to the strong polemic that follows in the letter. Swete drily observes that 'praise is more liberally given, if it can be given with justice, when blame is to follow' (*Apocalypse*, p. 42). It claims the readers' attention before John's criticism of them is imparted.

The criticism begins in 2.20. John complains that the Thyatirans 'tolerated that woman Jezebel' who 'calls herself a prophet' and 'is teaching and beguiling my servants to practise fornication and to eat food sacrificed to idols'. This recalls the criticism of 2.14 but uses different imagery. That the substance of the polemic remains constant but the titles of the opponents vary shows the true meaning of this material. This is given by the repetition of the reference to 'fornication' and 'food sacrificed to idols' in 2.20 (notice the rhetorical reversal of the noun order here from 2.14). Jezebel was the wife of Ahab, the king who introduced foreign cults into Israel (see 1 Kgs 16.31; 2 Kgs 9.22). The analogy is aptly chosen, for John thinks the present situation tantamount to idolatry. This New Testament Jezebel has been identified both with the Lydia of Acts 16.14-15 and with the Sibyl Samanthe but neither identification is convincing. The epithet probably refers to a specific person but her identity is unknown except for the fact that she claimed to be a 'prophet'. Female prophets appear in the Hebrew Bible (see, e.g., Isa. 8.3). As a prophetess, Jezebel doubtless claimed an authority similar to that of John of the Apocalypse. Her message was opposed to John's as the unflattering title indicates. She was evidently a settled figure in the Thyatiran church, and not a wandering prophetess, for otherwise John would have called for her ejection. For this reason John, perhaps himself a peripatetic, must have found her message difficult to counter.

John says that this Jezebel has been given time to repent but that she has scorned all such opportunity (2.21). This implies a prior warning, perhaps an oracle that the seer had imparted previously (when he was in Thyatira in person?). Since Jezebel was a prophet, she would doubtless have opposed John's criticism with oracles of her own. The text thereby conceals an interesting political agenda to which unfortunately we have no means of access. The possibility, if not probability, is that John was opposed by some church members when he visited this city. The unrepentant Jezebel is warned that Christ will throw her 'on a bed' together with those who commit adultery with her (2.22a). The reference is to a bed of sickness and not one of sexual indulgence. 'Adultery' has the same metaphorical sense as 'fornication' in 2.20. Its meaning is supplied by the wider context of the letters to the churches. The penalty may seem harsh, that of divinely instituted illness, but it has parallels in Paul's delivery of a notorious evil-doer to Satan 'for the destruction of his flesh' in 1 Cor. 5.5. It reflects the belief that physical illness can be caused (or removed) by supernatural intervention and that it is connected with 'sin' (cf. Jn 9.2). The point is that those who will not accept the hardship of following Jesus will suffer a divinely instituted punishment.

2.23a makes a still more shocking threat. Christ will strike Jezebel's children dead. 'Children' means 'disciples'. The reader instinctively winces in the hope that this is said metaphorically. Death by punishment in the lake of fire is, however, said to be the final fate of the ungodly in Rev. 20.15. There is a constant interplay between symbol and reality in the Apocalypse. Commentators compare this passage with the fate of Ahab's children in 2 Kgs 10.7. It recalls the destruction of the Egyptian first-born in Exod. 12.12. John uses the death of innocent children to emphasize the absolute undesirability of the behaviour he opposes.

The second half of 2.23 explains the purpose of this punishment. Christ says that 'all the churches will know that I am the one who searches minds and hearts'. This statement demonstrates God's unique majesty in a polytheistic situation. It recalls the Hebrew Bible's notion of punishment by the hand of Yahweh. This punishment is striking for the fact that it is directed towards Christians and not the world in general. This language used in 2.23b derives from Jer. 17.10 and signifies that each person's behaviour will receive an appropriate reward or punishment. Christians are reminded that they must not presume on their salvation but do the deeds that befit it.

2.24-25 commends the ethically scrupulous in the Thyatiran community. Christ says that on all who have not followed such teaching or performed what he calls 'the deep things of Satan' he lays no burden except to stay faithful until he comes. There is a problem of punctuation in this verse. The Greek could be taken to mean: 'You have not learned the deep things of Satan: *as they say*, "I do not lay upon you any burden."' There is, however, no evidence that the followers of Jezebel had argued in this way. The phrase probably represents an ironic reworking of their claim to disclose the deep things of God which John caricatures by his comment about the deep things of Satan (cf. 2.9). The phrase 'I do not lay upon you any burden' displays verbal similarity to the decree of the Jerusalem Council in Acts 15.28-29, where it was decided that no further burden should be laid on the Gentile Christians than the demand to abstain from fornication and from food sacrificed to idols. Revelation 2.24-25 possibly alludes to this edict which the author thinks has been obscured by the passage of time. He implies that those who hold to the teaching of the Council need no further ethical instruction except to persevere in what they know already. The implication is that not all Christians were abiding by the injunction and that these must be recalled to a stricter pattern of behaviour. The several possible references to this decree in Revelation 2-3 (principally 2.14, 20) suggest that John recalls his readers to these 'first principles'. It is not certain that John knows Acts, but he does seem to know the tradition on which Acts draws.

2.26 promises that those who 'conquer' and continue to 'do my works until the end' will 'have authority over the nations' and 'rule them with an iron rod'. 'Doing my works to the end', like 'conquering', means maintaining the author's desired position until the coming of Christ. This promise of eschatological reward is set in poetic terms that represent a loose citation of Ps. 2.8-9. The allusion is to the future reign of the Christians with their Messiah which John (like all first-century Christians) believes will be an earthly one (cf. 20.4; 21.1-22.5). Both Mt. 19.28 and 1 Cor. 6.3 expect the Christians to play a major role in the eschatological judgment. The eschatological subordination of the Gentiles to the people of God is a theme of wider Jewish literature which the Christians inherited and on which they drew (see, e.g., Isa. 61.5).

2.28 adds to this the promise that Christ will give his victors 'the morning star'. This is a biblical allusion whose source has been disputed. Isaiah 14.12 has been proposed but Num. 24.17 ('a star shall come out of Jacob') seems the more likely candidate. It gives the passage a messianic significance. On this interpretation, the promise is that Christians will share the Messiah's reign when he returns from heaven. This interpretation is supported by Rev. 22.16 where Christ describes *himself* as the 'morning star'.

Sardis

The letter to Thyatira is followed by the letter to the church in Sardis (3.1-6). Sardis was the capital of the ancient kingdom of Lydia, located 50 miles to the east of Ephesus and overlooking the Hermus valley. Sardis comes in for substantial criticism from John. He expresses his view of the church there bluntly. It has the name of being alive but is in fact dead (3.1b). John does not mention specific problems or make allusions as he does when addressing the other churches. This is a bad sign. The term 'dead' does not mean that the church has ceased to exist but that it has so far compromised with pagan standards that John thinks its Christian profession substantially called into question. 'Deadness' mocks the behaviour of those who claim to be Christians but think it acceptable to achieve a real compromise with urban society.

Also at variance with what he says elsewhere, John tells the Sardis Christians that he finds their works (i.e. behaviour) imperfect (3.2). John's criticism leads to an urgent call for action. Christians in Sardis must wake up and strengthen what remains and is on the point of death. The command 'wake up!' recalls Mt. 24.42, the saying of Jesus about watchfulness in view of the uncertain end. Ramsay (*Letters*, pp. 276-78) identifies two incidents in the history of Sardis that might have lent local meaning to this command, but these do not disguise its mainly rhetorical force. John acknowledges that vital Christianity can be restored at Sardis even though the initial diagnosis is poor; but he states that this will not be achieved without substantial effort on the community's part.

The command for watchfulness is accompanied by the command to

'remember…what you received and heard' (3.3). If the Christians in
Sardis refuse to do this, Christ says he will come to them like a thief
when they do not expect him. 'What you received and heard' refers to
the original evangelization of Sardis. John's words suggest that this had
been accompanied by teaching about the need for high social boundaries which the church had subsequently forgotten. The saying about
the thief derives from the tradition of the sayings of Jesus (Mt. 24.43)
and is found throughout the New Testament (e.g. 1 Thess. 5.2). It is
given a new shade of meaning here (characteristically in the Apocalypse) through the sinister implication that Christ will steal in to judge
the church in question. Those who refuse to repent will be punished by
Christ, despite the fact that they are Christians.

3.4 offers a partial qualification of this gloomy portrait. John says that
some in Sardis have not 'soiled their clothes'. These will walk with
Christ and dress in white for they are worthy. The author compares
ethical misdemeanours to dirty clothes in this passage (cf. 7.14; Jude
23). The colour white symbolizes purity, hence its frequent use in the
Apocalypse (cf. 2.17). There is a tradition in some texts that the resurrected righteous will resemble angels (cf. Dan. 12.1-3; *Asc. Isa.* 9).
Angels are often portrayed as clad in white garments in Jewish literature
(Dan. 10.5-6). It is not certain whether John's language here is purely
metaphorical or anticipates the resurrection but probably neither shade
of meaning should be entirely excluded from the passage. There is no
precise Jewish or Christian description of the resurrection from this
period (as may perhaps be understood). The eschatology of the Apocalypse is no exception to this.

3.5 tends towards the resurrectional interpretation of this passage. It
repeats the promise of white robes as if to emphasize it to a community
of renegades. John says that those who conquer will be clad in white
and have their names retained in the 'book of life'. This 'book' is a
reference to the heavenly ledgers that are familiar from other apocalyptic literature (e.g. *Asc. Isa.* 9.19-23). The idea derives ultimately from
Exod. 32.32-33 where Moses mentions a book that God had written and
which contains the names of righteous Israelites. In Revelation the
'book of life' contains the names of the followers of Jesus. Those who
refuse to repent will be blotted out of this book and miss the blessings
of the eschatological age. This ethical dualism, with its eschatological
basis, is further expressed by the promise that Christ will confess the
name of his faithful ones 'before my Father and before his angels' (3.5b).
This alludes to the saying about the Son of Man in Mt. 10.32 and shows a
further aspect of Christ's role as 'witness'. Christ says he will acknowledge those whose names are written in his book at the eschatological
assize. This understanding is close in meaning to the presentation of
Christ as the 'advocate' in 1 Jn 2.2 (cf. the similar language that is used
about the Holy Spirit in Jn 14-16).

Philadelphia

3.7 introduces the letter to the church at Philadelphia. Philadelphia lay on the southern side of the Cogamis valley. The city celebrated games in honour of Zeus-Helios and Anaeitis. It was struck by, but quickly recovered from, a disastrous earthquake in 17 CE. The difficulty for Christians in Philadelphia came from the Jews. The Jews were still causing trouble for the Christians when Ignatius wrote to Philadelphia more than a decade later (see Ignatius, *Phil.* 6). John's Philadelphian letter is often compared with his Smyrnaean letter as addressing a church that is singled out for praise. It opens with a poetic passage that explains the power of the heavenly Christ. Christ is said to be 'the holy one, the true one' (cf. Isa. 43.15) and to hold the key of David which no one can resist. The source for 'the key of David' is Isa. 22.22 which John understands messianically. In a context where Jews are causing trouble for Christians, Jesus is purposefully presented as Messiah. The 'opening and shutting' indicates Christ's ability to control entrance to his future kingdom. This phrase sounds a note of obvious foreboding in its negative aspect. The implications of this will be developed throughout the Apocalypse.

Christ says that he knows the works of the Philadelphian church (3.8). He sets before them an open door which no one can shut. This means that the Christians, although debarred by the Jews, cannot be debarred from God's kingdom if they remain faithful. The 'little power' of the Philadelphians has not prevented them maintaining high social boundaries. The phrase reveals their resilience. In 3.9 the phrases 'the synagogue of Satan' and 'those who say that they are Jews and are not, but are lying' recall John's earlier criticism of opponents. They denote a pattern of behaviour and not primarily an ethnic or religious identity.

3.9b reverses the status of the participants in this drama. Those who now gain much from social contact will be subjected to those who abstain from it: 'I will make them come and bow down before your feet.' This passage once again anticipates the eschatological supremacy of the people of God and strikingly casts the 'false Jews' in the subordinate role that Judaism reserved for the Gentiles. This identification is not developed here but it does provide a precedent for the more hostile picture of Judaism that we find in some second-century literature, not least the literature of Gnosticism.

Commentators sometimes suggest that the problem in Philadelphia was that the Christians were being excluded from the synagogue, but this is to impose (only) one interpretation of the Fourth Gospel on the Apocalypse in the absence of internal evidence for that identification. The description of the Jews as 'the synagogue of Satan' does imply that a formal breach between Judaism and Christianity has taken place but the comment is mainly symbolic and not necessarily an allegory of recent events. John here casts the faithful Christian in the role of the 'true Jew' and presents Christians opposed to his position as 'the synagogue of Satan' and the 'false Jew'. The language permits more then one interpretation. Sensitive exegesis will not rule out any of the likely possibilities.

3.10 alludes once again to the tradition of impending judgment and states that faithful Christians will be spared the 'hour of trial'. The notion of impending world struggle features in both Jewish and Christian apocalyptic literature (e.g. Dan. 11.2-45; *Asc. Isa.* 4). 3.11 predicts the return of Christ and combines it with a further call for perseverance. A non-specific eschatological prophecy (exemplified here by the 'soon' and the absence of a definite date) can never lose its currency. In the light of this hope, John asks his readers to maintain their distinctiveness in order to win the 'crown'. This denotes the eschatological future that is described in the rest of the Apocalypse.

3.12 promises further eschatological reward. Christ says that the person who 'conquers' will be made a 'pillar' in the temple of God. Christ adds that he will write on them the name of his God, the name of the new Jerusalem that comes down from heaven and his own new name. This passage alludes to the mystical names that will be revealed to the Christians in the eschatological age. It is clear that something more than the baptismal 'naming' is intended. These names are mystical names that can only be revealed at the end of human history. They imply an interest in mystical knowledge of which, as I said, we can now reconstruct merely the barest glimpses.

Laodicea

3.14 introduces the seventh and final letter to the church in Laodicea. The Laodicea in question is situated in the Lycus valley some ten miles from Colossae. It was a commercial and administrative centre that benefited from a good network of roads which provided ease of access and communication. In the Roman period Laodicea was the wealthiest city in Asia. Its wool and medical school were famous features of the region. Laodicea had a large Jewish community but this is (surprisingly) not mentioned in Revelation. The church in Laodicea was probably founded during Paul's third missionary journey (see Acts 19.10).

Laodicea is criticized for its lukewarmness (3.15). Several commentators note the presence of warm springs in nearby Hierapolis, but the primary focus of this reference is rhetorical and not merely antiquarian or topographical. John criticizes the church for its willingness to blow hot and cold according to circumstances. Because the church is lukewarm, Christ says, he will spew it out of his mouth (3.16). This vivid image symbolizes the humiliating rejection of a people who are neither one thing nor the other. The Laodicean church is criticized especially for its arrogance (3.17). It thinks it is rich and prosperous but it is in fact poor, blind and naked. The Laodiceans' blindness lies particularly in the fact that they are unable to perceive the true nature of their condition. This is presumably because many church members were willing to engage in the kind of integration that John deems wrong.

In 3.18 the imagery of 3.17 is developed in riposte. Christ advises the Laodiceans to buy from him gold, white garments and salve to anoint their eyes. The notion of buying was suggested by Isa. 55.1. The artefacts mentioned here contrast with the condition described by 3.17. 'Gold' incorporates elements from the description of Christ in Rev. 1.12-16; 'white' from that passage and from the garments of the worthy in 3.4. The implication is that only Christ can heal the condition John diagnoses. This is a way of saying that the Laodiceans must do what John requires if their cure is to prove effective.

In 3.19 the letter moves towards its conclusion. Ramsay (*Letters*, pp. 318-19) sees 3.19-22 as the conclusion to *all* the letters and not just the Laodicean letter. This seems a plausible view, especially if the churches addressed have representative significance. Christ says that he reproves and disciplines those whom he loves. This is said about God in other Jewish literature (see Prov. 3.11-12; *Pss. Sol.* 10.1-3; Heb. 12.5-6) so that Christ is here shown to be discharging a divine task. This statement is combined with a further exhortation to repent.

3.20 is a much-quoted verse. Despite its frequent use in Christian evangelism, it is addressed to Christian readers and not to people outside the church. Christ says that he stands at the door and knocks. If the door is opened, he will come in for dinner. This image has a particular force given the setting of the Apocalypse in a situation where the question of dinner-parties was a particular problem. John states that when Christians gather, Christ himself joins them. This more than compensates for the required absence of Christians at pagan banquets by saying that they entertain the most important guest at their *agapes*. Their gathering for the common meal is thus not inferior to the pagan dinners which seemed more tempting. Revelation 3.20 is a vivid assertion of the *agape*'s true significance.

3.21 returns to the theme of 'conquering' in summary of the letters. It sets the tone for what follows in the Apocalypse. Christ says that those who conquer will have a place on his throne just as he himself has conquered and sat down on the throne of his Father. 'Enthronement' symbolizes future victory which the author understands as the earthly reign of Christ and the recreation of heaven and earth (chs. 20–22). We should not suppose that this verse makes a literal prediction of future heavenly enthronement for the righteous. The language is symbolic and does nothing to contradict the hope for the *earthly* reign of the saints which is a prominent feature of the Apocalypse (see esp. 20.4). Other enthronement passages in Jewish literature provide the source for this saying: Moses in Ezekiel the Tragedian's *Exagoge* and the description of the Son of Man-Elect One in the *Similitudes of Enoch* (*1 En.* 37-71) are examples of this. John is possibly thinking also of the saying of Jesus in Mt. 19.28 that the Twelve will occupy thrones in the eschatological age and judge the tribes of Israel. There is a good parallel for this passage in *1 En.* 51.2-3:

> And he shall choose the righteous and the holy ones from among (the risen dead), for the day when they shall be selected and saved has arrived. In those days, (the Elect One) shall sit on my throne, and from the conscience of his mouth shall come out all the secrets of wisdom, for the Lord of the Spirits has given them to him and glorified him.

The thought is of a future and earthly transformation, including the hope for resurrection, in which the righteous surround the Messiah on his throne.

This verse clearly identifies Jesus with the throne of God. That is an important exegetical insight with which to approach 5.6 where scholars are divided in their exegesis as to whether or not the Lamb occupies the throne of God. It seems indisputable that he does so in 3.21. The letters close by promising future victory for the faithful and by emphasizing the truth of John's promise in what has almost become the refrain of the letters: 'Let anyone who has an ear listen to what the Spirit is saying to the churches...'

In Retrospect

The letters have an important function in the Apocalypse. They introduce the reader to John's special language and explain, both in symbol and explicitly, the problem that the Apocalypse addresses. I have argued that this situation is given by the references to (fornication and) meat-eating in 2.14, 20.

My reading of the letters takes the view that the seven churches have representative significance and that the material gains its effect from its symbolism with the occasionally clear punctuation. It would be wrong to look either for precisely described situations or even, I think, for substantially different situations in the churches addressed. The symbolism is allusive. John thinks in typical categories. This means that we must take special note of those places where the symbolism parts to reveal explicit criticism. I have identified 2.14, 20 as the places where this is found.

The letters set the scene for everything that follows in the Apocalypse. They set the terms for John's dualism and explain that this has both ethical and eschatological implications. John says that those who will not do what he asks are a 'synagogue of Satan' (2.9; 3.9). Such people ally themselves with the dragon and the beast who appear later in the Apocalypse. They will follow their masters into the lake of fire (22.15). By contrast, the Christian eschatological hope is presented as the promised destiny of the faithful. Readers are reminded of what they know already to recall them to a stricter pattern of behaviour. They must be wary of full integration with the urban social world. Once we recognize that the eschatology undergirds the ethical appeal, we can understand the entire message of the Apocalypse. In a sense, everything that follows in the text is commentary. It is no doubt encouraging to remember that those who understand the (relatively simple) message of the letters already understand the (much more complex) contents of the Apocalypse proper, to which we now turn.

Revelation 4 and 5

Chapters 4 and 5 also belong together. They move the readers' attention from earth, where the seven churches are located, to heaven through the description of John's ascension with which the Apocalypse proper begins (4.1). The shift from earth to heaven is a significant one in terms of John's apocalyptic outlook. The heavenly world is the location of the throne of God and the place where the secrets of the universe are stored. The rest of the Apocalypse describes a sequence of visions which John receives by means of revelation from heaven. As in other apocalypses (notably *1 En*. 14), John's vision of the throne of God (chs. 4-5) is presented as the first and most important aspect of the heavenly mysteries that are revealed in this way.

This section draws extensively on the Jewish theophanic tradition. Meditation on the biblical theophanies possibly even helped to *induce* a mystical experience of this kind. It would be foolish to discount this possibility even if in practice the point cannot be proved. John introduces some new elements into the theophanic tradition, notably his reference to the Lamb and the worship of the heavenly Christ which are clearly Christian features. The liturgical elements in this section (and elsewhere in the Apocalypse) do not necessarily reflect the actual worship of the churches addressed but they do represent John's creative attempt to describe the heavenly liturgy. At critical places, the heavenly chorus discloses the truth about the readers' situation and gives an authoritative perspective on it. This function is used to great effect in the seer's vision of the throne of God where the chorus sings that God and the Lamb are invincible.

The Throne of God

John's vision of the heavenly throne-room begins with a reference to the door which he sees open in heaven (4.1). This conventional theme (cf. *1 En*. 14.15) emphasizes the esoteric nature of the revelation through the suggestion that the seer has pierced the vault of heaven. The phrase 'I saw' is used elsewhere in Christian literature to describe apocalyptic experience (Mk 1.10; Acts 7.55). It denotes especially visionary experience (Revelation is strong on visual symbolism). The phrase has a background in Jewish apocalyptic literature (see Dan. 7.2).

Through the open door John hears the voice that addressed him at the beginning of the Apocalypse (4.1). This is the voice of the heavenly Christ (1.12). Christ instructs the seer to pass through the open door to learn 'what must take place after this'. Heavenly ascension is described a number of ways in apocalyptic literature. Here, John is invited to step through the door himself. He has already entered a trance in 1.17. In other texts, especially those with a more complicated cosmology, the seer is accompanied by an angel guide (e.g. *2 Enoch*; the *Apocalypse of Abraham*; the *Ascension of Isaiah*). The statement that John will learn 'what must take place after this' shows the essentially eschatological nature of the revealed mysteries in the New Testament Apocalypse.

In 4.2 John finds himself in heaven. The statement that he is 'in the Spirit' confirms he is in a trance. The first thing that John sees in heaven is a throne. This is the *merkabah*, the throne-chariot of God. The *merkabah* features in earlier Jewish visions of God (see Ezek. 1; 1 Kgs 22.19; Isa. 6.1-4; and Dan. 7.9-14). Ezekiel 1 and Daniel 7 both describe God in anthropomorphic form (as if he resembles a human being). The author of Revelation is reluctant to describe the form of God (cf. *Apoc. Abr.* 16.3) but elsewhere he describes the heavenly Christ (e.g. 1.12-16) as if to compensate for this reserve. In one strand of Johannine Christology the Son is presented as the visible aspect of God (Jn 14.9; cf. Jn 6.46). The Christology of the Apocalypse seems related to this conviction. All such language reflects the binitarian convictions that sustained early Christianity.

4.3 offers a short and unornate description of God. The language is heavily qualified. God is said to resemble 'jasper and carnelian'. The throne is surrounded by a rainbow that looks like an emerald (cf. Ezek. 1.26-28). The seer's reluctance to describe the form of God leads him to describe God by analogy with precious stones. Commentators often point to Ps. 104.2 (which says that God wraps himself with 'light as with a garment') to explain the basis of this passage, but the identification of the stones remains uncertain. Sardis was a red stone; jasper may have been translucent rock crystal. Emerald is of course green. If so, this means that the stones contain the principal colours of the rainbow. These colours are mentioned together in Jewish (Ezek. 28.13) and classical literature (see Plato, *Phaed.* 110e) so that John employs a familiar combination. The description of the primal person in Ezekiel 28 may have contributed more to this passage than some commentators are prepared to acknowledge.

It would be wrong to treat this colourful description as an allegory of the different facets of God's character. That would detract from its mystical impact which resembles a kaleidoscope and not a telescope. The passage demonstrates John's mystical imagination. It is not an early philosophical theology. It is nevertheless true that we find here an early version of what would come to be known as the 'analogical argument'. The Apocalypse embodies the recognition that, since God cannot be fully described in human language, he must be described by analogy with entities that are known to human beings. Earlier apocalyptists (e.g.

the author of *1 En.* 14) are more willing than John to describe the form of God. John's reserve is to be explained with reference to the growing understanding of divine transcendence in the first century CE and also to his conviction that the vision of Christ (ch. 1) is itself the vision of a divine being.

Around the throne of God sit 24 elders (4.4). These elders are clad in white and wear golden crowns. Some commentators see the elders as an editorial insertion but they appear later in Revelation (e.g. 7.11) and clearly belong in the Apocalypse. Their white dress means that they resemble angels. Their human form and crown distinguishes them from the angels. The elders to this degree transcend the angels through their connection with the human world. The presentation may thus be called an 'angelomorphic' one according to the definition of this term that I offered in the Introduction. Some apocalypses describe the transformation of exceptional humans into angel mediators (e.g. *1 En.* 71.14); but John has no such description, and this view is not obviously intended in the Apocalypse. The elders are symbols of faithful Christians. They are modelled on the 24 heads of the priestly families in 1 Chron. 24.4-6. They are priestly figures just as Christians are called to be 'priests' in the Apocalypse (see 1.6; 5.10 and 20.6). Their enthronement symbolizes the future victory of the people of God.

As with 3.21, however, we should not assume that the elders symbolize a future *heavenly* destiny for the faithful. This view finds no support in the Apocalypse. John expects the kingdom of Christ to be an earthly one (20.4) and that it will be followed by the recreation of heaven and earth in which the barrier between the two different realms is removed (ch. 21). The elders symbolize by their enthronement in heaven what will prove to be true at some future point for the faithful on earth. This is that those who conquer—which for John is linked to ethical strictness—will enjoy the Messiah's kingdom when the priestly people of God comes into its own.

From the throne issues lightning and thunder (4.5). Before it burn seven torches of fire which are the seven spirits of God (cf. 1.20). This description of the throne has a traditional nature and it initially represents what any Jewish reader would expect to find in a theophany. There is an echo here of Ezek. 1.13 (cf. *Jub.* 2.2) where fire burns in the middle of the living creatures. The author of Revelation takes up this tradition and modifies it by the inclusion of the number seven. This, too, derives from earlier literature (Zech. 4; Tob. 3.16-17).

Before the throne stands a sea of glass that resembles crystal (4.6). Two Hebrew Bible passages have resourced this description. Ezekiel 1.22 says that over the heads of the cherubim stands 'something like a dome, shining like crystal'. Also relevant is the statement of Exod. 24.10 that a sapphire pavement undergirds the throne of God. It is difficult to resist the conclusion that the primary reference in Rev. 4.6 is to the sky which features in much apocalyptic literature as the entity that divides the heaven(s) from the earth. Such a reference is important hermeneutically because apocalyptic literature promises to disclose what stands above the sky—what is ordinarily inaccessible to the human understanding. It is possible, given the complex nature of John's imagery, that other shades of meaning can be found in this reference to the crystal sea. Of the interpretations that have been proposed, a reference to the sea of chaos seems the most plausible. This features extensively in Mesopotamian mythology (cf. also *2 En.* 3.3) and would signify that God restores harmony from disorder. This is a prominent theme in the Apocalypse (see esp. chs. 21–22). But the primary meaning is surely the sky, on which God's throne is said to rest.

In 4.6b John describes the four living creatures who attend the throne of God. In the logic of his vision, the creatures surround the chariot (one perhaps at each corner) and the elders and angel-spirits stand before it. These creatures have been developed from Ezekiel's throne-theophany where four such beings are mentioned (Ezek. 1.4-13). There are some important differences from Ezekiel's theophany. One such difference is the fact that eyes are assigned to the creatures in the Apocalypse but to the wheels of the throne-chariot in Ezekiel's vision. Another is the fact that only one creature in Rev. 4.7 has a face. Sweet cites the evidence of the (late) *Midrash Shemoth R.* 23 to explain this passage: 'Man is exalted among creatures, the eagle among birds, the ox among domestic animals, the lion among wild beasts...Yet they are stationed below the chariot of the Holy One' (*Revelation*, p. 120). The creatures symbolize the whole of creation; their subordination to God reflects his transcendence of it. Their ever-present eyes are a picture of divine omniscience. The attempt that Irenaeus made in the second century to identify these creatures with the four Evangelists (*Adv. Haer.* 3.11.11) is inventive but must be regarded as fanciful.

That the creatures have wings (4.8) again has foundations in Ezekiel and should occasion no more surprise than any other detail of the theophany. Their *six* wings embodies a detail from Isa. 6.1-4; John draws on more than one passage to construct his theophany. The creatures offer the heavenly liturgy: 'Holy, holy, Holy, the Lord God Almighty, who was and is and is to come.' The threefold 'Holy' comes from Isa. 6.3 (liturgists often call it the 'Trisagion'; it has trinitarian overtones). The rest of the acclamation is composed by John and repeats convictions that are expressed earlier in the Apocalypse (e.g. 1.4). John's disclosure of the heavenly liturgy is a natural concomitant to his vision of the throne of God. This is an audition as well as a vision. This liturgical passage is exclusively monotheistic and it makes no reference to the heavenly Christ. The liturgy becomes binitarian in ch. 5, but only once the sovereignty of God has been established.

In 4.9-11 the elders join the heavenly liturgy. Their language is formal (as is their prostration which is mentioned in 4.10). It reflects ancient kingship ritual. This scene impacts on the readers because it is so visually different from the normal worship routines of the churches addressed. It encourages them to think in different terms, in line with John's ethical admonitions. 4.11 preserves the liturgy that is uttered in this context. The language again reflects elements of the imperial court, possibly the 'Lord and God' title which was addressed by sycophants like Martial to Domitian (see Suetonius, *Dom.* 13). In a context where some Christians are tempted to compromise with pagan standards, even with the conventions of pagan worship, John reminds his readers that the God of Israel alone is truly 'Lord and God' and that he uniquely deserves 'glory and honour and power'. The difference between the Jewish God and the pagan deities is that (only) the former created the physical universe (4.11). It is implied again by this assertion, in the spirit of Hebrew literature (e.g. Pss. 115.4; 135.15), that idols have no real existence. Revelation 4.11 is an important early Christian statement of belief about creation. It asserts that God created the world and implies that he sustains it through his will. But there is no reference here to the idea of creation *ex nihilo* which Christian theology came to adopt in the patristic period and thereafter.

Behold, the Lamb of God!

Chapter 5 develops this (essentially Jewish) vision of God with material about the Lamb who shares the divine glory. The worship of Jesus marked a substantial difference between early Christianity and the devotional practices of Judaism. This difference is well exemplified in Revelation 5. This chapter describes the vision and worship of a *second divine being*. God is an enthroned deity. The Lamb is next to him (see below on 5.6). Both receive the worship of the creation (5.13), God as creator (4.11) and the Lamb on the grounds that he has 'ransomed for God saints from every tribe...' (5.9). The author of Revelation was not the first Christian to speak about Christ in this way. The view that Jesus is a divine being, entitled to worship, is found in one of the earliest christological confessions that we have: 'every tongue should confess that Jesus Christ is Lord, to the glory of God the Father' (Phil. 2.11; cf. 1 Cor. 8.6). We can only now ponder what prehistory the material in chs. 4 and 5 enjoyed before its inclusion in the Apocalypse. It seems unlikely that John composed this material in a single sitting. It may well have a complex history of development.

5.1 allows the prophet to see the hand of God. God's hand holds a scroll which is written on both sides and has seven seals. There is a manuscript problem at this point. Some manuscripts have the words 'written on the inside, and sealed on the back'. This reflects the Latin *diploma* or sealed document. But the reference to writing on both sides is probably the original form of words. The image of the proffered scroll embodies the assertion, associated with the notion of creation, that everything is known to God and rests within his will and control. This scroll has sometimes been identified with the Torah but that identification is by no means obvious. It is an apocalyptic symbol which contains the disasters that follow. The scroll provides a transition to the next part of the Apocalypse where the Lamb opens the seals to reveal a sequence of events.

An angel asks a rhetorical question (5.2): 'Who is worthy to open the scroll ánd break its seals?' The impression is that no angel is equal to this task, not even the 'mighty angel' who is mentioned here (5.3). This shows that knowledge of the human world is a divine prerogative. No one in heaven, earth or hell can open or read the scroll. The seer weeps because no one can do this (5.4). This rhetorical question replaces the dialogue between the seer and the angel which occurs in other apocalypses.

The seer's weeping, with its dramatic effect, is short lived. One of the elders proclaims that the 'Lion of the tribe of Judah, the Root of David, has conquered, so that he can open the scroll and its seven seals' (5.5). This Lion is the heavenly Christ. His title has messianic connotations. In Gen. 49.9 Judah is called 'a lion's whelp'. Genesis 49.9 was interpreted messianically in the post-biblical period as we know from *T. Jud.* 24.5 and other passages. The title 'Root of David' reflects the influence of Isa. 11.1 (cf. Rom. 15.12) which describes the Messiah's Davidic descent. Revelation 5.5 thus uses two messianic titles to say that the Christian Saviour can open the scroll because he has 'conquered'. His 'conquering' (like the 'victory' motif in the Fourth Gospel) is an allusion to the cross as the 'Lamb' imagery makes clear. The victory was won on earth. Its authoritative interpretation is now promulgated in heaven. It is implied that the *full effects* of the victory will be disclosed at some future point on earth. The unswerving witness of the Lamb is made the pattern of behaviour that the readers must adopt.

There is a powerful subversion of reality here, as throughout the Apocalypse. The death of Jesus posed a problem for the early Christians because Jesus had been executed as a criminal by the Romans. Crucifixion offended the Jews because it infringed the Deuteronomistic prohibition against exhibiting the bodies of those who had been executed by stoning (see Deut. 21.23 and Gal. 3.13). It reinforced for pagans the seeming strangeness of the Christian religion with its claims for the divinity of a would-be insurrectionary whom the authorities had executed. The Christians responded by turning this criticism on its head. Paul told the Corinthians that what seemed like folly was in fact the wisdom of God (1 Cor. 1.18-25). The deutero-Pauline author of Col. 2.15 says that even on the cross God in Christ had robbed the 'rulers and authorities' (i.e. cosmic spirits) of their power. Similarly, the author of

Revelation calls the cross an act of victory through his 'conquering' terminology. This understanding of the death of Jesus explains why the Apocalypse contains so many allusions to martyrdom when it comes from a situation where martyrdom was not a significant factor. The imagery reminds readers to maintain high social boundaries through the stark image of the suffering Christ. The bitterness of the death of Jesus is allowed to exercise a full rhetorical appeal.

The portrayal of Christ as a 'lamb' is found both in Johannine (Jn 1.29, 36) and in other New Testament literature (Acts 8.32; 1 Cor. 5.7; 1 Pet. 1.19). In this context, the reader thinks immediately of the sacrificial lamb, for John the Apocalyptist's Lamb stands 'as if it had been slaughtered' (5.6). Commentators note a number of Hebrew Bible analogies, not least Isa. 53.7 ('like a lamb that is led to the slaughter'). Lamb imagery features in post-biblical literature too (*1 En.* 90.9; cf. *T. Jos.* 19.8). John's imagery is sufficiently imprecise to let readers form a variety of mental associations concerning this image. The shift from the lion to the lamb is striking. It prompts readers to think about the status of the Messiah who is described in this way. The fact that the Lamb has 'seven horns' (cf. *1 En.* 90.9) indicates his almighty power which is the power of God himself (cf. 4.5).

5.6 contains a significant problem of translation. Does the Lamb stand in the *middle* of the throne or *between* the throne and the 24 elders? The Greek has been taken to support both views. The NEB preserves the first translation ('standing in the very middle of the throne') which is suggested also by 3.21. There is a background to such Christology in Jewish apocalyptic literature, especially in the *Similitudes of Enoch* (*1 En.* 37-71) where the Son of Man-Elect One is seated on the throne of God. On the other hand, early Christian literature generally gives Jesus his *own* throne in heaven on the grounds that he is a second divine being (see 1 Pet. 3.22; *Asc. Isa.* 11.32-33). The problem is a finely balanced one which should probably be answered internally through the evidence of 3.21 where the Lamb does occupy the throne of God (and for which the *Similitudes* provide Jewish corroboration). Even if this translation is rejected, however, the passage asserts that the Lamb stands nearer the throne than do the 24 elders. This is a visual demonstration of the Lamb's close affinity to God—his divinity—which will now be affirmed through his reception of universal worship.

The Lamb takes the scroll from the right hand of God (5.7). The elders and throne-creatures prostrate themselves before him in worship (5.8a). They hold a harp and bowls of incense (5.8b). The latter is called 'the prayers of the saints'. The harp appears in the Psalms (e.g. Ps. 33.2). Incense was used in the temple ritual. The incense either represents or accompanies the prayers of the saints (probably the latter). The notion that the angels present the prayers of the righteous before God derives from post-biblical Judaism (see Tob. 12.15; cf. *3 Bar.* 11). This function is here attributed to the elders.

John describes the 'new song' sung by the elders (5.9-10). They sing that the Lamb is worthy to open the scroll because he has been slain and ransomed people for God from every 'tribe and language and people and nation'. The opening words ('you are worthy') provide a form of parallelism with the worship of God in 4.11. They designedly present the heavenly Christ in the same terms as God. The concept of a 'new song' derives from the Psalter (e.g. Ps. 33.3) but the adjective has a Christian connotation. This song is 'new' because it describes the triumph of the Lamb which has made possible the state of being 'ransomed' for God. That is how John understands the constitution of the church (5.9).

John does not say *how* the Lamb's death has achieved this effect, only *that* this has happened. Jesus' death, including the shedding of his blood (see above on 1.5b-6), has given the Christians a new status (cf. 2 Cor. 5.17). This status is described in 5.10 as being that of 'a kingdom and priests serving our God'. 'Ransoming' as a metaphor comes from the slave market. It signifies acquisition by a new master. The new master is God (cf. 1 Cor. 6.20). John presents Christ as the agent and price of the ransoming, as does the author of Hebrews with his identification of the priest and the victim (Heb. 9.12). That the redeemed come from every 'tribe and language and people and nation' emphasizes the cosmopolitan nature of the Christian religion which cut across social divisions and attracted people of different backgrounds. It is said that 'they will reign on earth', as they do at the conclusion of the Apocalypse (20.4).

John hears the angels' chorus (5.11-14). The almost indescribable number of angels (5.11) agrees with information about them in other apocalyptic literature (e.g. *1 En.* 14.22). The angels sing that the Lamb is worthy to receive 'power and wealth and wisdom and might and honor and glory and blessing!' It would be fruitless to distinguish between these nouns. They all designate the universal authority of the Lamb which is related to the fact of his vindication through slaughter. From this belief stems the peculiar status of Christians redeemed as a priesthood who must demonstrate their sanctity in their behaviour. At the close of ch. 5, all the inhabitants of the earth and the underworld join the chorus which now has a binitarian focus, singing, 'To the one seated on the throne and to the Lamb be blessing and honour and glory and might, for ever and ever!' (cf. Phil. 2.9-11). The creatures add the 'Amen!' to this song to emphasize their assent. The elders fall down and worship so that the scene ends with prostration, calling to mind once again the ritual of the royal court.

In Retrospect Again

We should ask about the function of chs. 4-5 in the Apocalypse. Chapter 1 introduces the Apocalypse. Chapters 2-3 introduce the readers to the seer's special pattern of language and identify the problem that the text is going to address. Chapters 4 and 5 follow on from this scene-setting. Their function is to provide authentication for the sequence of visions which begins in ch. 6 and thus to authenticate the rest of the Apocalypse. That John sees the throne of God, following his commission by Christ, is a rhetorical assertion that what he says is true and comes direct from God. That the Lamb will open the seals shows that the future is under God's control. The almost incidental comment 'they will reign on earth' (5.10) turns out to be rhetorically significant as the Apocalypse unfolds. John anticipates the eschatological future which *only* the faithful will share with Christ on earth. Chapters 4-5 thus demonstrate John's authority as an apocalyptist which is related to his commission by Christ and his vision of the heavenly mysteries.

Revelation 6

Chapters 6 to 8 describe what happens when the seals of the scroll are opened. Chapter 6 narrates the opening of the first six seals. We must wait until 8.1 to see what the seventh seal discloses. Chapter 7 is an interlude in this wider section that describes the sealing of the servants of God. In the meanwhile, ch. 6 has some surprises.

John's language is pictorial. We should no more expect to find here a literal description of the end than in any other part of the Apocalypse. But this is not to say that the symbols are entirely distant from the situation that John addresses, or that the material lacks a practical application. This part of the Apocalypse describes the judgment which awaits those who do not do what God requires. The symbolism makes a clear distinction between the followers of Christ and all other people. This leaves readers in no doubt about the clear-cut choice that they must make in terms of their social behaviour.

The strength of John's symbolism lies in its starkness. Its sharp focus makes the readers consider the meaning of the different symbols employed. This encourages them to create a mental link between the symbolic world of the Apocalypse and their own situation. To this extent the meaning of the symbols lies in the reader's response to them. The dissonance between the two world-views (John's mythological world and the readers' actual world) allows the criticism of the latter through what happens in the former. It is inevitable that readers' minds should wander from one world to the other. That the symbols are so bizarre is an aid and not a hindrance to understanding.

The theme of chs. 6 to 8 is the wrath and judgment of God. This is introduced very forcefully in 6.1-2 as the white horse gallops onto the stage when the first seal is opened. He is the first of four horses and horsemen in the Apocalypse. The scene as a whole is modelled on Zech. 1.8; 6.1-8. The four forms of destruction derive from Ezek. 14.21. The drama is carefully staged. The horse is *permitted* to enter by the heavenly voice (6.1). He does not enter of his own accord. 'A crown was given to him, and he came out conquering and to conquer' (6.2). This reference to 'conquering' shows that the horseman is a servant of God. It is not said in more detail what 'conquering' involves and what the first horseman conquers. We are not shown the world as it is but given a picture of the world as it stands under God's judgment. Into this picture readers must insert their own understanding of their situation. This reacts with the imagery that the seer constructs for them.

The first horse's white colour led patristic commentators (e.g.

Victorinus) to identify its rider with Christ. There are obvious reasons for rejecting this interpretation. It is difficult to see how Christ can be a character in the story when he himself opens the seals and stands, so to speak, behind and not within the action. This horseman is an agent of divine destruction like his fellows who appear next.

6.3 describes the opening of the second seal. The second living creature calls 'Come!' A bright-red horse appears. Its rider is permitted (sc. by God) to take peace from the earth so that men begin to kill each other. The red colour symbolizes blood for this reason. To emphasize his power of destruction, this horseman is given a sword. Again, the thought is that God permits the destruction and that the horseman is the agent and not the source of the destruction. The fact that judgment happens (only) on the opening of the seal shows its essentially determinate nature.

On the opening of the third seal (and the words of the third creature) a black horse enters the arena (6.5-6). Its rider holds a balance. A voice from among the creatures pronounces the words, 'A quart of wheat for a day's pay, and three quarts of barley for a day's pay; but do not damage the olive oil and the wine!' The reference to scales and inflation show that famine is expected (cf. Mt. 24.8). Famine was the scourge of the ancient world. It was exacerbated by the agrarian nature of the ancient economy. To judge from information provided by Cicero (*Verr.* 3.81), the price for these commodities was ten times what it should have been given that a denarius was the daily wage for a workman. Commentators note that oil and wine have deeper roots than corn and survive when corn fails, but John's interest is more symbolic than horticulturally precise. 'Oil and wine' are symbols of the messianic age in Jewish literature (see Jer. 31.12; Hos. 2.22; Joel 2.24). The command not to harm them shows that the blessings of the eschatological age are preserved by God even though he permits the destruction.

The opening of the fourth seal produces a pale horse whose rider is Death (6.7-8). Death is followed closely by Hades. Death and Hades are given power over a quarter of the earth to kill by various forms of destruction ('sword, famine and pestilence, and by the wild animals of the earth'). The reference to 'a quarter' is limitative. It emphasizes the point that the destruction is controlled by God. 6.1-8 shows signs of careful construction. The notion of God's control is progressively reinforced as the different misfortunes are described. The four means of destruction are all commonly encountered features of ancient life. They have a biblical foundation and are set within the purposes of God.

The Martyrs

There is a profound change in tone in 6.9-10. After the opening of the fifth seal, John sees 'under the altar the souls of those who had been slaughtered for the word of God and for the testimony they had given' (6.9). The martyrs contrast with the horsemen. They are victims (but not passive victims) and not aggressors. Their presence in heaven is a sign of the messianic victory. The martyrs intrude into the portrait of destruction to set things in their true light. They show that the destruction is permitted by God and that those who wear white—which for John has ethical implications—will be kept safe by God.

The reference to 'souls' (6.9) suggests an anthropology in which the death of the human person allows the soul to ascend to heaven. There are superficial parallels for this in Platonic eschatology but the closest parallels are with Jewish views about martyrdom. Several texts indicate that resurrection or immortality is the reward for the martyrs (see, e.g., Dan. 12.1-2; *4 Ezra* 7.32; *Wis.* 5.15). Paul and Ignatius evidently shared this view (see Phil. 1.23; Ignatius, *Eph.* 12.2). This passage is a symbolic assertion that the martyrs are dear to God and that their deaths will be avenged. It uses the same imagery as the rabbinic text *b. Šab.* 152b ('the souls of the righteous are kept under the throne of glory') to explain that God preserves his faithful servants. Later in the Apocalypse, the martyrs are resurrected for the thousand-year reign on earth (20.4). The thought here is that they are kept safe in anticipation of that event.

In 6.10 the martyrs cry to God for vengeance ('how long will it be before you judge and avenge our blood?'). Some commentators dislike this notion of revenge and contrast it with the recorded words of Jesus (Lk. 23.34) and Stephen (Acts 7.60). Yet the idea of vindication is prominent in the Hebrew Bible (e.g. Ps. 79.10) and in post-biblical Judaism (see *1 En.* 47.2, 4; *4 Ezra* 4.35). It features in the Christian eschatological tradition in 2 Thess. 1.8-10 (quite strikingly so). The author of Revelation is doing nothing exceptional in attributing this request to the martyrs. More than anything else, their cry reflects the perceived injustice of their death. This provokes empathy in the readers and makes them consider why the martyrs died. It is implied that they died because they stood out against a God-opposing system and provoked the vengeance of that system by their refusal to acquiesce with it. This call for cognitive resistance will be made time and again in the Apocalypse, most notably in the symbolism of the Beast (ch. 13). Martyrdom for John is the ultimate act of commitment which illustrates the need for separate existence from the world. The martyrs are given a white robe and told to wait until their number is complete (6.11). The white robe demonstrates the need for separate standards *in nuce*.

Further Destruction

6.12-17 describes what happens when the Lamb opens the sixth seal. John sees a great earthquake. The sun becomes like sackcloth and the moon turns to blood. These are signs in the natural order that the last days have begun. Earthquakes are a feature of the Hebrew Bible (Amos 8.8; Joel 2.10) and the New Testament (Mt. 28.2). In 6.13 the stars fall like fruit from a tree (cf. Isa. 34.4). This calls to mind Jesus' cursing of the fig tree in the Synoptic Gospels (Mk 11.12-14 and par.; cf. Mt. 24.32-35). The sky is rolled up like a scroll and every mountain and island is removed from its position (6.14). This reference to the sky is an interesting one. Sweet mentions the possibility that it signifies the eschatological removal of the veil between God and man (*Revelation*, p. 145). With this we might compare the Pauline hope that God will be 'all in all' (1 Cor. 15.28), and again the thought-world of Hebrews (esp. Heb. 6.19-20; 10.19-20). Commentators observe that there is no parallel in apocalyptic literature for the second half of this verse (the removal of the mountains and the islands), but its thought may have been suggested by Nah. 1.5 or Jer. 4.24.

6.15-17 describes the effect that this activity has on the inhabitants of the earth. Led by the kings, the people run to the caves to take shelter from the destruction that has been unleashed upon them. The flight starts with the powerful because not even they can withstand the wrath of the Lamb. This passage is based on Isa. 2.20-21 which anticipates that people will hide themselves on the Day of the Lord. There is an important parallel in *1 En.* 62.3 where the enthroned mediator begins his judgment with the kings and mighty ones. In 6.16 people call to the rocks to fall on them to provide shelter from the face of God and the wrath of the Lamb (cf. Hos. 10.8). This is the first reference to the 'face' of God in the Apocalypse. This was not mentioned in ch. 4. It is in every sense an angry face. Behind this passage stands the fearful warning that 'you cannot see my face; for no one shall see me and live' (Exod. 33.20b). John has not seen the face of God himself but he knows that those who deserve divine vengeance will see it clearly enough. The 'wrath of the Lamb' in this passage signifies retribution and not just displeasure.

6.17 brings the chapter to a conclusion with a rhetorical question, 'Who is able to stand?' (cf. Mal. 3.2; Nah. 1.6). The breaking of the sixth seal reveals a time of horror for the world for which the first five seals have served merely as the preparation. The description of this misfortune gains a cumulative effect as the chapter gathers pace. John challenges the prevailing standards of the readers' society by showing that it falls under divine condemnation. His rejection of the world at large is particularly obvious in the shift from the fifth to the sixth seal. This juxtaposes the image of the martyrs in glory with the image of the kings in their terror. The message of the chapter is that only those who maintain a rigid separation, symbolized under the image of martyrdom, will escape the fate of the kings. The author uses the threat of judgment to make readers consider where they stand.

Revelation 7

Chapter 7 is an interlude between ch. 6 and the opening of the seventh seal in 8.1. The interlude reinforces John's call for separateness with a different image. John now describes the sealing of the people of God (notice the rebirth of imagery from ch. 6). This sealing is a symbolic demonstration of the need for separateness by which John again reminds his readers of what they should be doing. The implication is that separate religious identity requires distinctive behaviour among the people of God. Much of this material has a Jewish origin, not least the list of tribes in 7.5-8.

In 7.1 John sees four angels standing at the corners of the earth. They restrain the winds for a time, by implication under divine control. Apocalyptic literature often assigns natural phenomena to the supervision of the angels (see, e.g., *1 En.* 75.3). The thought is that the wind will be prevented from exercising a harmful effect until the servants of God have been sealed. Their sealing is the main theme of this chapter.

In 7.2 another angel ascends from the sun with the seal of the living God. He tells the angels not to 'damage the earth or the sea or the trees' until the servants of God have been sealed on their foreheads (7.3). There is a Hebrew Bible background for this passage in Ezek. 9.4 where the linen-clothed man is told to mark those who grieve over the abominations in Jerusalem. It also recalls the blood that was placed on the Israelite lintels at the time of the Exodus from Egypt (see Exod. 12.21-27). We can hardly ignore the possibility that the sealing also symbolizes baptism since Christians were signed with a 'T' at the moment of their initiation. Baptism, however, does not exhaust the meaning of this passage which suggests a special demarcation of the people of God in language that is familiar from biblical literature.

7.4-8 describes the number and the tribes of the sealed. The figure 144,000 prompts much discussion in the commentaries. It is clearly symbolic. Twelve was the number of the tribes of Israel (and the main disciples of Jesus). Numerical symbolism plays its part in this passage. The figure 12 is squared and then multiplied by a thousand in a calculation whose full significance remains obscure. Much light can be shed on this section by comparison with the Qumran *War Scroll* (1QM). The Qumran community were Jewish sectarians who inhabited a desert retreat on the shores of the Dead Sea between approximately the middle of the second century BCE and the First Jewish War against Rome (66-70 CE). They are often but not universally identified with the Essenes who are mentioned by Philo and Josephus. Their *War Scroll* describes the preparations for the final war between the Sons of Light and the Sons of Darkness in which the former are to prove victorious. Eschatological victory is the theme of Revelation 7. Comparison with the Qumran text suggests that the numbers specified by Rev. 7.4-8 are adult male warriors who constitute the Christian army that fights against the forces of Satan (see Bauckham, *Climax of Prophecy*, p. 217). In this case the number 1000 evidently designates an army division under the belief that each tribe will supply 12 such divisions. The language is symbolic but it probably implies the belief, inherited from Judaism, that the 12 tribes will be reconstituted in the eschatological age.

The force of this passage is that membership of the Christian church confers a separate status that must be demonstrated in people's behaviour. The military imagery gives this expectation added edge. Far from being comfortable, readers are reminded that they are engaged in a conflict. Chapter 7 is an apocalyptic vision of perfection that reveals the truth about what people should be in order to confront the truth of what they are at present. It is inconceivable that this vision of the elect people of God can be addressed to people who need no reminder about what they should be doing. The author provokes them to fresh thought and action through the juxtaposed images of chs. 6 and 7. 'Sealing' means election; election requires a different kind of life.

The list of tribes in ch. 7 is not without problems. It corresponds to no other known Jewish list. The inclusion of both Joseph and Manasseh is difficult. Judah is placed at the head of the list because this is the tribe from which Jesus came (cf. Heb. 7.14; Rev. 5.5). Dan is omitted and Manasseh perhaps included to compensate for this omission. Irenaeus preserves the tradition that Dan was omitted because Antichrist was supposed to come from that tribe (*Adv. Haer.* 5.30.2), but we have no way of telling whether this information was known to the author of the Apocalypse.

7.9 significantly adds the whole number of the Christian redeemed to these adult male warriors. John sees a great multitude that cannot be numbered. This multitude is taken from 'all tribes and people and languages'. It stands before the throne and the Lamb. The multitude is clad in white robes. People hold palm branches in their hands. The branches make it a victory procession. Palm branches are mentioned in the Maccabaean literature as a symbol of victory after war (see *1 Macc.* 13.51; *2 Macc.* 10.7). There is doubtless also an echo of the 'triumphal entry' of Jesus into Jerusalem (Mk 11.1-10 and par.). The major exegetical question that this passage raises is whether this multitude are identical with the 144,000 of 7.5-8 or different from them. This point probably did not trouble John's fertile mind as much as it troubles some of his commentators but the answer is surely that, if 7.5-8 refers to adult male warriors, 7.9 should be taken to designate the wider Christian body. These are innumerable and cosmopolitan like Abraham's promised descendants

(Gen. 17.4-5). In the logic of the chapter, this indicates that there is no restriction on the numbers who can be saved. Neither group is of course an allegory of divisions or parties in the readers' communities. The language insists that the final conflict is near and that the redeemed must stand their ground through careful attention to their behaviour. My interpretation of 7.9 finds no textual basis for the opinion of some sectarian groups that only a predetermined number will inherit the kingdom.

The innumerable multitude worship God and the Lamb (7.10). They sing, 'salvation belongs to our God who is seated on the throne, and to the Lamb' (7.9-10). The angels fall down in worship and sing a song. Its words resemble the liturgy of chs. 4-5 (7.11-12). The effect of this material is to insist that God's victory is assured and to imply that those who turn their backs on John's required lifestyle thereby place themselves outside the boundaries of salvation. The chorus pronounces the truth of the situation which the readers must apply as they see fit.

In 7.13-17 an elder asks John a question in order to supply the correct answer himself (other apocalypses describe the seer's dialogue with an angel). The elder asks John: 'Who are these, robed in white, and where have they come from?' (7.13). He tells John that 'these are they who have come out of the great ordeal; they have washed their robes and made them white in the blood of the Lamb' (7.14). If this reference to the 'great ordeal' signifies some kind of persecution, John has not made this obvious in the Apocalypse. His language is principally symbolic as the clash of imagery (red–white) indicates. The elder's reply *encourages* the readers to believe that they are engaged in a conflict which this reference to the 'great ordeal' suggests. The depiction of the conflict demands a distance from the world which is portrayed in hostile terms. It is implied that *only* those who undergo the conflict will share the rewards of the victory. This means we should consider the purpose of this passage as 'consciousness-raising', not as descriptive of the actual situation addressed by the Apocalypse.

John's imagery is strikingly vivid. He mixes familiar symbols (white–blood) in a bizarre fusion to commend this perspective to the readers. The image of 'washing robes' foregrounds the clash of colours because it calls to mind the ritual of baptism with its linkage of water and blood (cf. Rom. 6.3; Isa. 1.18). The mingling of the white and red demonstrates the belief that the death of Jesus has provided eschatological security for his followers. It reminds readers that those who want the triumph of the white must bear the isolation symbolized by the red. What we know about John's use of Scripture indicates that he was thinking of Isa. 1.18 and gave that passage a new twist of meaning through his meditation on the passion of Jesus.

The concluding song celebrates the benefits of Christian redemption (7.15-17). It is said that the redeemed worship God day and night in the temple, and that the One who is seated on the throne (presumably Christ; cf. 3.21) will shelter them (7.15). The song anticipates a forth-coming time of reversal: 'they will hunger no more, and thirst no more...for the Lamb at the centre of the throne will be their shepherd' (7.16-17; cf. Ps. 23.1; Isa. 40.11). John's Gospel portrays Christ as the Good Shepherd (Jn 10.1). This Johannine image may have influenced the Apocalypse at this point. Elsewhere in Revelation, Christ is assigned a quite different 'shepherding' role in respect of the nations. In 12.5 (cf. 19.15; 2.27) he 'shepherds' them with a rod of iron. In this passage the Lamb's care for his people leads him to ward off those who would harm them. God's providential care is further illustrated by his wiping away of tears from their eyes (7.17).

Revelation 8

The interlude of ch. 7 creates a dramatic tension between the opening of the sixth and the seventh seals of the scroll. Chapter 8 describes what happens when the Lamb opens the seventh seal. This results in a sequence of plagues that are heralded by the prayers of the saints (8.3-5) and the blowing of trumpets by the angels (8.6). The plagues recall the miseries of the Egyptians in the book of Exodus. They refused to allow the Israelites their freedom and suffered in consequence a series of punishments by God. John freely reworks this material to produce a new patchwork of imagery which describes a further sequence of misfortunes that are unleashed upon the earth.

Chapter 8 opens with the statement that silence prevails in heaven for half an hour after the Lamb opens the seventh seal (8.1). This heightens the drama by contrasting with the noise of the heavenly chorus. This silence is a sharp (if not eerie) intake of breath. It warns the reader that something sinister is to happen in this chapter.

Seven angels are given trumpets in 8.2. These are 'the seven angels who stand before God' (cf. Tob. 12.15). Before they blow their trumpets, there is another dramatic interlude in 8.3-5. John is nothing if not a careful artist. Another angel with a golden censer stands at the heavenly altar. He mingles his incense with the prayers of the righteous. All attempts (of which there have been several) to identify this angel with Christ are misplaced. Some scholars try to distinguish more than one heavenly altar on the basis of this passage, but this is also unlikely. It has been disputed (as in 5.8) whether the incense is mingled with the prayers of the saints or merely represents the prayers of the saints. Bruce ('Revelation', p. 646) argues that the phrase preserves an underlying Semitic original which suggests the second meaning, but the former is the better explanation. One should not reduce apocalyptic symbolism to rational explanation.

This second interlude presages further destruction (8.5). Smoke rises from the altar. The angel throws hot coals down to earth. This makes a clever contrast in the direction of movement. Prayer rises; divine judgment falls from heaven. It results in 'peals of thunder, flashes of lightning and an earthquake'. This scene is suggested by Ezek. 10.2-7 where the linen-clothed man scatters coal from between the cherubim over the city of Jerusalem.

8.6 describes how the angels stand ready to blow their trumpets. The blowing of their trumpets results in a further series of calamities. At the blowing of the first trumpet, there appears hail and fire mixed with blood (8.7). This is hurled to earth and a third of the earth is destroyed, together with a third of the trees and all the grass (cf. Exod. 9.13-35; Zech. 13.8-9). The fraction seems odd but it indicates that the full force of God's wrath has yet to appear.

On the blowing of the second trumpet, something like a mountain, burning with fire, is thrown into the sea (8.8-9). A third of the sea turns to blood, a third of the fish die and a third of the ships are destroyed. Commentators have sometimes explained this imagery with reference to the natural phenomena of Asia but once again it would be unwise to attempt an overly 'rationalistic' interpretation of the passage. The burning mountain derives from *1 En.* 18.13 or 21.3 (cf. 108.4); Amos 7.4 forms a remoter parallel. The turning of the sea to blood recalls Exod. 7.20 (cf. Ps. 78.44). The destruction of the fish comes from Zeph. 1.3. We find here another example of the way in which John's apocalyptic imagination has blended together a medley of biblical imagery to yield a new pattern that is germane to the matter in hand.

When the third trumpet is blown, a star called Wormwood falls from heaven, blazing like a torch (8.10-11). It falls on a third of the rivers and their fountains. A third of the waters turns to wormwood; a third of humanity dies from drinking the polluted water. Wormwood is a bitter herb (cf. Lam. 3.19). The falling star recalls the fate of Lucifer, the Day-Star, who falls from heaven in Isa. 14.12. This Isaianic passage has a history of exegetical development in early Christianity as we know from Lk. 10.18 where Jesus sees Satan fall like lightning from heaven (cf. *Asc. Isa.* 4.1-4). The contamination of the water recalls the first Egyptian plague in Exod. 7.20. It is through this contamination of the natural order that humanity is adversely affected. This is the reverse of the nature miracle described by Exod. 15.25.

8.12 describes the effects of the fourth trumpet. A third of the sun is struck, as of the moon and stars. A third of their light is darkened. This change affects the natural order of day and night. The passage recalls the third Egyptian plague (Exod. 10.21-23) but does not form a precise parallel. Darkness is a well-known symbol of destruction in the Hebrew Bible, most obviously in Amos 5.18 (cf. Joel 2.2). Darkness in both early Christian and Qumran literature is understood as the property of the powers opposed to God (see 2 Cor. 6.14-15 and 1QM). The Synoptic eschatological discourse anticipates darkness at the end times (Mk 13.24). In Rev. 8.12, the darkness is caused by the action of *God*. This is the significant feature of the passage. It reinforces the point that God holds the final authority, even over the eschatological disasters. This point is foregrounded in the Apocalypse where disaster is a stock item. That is why, at the end of the text, the disasters cease with the advent of the kingdom of God.

The chapter closes with a reference to an eagle flying in heaven (8.13). This eagle pronounces woes on the inhabitants of earth because the last three trumpets have yet to be blown. This comment sets the scene for the next part of the Apocalypse where the three 'woes' are mentioned.

Uncomfortable Reading

Chapter 8 does not make for comfortable reading. It describes an unmitigated vision of disasters that are said to be caused by the will of God. We should approach this material by recognizing that John is not so much describing what will happen in the future as commenting on the reality that exists now. This is not an inevitable prediction of wide-scale destruction but a rhetorical condemnation of the existing situation through which John encourages his readers to see their society in a hostile light. It is because life has become too comfortable that they are warned of impending destruction. The *warning* of disaster (and not the disaster itself) makes them sit up and think about what should be done.

The dramatic pauses assist this reflection. At the beginning of the chapter, we read of silence in heaven for half an hour; at the end, of a pause before the last three trumpets. This makes the reader wonder that will happen next. The point is that nothing in creation is exempt from the wrath of God. The binary oppositions in 8.3-5 (heaven/prayer-earth/judgment) give the rationale of this view. The passage knows of only two reactions—faithfulness and punishment—which are symbol-ized by the upwards and downwards movement respectively. People must choose whether they will be faithful—the meaning of which is defined in the letters to the churches—or whether they will determine their own punishment. This is the significance of the shift from chs. 7 to 8. It has both ethical and eschatological implications.

Revelation 9

The trumpets and the judgment continue in ch. 9. At the blowing of the fifth trumpet, a star falls to earth (9.1). It is given the key to 'the bottomless pit'. This star's identity is much discussed in the commentaries. It appears to be an (otherwise anonymous) angel who carries out the function of judgment. There was a cycle of stories about the fallen angels in Jewish literature, stemming from Genesis 6 but that material is not obviously reflected here. This angel acts in accordance with the divine purpose and not against it. The verb, 'had fallen', lacks a sinister sense altogether. Charles provisionally identifies this angel with Uriel (on the basis of *1 En.* 20.2) but this is to say more than does the text itself (*Critical and Exegetical Commentary*, I, p. 239). The 'abyss' or 'bottomless pit' is understood in the Apocalypse as the place of preliminary punishment (see 9.1; 11.7; 17.8; and 20.1-3). It is distinct from the final place of punishment which is the 'lake of fire' mentioned in Rev. 20.10-15. The adjective 'bottomless' indicates there is no possibility of escape from this punishment.

The angel opens the abyss (9.2). From it rises smoke that fills and darkens the atmosphere. Out of the smoke flies a swarm of locusts (9.3). The locusts are given power like scorpions. Two Hebrew Bible passages stand behind this passage. Exodus 10.1-20 describes the plague of locusts that devoured the vegetation of Egypt. Joel 1.4 mentions locusts in its portrait of the eschatological vengeance. Once again, John's material represents a fusion of imagery. Locusts are unpleasant enough. Their comparison with scorpions heightens the terror of this plague.

The one redeeming feature of the passage is that the locusts are told not to harm the vegetation and to destroy only those who do not bear the seal of God (9.4). Those who were sealed in ch. 7 are exempted from this punishment. John clearly knows that the Israelites went unharmed in the Exodus story. It must not be different for the latter-day Israel of God. That the locusts attack human beings (against the course of nature) reflects the horrific nature of this plague. Its terror derives from the hybrid quality of the imagery. The damage inflicted by the locusts is made worse by the command that they must not kill their victims but may torture them for five months. This passage is sometimes held to be determined by the life-cycle of the locust which is apparently five months. But the figure probably has the same symbolic function as the earlier references to one-third in that it leaves scope for further torture and destruction.

9.6 expresses the horror that this plague brings. John says that people

will seek death but will be unable to find it. This recalls the panic of
6.15-17. It shows the effect of the Lamb's wrath displayed in this metamorphosis of the natural order. As if to reinforce this point, 9.7 describes
the locusts in more detail. They are compared to horses arrayed for
battle. This reflects their size and strength. They wear what appear to be
golden crowns and have human faces (cf. Joel 2.4). The crowns signify
that they are divinely commissioned agents of destruction. Their human
faces suggest a special note of cruelty given that they resemble people
but behave with purely animal destructiveness. They have women's hair
and lions' teeth (9.8; cf. Joel 1.6). This description resembles the Furies
from Greek mythology and gives the passage anything but the air of
gentle femininity. Their scales resemble iron breastplates; the noise of
their wings is like chariots and horses as they rush into battle (9.9; cf.
Joel 2.4-5). Their tails are like scorpions; their sting lasts for five months
(9.10).

9.11 describes the locust chief. He is called 'the angel of the bottomless pit'; Abaddon in Hebrew and Apollyon in Greek. The title 'Abaddon'
appears in the Wisdom literature (e.g. Job 26.6; Prov. 15.11) where it
means 'destruction'. It is used in parallel with 'Sheol' in Job 26.6 and
other references. Apollyon in Greek means 'Destroyer'. Some commentators play off the name Apollyon with the Greek god Apollo and see an
implicit downgrading of the latter in this passage. This may be a feature
of John's imagery, given the social setting of the Apocalypse, but the
primary meaning of the noun is supplied by the present context and not
by external allusions. This Apollyon is a destroyer who leads his locusts
into battle.

Chapter 9 is one of the most vivid passages in the Apocalypse. John
clearly has a biblical source—several passages from Joel—but he is no
slavish tradent who lacks the imagination to recast his material. We
might say even that this passage represents a form of biblical *midrash* in
which John gives new depth and meaning to the Hebrew text. John is
helped by the fact that he is not restricted to the level of prosaic or
literal repetition. John's portrait of the locusts gains its strength from its
mutational obscenity. These locusts are specially empowered agents of
destruction. Their unnatural properties come from the creator himself.
Their divinely willed origin is signified by the fact that they come from
the bottomless pit which is opened by the angel. Their appearance is,
however, an intermediate affliction. 9.12 announces ominously: 'The
first woe has passed. There are still two woes to come.'

The three 'woes' are among the most difficult features of the
Apocalypse. It is clear that the first woe is the appearance of the locusts
in 9.1-11. In 11.14 we read, 'the second woe has passed. The third woe
is coming very soon.' This 'second woe' seems to be the *entirety* of the
material in 9.13–11.14. It is difficult to restrict it to only part of that
material given the flow of the text. The 'third woe' is not formally held

accomplished in the Apocalypse, but the most obvious interpretation of
11.14b is that it is in turn the entirety of the material between 11.15 and
15.4. This is introduced and concluded by a liturgical section. On this
reading of the text, the similarity between 11.19 and 15.5 serves as a
structural marker. In any event, the sequence of three woes shows that
John is looking towards the conclusion of his Apocalypse. In a text
where numerical symbolism is important, we are probably right to
discern trinitarian significance in the woes. They reinforce the point that
the destruction is permitted by God and furthers his eschatological
purpose.

The sixth angel blows his trumpet (9.13). A voice comes from the
altar and instructs the angel to release the four angels who are bound at
the river Euphrates (9.14; cf. Gen. 15.8; Deut. 1.7; Jos. 1.4). This again is
a divine command. These four angels are angels of destruction. Their
identity has intrigued the commentators. It is impossible to identify
them with a known quartet of angels from Jewish tradition, and probably mistaken to try to do so. They are unnamed angels of destruction.

9.15 states that these angels are released and that they have been kept
ready 'for the hour, the day, the month, and the year' to kill a third of
humanity. This means, a further third of the three-quarters who were
left undestroyed by Rev. 6.8. The precision of the date is part of the
familiar determinism in apocalyptic literature.

9.16 is awkward in its present form. The angels suddenly become a
vast cavalry force without any textual indication of the change. This is a
further example of John's kaleidoscopic imagery. The number of the
angels is deliberately vast: twice ten thousand times ten thousand. This
designates the almost innumerable force that operates under the divine
command. 9.17 describes the cavalry. The riders wear breastplates the
colour of fire, sapphire and sulphur. The heads of the horses are like
lions' heads. Fire, smoke and sulphur comes from their mouths (cf. Gen.
19.24). This description makes the riders almost passive actors as the
horses effect destruction. 9.18 states that these plagues killed a third of
humankind. 9.19 reinforces the warning by describing once again the
power of the horses which lies in their mouths and their tails. The
imagery is almost deliberately bizarre. John's visionary perception is
what gives the Apocalypse its power.

9.20-21 states that the rest of humankind did not repent despite these
plagues. They continued to worship demons and idols. John adds the
traditional Jewish view that idols cannot see, hear or walk. People stub-
bornly persist in their murder, sorcery, fornication (cf. 2.14, 21) and
theft. The reader marvels at their folly. This implied response sets the
Asian social world in a negative light. Three of the four offences in 9.20
are proscribed by the Ten Commandments (murder, adultery, theft); the
fourth (sorcery) is proscribed by Deuteronomy 13. The list is symbolic

of the behaviour that is adopted by people estranged from God (cf. Gal. 5.19-21). From it, readers draw their own conclusions about the kind of behaviour that is required of them.

Revelation 10

The clue to understanding ch. 10 lies in the reference to the woes in 9.12. We might have expected the reference to the second woe at the end of 9.13-21 which describes the effects produced by the blowing of the sixth trumpet. But this is deferred until 11.14. 10.1-11.13 must therefore be part of the second woe, although some commentators think that it is a further interlude between the blowing of the sixth trumpet and the announcement of the third woe. It is pedantic to press this distinction too far. 10.1-11.13 is clearly associated with the second woe. The material must be considered in that context, even if John's structural scheme is perhaps somewhat difficult to follow here.

In 10.1 John sees another angel descend from heaven. This angel is wrapped in a cloud. He has a rainbow over his head. His face is like the sun and his legs like pillars of fire. John's vision of this angel 'coming down' implies that the seer is now on earth, but nothing has been said to indicate this in the text of the Apocalypse. This problem evidently does not trouble the author who introduces a number of abrupt transitions in his work. As with the other angels in Revelation the angel of 10.1 has sometimes been identified as Christ, but this is as unlikely here as it is in 8.3. His description nevertheless incorporates elements from the biblical theophanies. The cloud derives from Dan. 7.13 and the rainbow from Ezek. 1.28. The shining face includes a detail from *1 En.* 14.20. The description of his legs probably comes from the description of Israel's wilderness wandering (Exod. 14.19, 24) where the pillar of fire symbolizes the divine presence. This language means that the angel bears something of the visual majesty of God but without the suggestion that he is a divine being.

The angel holds a scroll in his hand (10.2). He shouts with a voice as loud as a lion's (10.3). The roaring of the lion is used in Jewish literature as a description both of Yahweh (Hos. 11.10) and the Messiah (*4 Ezra* 12.31-32). Given the symbolism of 5.5 ('the Lion of the tribe of Judah') it seems likely that this detail links the angel with Christ to demonstrate the divine origin of his message (10.7).

When the angel speaks 'the seven thunders' sound (10.4). Thunder is associated with divine vengeance elsewhere in the Apocalypse (see 8.5; 11.19; 16.18). But this reference to the 'seven thunders' is probably another mystical allusion. It draws attention to the significance of what is to follow. John is about to write down the vision when a voice comes from heaven with the command to seal up what the thunders have disclosed and not to write it (10.4). Commentators are puzzled by the contrast between this passage and 1.19 (where the seer is commanded to write down what he sees), but the reference to 'sealing' is commonly found in the apocalyptic tradition (e.g. Dan. 12.9). 22.10 makes for a further contrast with this passage, but for agreement with 1.19, when it forbids any 'sealing'. The Apocalypse is not consistent on this issue. It is possible that the command of 10.4 is deliberately countermanded by 22.10 to form an eschatological declaration of hope. 10.4 implies a wider body of apocalyptic knowledge that goes beyond the contents of the Apocalypse and is not made public there. John may or may not have disclosed this to his churches on other occasions.

Many commentators compare this passage with 2 Cor. 12.3-4 where Paul briefly describes a mystical experience. It is perhaps not surprising that John does not reveal all that he has learned through revelation. 10.4 implies that the Apocalypse is carefully honed to suit the present situation and that John could say more than he does to the churches. One wonders what it would have been like to hear this prophet in person!

In 10.5-7 the drama reaches a critical moment. The angel lifts up his right hand and swears by God that there will be no more delay: 'the mystery of God will be fulfilled, as he announced to his servants the prophets' (10.7). The upraising of the hand is part of the oath in Jewish practice (see, e.g., Gen. 14.22-23). The immediate source for this passage is Dan. 12.7 where the linen-clothed man raised up his hands to predict that the 'power of the holy people' would no longer be dispersed. The mystery mentioned here (in line with the contents of the Apocalypse) is an eschatological one. It signifies the final moves towards the end which will yield the Messiah's kingdom and the recreated heaven and earth. It is not accidental that John's language becomes more conspicuously mysterious as he begins to describe the final things. As before, this heightens the dramatic tension and tells the reader that significant things will follow.

In 10.8-9 the heavenly voice tells John to take the scroll from the angel's hand and eat it. The angel says that it will taste as sweet as honey to his mouth but bitter to his stomach. This reference to eating (which derives from Ezek. 2.8–3.3) signifies that John will become the embodiment of his message by digesting the contents of the scroll. The thought is not that bitter revelation is presented to John in the form of a sugared pill. The sweetness signifies the divine origin of the message. The Hebrew prophets were often instructed to proclaim a message that they found unpalatable. In this case, the message is a hopeful one because Christians are promised the blessings of the eschatological age. It may be that 11.1-13 provides the content of this scroll, especially since there (as in the letters) we find the 'message' of the Apocalypse in microcosm (see below). The scroll would then promise that the person who 'conquers' (with its ethical implications) will share the victory of Christ.

John does as he is told (10.10). The scroll produces its projected effect. John is told that he must prophesy about 'many people and nations and languages and kings' (10.11). As in 1.5, the piling up of nouns demonstrates the universality of the knowledge (knowledge about *all* people) that is granted to the seer through revelation. The reference to 'nations and kings' leaves little doubt that their fate will be described, together with the victory of the followers of Jesus.

Revelation 11

Chapter 11 falls into two main parts. 11.1-13 describes what happens when John eats the scroll. He sees two witnesses whose martyrdom terrifies the world (11.13). This is followed by the announcement of the third woe in 11.14. That in turn leads to the celebration by the heavenly chorus of the coming of the kingdom of God (11.15-18). In this way, ch. 11 provides the transition to the middle section of the Apocalypse.

The Temple

In 11.1 the seer is given a measuring-staff and told to measure the temple, the altar and those who worship there. It is clear from what follows that this is a symbol of the temple's preservation, despite the statement that part of the building will be trampled underfoot by the Gentiles (11.2). The question arises of why a Christian author should write about the temple in this way in the late first century CE in the years following the Roman destruction of Jerusalem in 70 CE. It is insufficient to say that John is merely reflecting this act of destruction. Revelation 11 is not a prediction made in the light of history but an apocalyptic prophecy that reveals the divine will for the temple. It reflects the Jewish tradition that the new temple will be introduced in the eschatological age by God. This idea has biblical foundations in Deutero-Isaiah (e.g. Isa. 60.3-7, 10-14) and Ezekiel 40–42, and it is evidenced in Jewish apocalyptic literature (e.g. *1 En.* 90.28-36; cf. *T. Benj.* 9.2; 11QT 29.8-10). This expression of hope was felt particularly appropriate in the period after 70 CE, as two other apocalypses show (see *4 Ezra* 10.44-59; *2 Bar.* 4.2-6). John here anticipates the preservation of the temple through conflict as an eschatological sign.

The close of the Apocalypse, however, says that the new Jerusalem has no temple and that the Lord God and the Lamb have taken the place of the temple (21.22). We should not look for complete consistency in the Apocalypse. The temple of 11.1-2 is understood as a symbol of the divine presence which the author expects to disappear when the divine presence itself is revealed from heaven (21.22). John thus measures the temple in preparation for its interim preservation but in the actual expectation (not disclosed until ch. 21) of its replacement by God in the eschatological age. The command to measure the temple involves John in the drama of his own vision, just as Ezekiel and Hosea similarly became involved in their own prophecies.

The question has often been raised of whether John employs a source in 11.1-13. The answer is that he may have done so but that it is more important to understand how this material is used in the Apocalypse than to speculate on the precise nature of the source from which it was derived. The present form of material speaks with a Christian voice (especially in 11.8). It would be unwise to ignore this observation even when a Jewish origin is posited.

The seer is told to ignore the outer court of the temple because this will be given over to the nations (11.2). This is a reference to the court of the Gentiles beyond which only Jewish people were allowed to pass (see Josephus, *War* 5.5.2). That the court of the Gentiles is excluded from the calculation makes the point that Gentile practices (but not, of course, Gentiles themselves) have no place in the church. 'Measuring' in this passage is the symbolic equivalent of the 'sealing' in 7.3-8. There is possibly a distant echo of Caligula's attempt to erect his standards in the temple in 39 CE. The timescale placed on the 'trampling' is equivalent to the three-and-a-half times (i.e. three-and-a-half years) of Rev. 12.14. It derives from the symbolic eschatology of the book of Daniel (Dan. 7.25).

The Two Witnesses

Two witnesses now appear (11.3). John says that these will be clothed in sackcloth and have the power to prophesy for 1260 days. These witnesses are generally interpreted as Moses and Elijah on the basis of what is said about them in 11.5-6. This passage states that fire pours from their mouths; that they have the power to stop the rain; that they can turn water into blood; and that they can strike the earth with plagues. Such information recalls the stories about Moses and Elijah in Exodus 7-8, 1 Kings 17 and 2 Kings 1. John himself does not name the two witnesses. He does this perhaps to tease his readers into thought; but his silence means we cannot be sure that the witnesses' identity is *precisely restricted* to the two figures mentioned. Symbolism comes first in the Apocalypse; identification follows behind.

Moses and Elijah (if this is who they are) are recalled for their eschatological significance in Judaism. Elijah is the expected prophet of the end time (see Mal. 4.5); Deuteronomy 18.15 predicts the appearance of a 'prophet like Moses' at some future point. That the figures are not named means they are symbols in a vision who make a point on one level which can (and does) have meaning on a range of other levels. The basic meaning of this passage is the indestructibility of their witness which symbolizes the witness of the church (or, more probably, the witness that the church should be making). The portrait is to this extent an idealizing one. This is why the witnesses are empowered to destroy those who would harm them or hinder their message (11.5-6).

The two witnesses are identified as two olive trees and lampstands which stand before the Lord (11.4). The background to this identification is Zechariah 4, where a lampstand is flanked by two trees. There is an obvious link with the lampstands of chs. 2–3. This identifies the witnesses—whatever else they are—as symbols of the church. 11.4 is a symbolic repetition of the point that the church's witness cannot be snuffed even if in places it burns quite dimly. If the olive tree suggests peace, this image is shown to be deceptive (or at least implicitly malleable).

The time will come when the witnesses have 'finished their testimony' (11.7). This will be when the 1260 days of 11.3 are completed. Then the beast will ascend from the bottomless pit, make war on them, conquer them and kill them. This passage anticipates the beast's appearance in chs. 13 and 17 of the Apocalypse. It is a variation on the early Christian theme of eschatological opposition to the righteous which is found in the Synoptic Eschatological Discourse (Mk 13 and par.), 2 Thessalonians 2 and several other passages. Neither Moses nor Elijah was killed in this way, but this does not matter for John's imagery. John adds that their bodies will lie unburied in the street of that great city which is 'prophetically called Sodom and Egypt, where also their Lord was crucified' (11.8).

Many commentators identify this 'great city' as Jerusalem on the basis of the last clause ('where their Lord was crucified'), but this is probably an over-literal reading of the passage which belittles John's allusive mind. The city's identification as 'Sodom and Egypt' is called 'prophetic' or 'symbolic'. This prevents any single or exclusive identification of it. Sodom and Egypt were notorious places of rebellion against God. John does not tell his readers the obvious fact that Jesus was crucified in Jerusalem. The symbolism implies that Jesus is crucified in every city and by every person who is opposed to Christian standards (including, no doubt, John's Christian opponents). Readers are invited to identify themselves with the shame of the witnesses who followed the Lord's example and perished as he had done. As elsewhere in the Apocalypse (e.g. 16.19; 17.18, etc.), 'the great city' primarily designates Rome but it also denotes all those other cities (including the cities of the seven churches) where Roman influence was prominent.

In 11.9 people are said to gaze on the bodies of the witnesses for three and a half days and to prevent their burial. This is a deliberate mark of disrespect to the servants of God (cf. Tob. 2.1-7). 11.10 describes the mirth that is raised over their bodies. People celebrate and exchange presents because the witnesses have been a torment to them. But, as John tells their story, it is the witnesses who call the tune by their faithfulness to death. People react to them; how they lived made a difference. 11.11 duly vindicates the martyrs (as we should now call them, although the Greek word is the same). After three-and-a-half days, a 'breath of life' from God enters them and they stand on their feet. This resurrection terrifies those who see it. There is an echo here of the Valley of Dry Bones (Ezek. 37) where human bodies are reconstituted by the spirit of God.

Revelation 11.11 is one of the most vivid descriptions of the resurrection in the New Testament literature. It conceivably anticipates the process that John expected in the eschatological future, but we should remember that all descriptions of the resurrection in New Testament literature are speculative. It would be wrong to expect an entirely literal description in Revelation 11. The symbolism does however recall the 'physicality' that other passages expect of the resurrection (e.g. 1 Cor. 15.44b).

The martyrs are addressed by a voice that calls them to heaven (11.12). They enter heaven 'in a cloud' as their enemies look on. There are echoes here of the ascension of Jesus; the verse mirrors Jewish beliefs about the immortality of martyrs and other exceptional people. This description of their vindication, like John's earlier portrait of the elders, is not so much a promise of heavenly immortality to the readers as a symbol of the fact that death cannot deprive people of their eschatological destiny. The passage recalls Paul's assurance in 1 Thessalonians 4 that in this sense it makes no difference whether one is dead or alive at the return of Jesus to earth. The eschatological benefits are assured for both alike. At the end of the Apocalypse, the martyrs are resurrected to reign on earth with Christ (20.4) as a prelude to the recreation of heaven and earth. 11.12 anticipates this future hope.

At the moment of their ascension, there is a great earthquake (cf. 6.12). A tenth of the city falls (11.13). Seven thousand people perish in the earthquake. The rest give glory to 'the God of heaven'. An earthquake is an eschatological sign in the Hebrew Bible (see Ezek. 38.19-20; Zech. 14.15; Hag. 2.6-7). This scene is reminiscent again of the book of Daniel where those who are confounded by the miracles acknowledge the power of the Jewish God (see esp. Dan. 2.17-19). The title 'God of heaven' deliberately recalls this Jewish background.

This part of ch. 11 describes what can only be called a process of conversion. The earthquake leads people to glorify God (11.13). It concludes the story of the martyrs, so that we are probably right to suppose it is the death of the martyrs (and not the earthquake in the limited sense) that leads people to glorify God. This means that their witness achieves what the plagues did not. That is in every sense a significant assertion. John implies that the plagues might not bring conviction but that the witness of the church will have this effect. Through the church's witness, the Gentiles will be turned. The witnesses remind the readers what effect their behaviour will have in their society. Chapter 11 is an ethical appeal in miniature.

11.14 states that the second woe has passed and the third yet to come (cf. 9.12). I have suggested that the content of 'the second woe' is given by the entirety of the material in 9.13–11.13, which is introduced by the blowing of the seventh trumpet. 10.1–11.13 is clearly connected with the preceding material and must be considered in that light. 11.13, like 9.13-21, has the nature of a 'woe' because it describes how seven thousand people were killed and the rest glorified God. This is the reversal of the situation described by 9.20-21 where people refused to repent and foolishly persisted in their idolatry.

The Seventh Trumpet

11.14-19 is a transitional section that introduces the second half of the Apocalypse. It is introduced by the statement that 'the second woe has passed. The third woe is coming soon.' The third woe is concluded at the end of ch. 15 (15.8) which looks back retrospectively to 11.19 and uses similar language. In 11.15 the seventh angel (finally) blows his trumpet. Now comes a further surprise. Readers instinctively expect calamity. Instead, loud voices are heard in heaven. These voices proclaim that 'the kingdom of this world has become the kingdom of our Lord and of his Messiah, and he shall reign forever and ever' (11.15). The seventh trumpet is thus followed by a victory chorus. It is, of course, true to say that chs. 12–14 will disclose further calamities, notably the opposition of the dragon and the two beasts. This raising of the heavenly chorus is an unexpected element that sets what follows in relief.

The heavenly chorus once again discloses the true meaning of the drama. The song sets the tone for the dénouement of the Apocalypse by asserting the triumph of the Christian God and his followers over the forces arraigned against them. The raising of the victory cry in heaven gives to earthly events the nature of a 'mopping-up' operation in which the eventual outcome is not in doubt even if initial difficulties are encountered. The chorus reveals what is now true in heaven and that will soon come to pass on earth. Encouragement is thereby added to the exhortation that is imparted in the earlier part of the chapter.

The heavenly voices belong to angels; the elders do not join the chorus until 11.16. There, the elders praise God that he has 'taken his great power and begun to reign'. The aorist tense here and in 11.15 is a significant usage. It implies a sense of fulfilment despite the fact that God's rule has yet to be realized on earth. The heavenly liturgy challenges the readers' perception of their situation and prompts reflection about the relationship between Christian hope for the reign of God and Christian behaviour in a pagan environment. This is done with allusion to biblical language. The contrast between the raging of the nations and the wrath of God in 11.18 shows the choice that confronts readers. They can *either* go along with the nations *or* enjoy the reward provided by God. Between the two there is no possible compromise. Each brings its own destiny. John promises reward or punishment in polarized terms. Destruction will be the punishment for those who have worked destruction (11.18; cf. 1 Cor. 15.24).

11.19 authenticates this statement by describing the opening of the temple and John's vision of the ark of the covenant. This is accompanied by natural portents: lightning, thunder, earthquake and hail. The opening of the temple and ark (God's heavenly seat) reveals God's judgment. The natural portents confirm that the judgment is now beginning. This is a further reminder of the choice that readers must make.

Revelation 12

The scene is set for the description of the events of the end. Chapters 12–15 begin this description with the mythological narrative of the supernatural opposition unleashed against the Christians. There is a clear structural marker in 15.5-6 that looks back retrospectively to 11.19 and binds this section together. This is the third woe of the Apocalypse. Chapter 12 describes the portents that herald the end. We read here of the woman and the dragon (12.1-6); of the dragon's expulsion from heaven (12.7-12); and of the woman and the dragon again (12.13-17). The blowing of the seventh trumpet in 11.15 marked the start of the eschatological climax. This is now described in symbolic form.

The Woman and the Dragon

In 12.1 a portent appears in heaven: a woman clothed with the sun who stands on the moon. She wears a crown of 12 stars. Portents were a familiar feature of Graeco-Roman and Jewish religion. The twelve-starred crown identifies this woman as a symbol of Israel. This is a more convincing explanation of this symbol than Mary, the mother of Jesus, who has sometimes been proposed to explain it. Zion is often called the mother of the faithful in Jewish literature (e.g. Isa. 54.1; *4 Ezra* 10.7; Gal. 4.27). That explains the female imagery here. The notion of the 'star' suggests a messianic significance on the basis of Num. 24.17 ('a star shall come out of Jacob'; cf. 2.28). This passage thus celebrates the supremacy of (the true) Israel by analogy with the two main planets.

In 12.2 the woman is in childbirth. This too has messianic significance. It recalls the prophecy of Hezekiah's birth which Matthew also utilized (Mt. 1.23; cf. Isa. 7.14; 26.17; Mic. 4.10). Nothing, however, in John's symbolism is uncomplicated. The story of the childbirth is compounded by the appearance of another portent (12.3). This is a red dragon with seven heads and ten horns, and seven crowns on its head. The figure 'seven' identifies this dragon as a symbol of Rome, the city that was built on seven hills. The ten horns represent the Roman emperors, as they will do later in 13.1. The source for this symbol is the mythical dragon of ancient Near Eastern mythology and the description of the fourth beast in Dan. 7.7, 24, which John has fused together. The impression is once again a dualist one as messianic and demonic symbols come into open conflict on the stage of the Apocalypse.

The dragon's tail sweeps down a third of the stars to earth (12.4; cf. Dan. 8.10). He stands before the woman to devour the child whom she bears (i.e. the Messiah). This is a symbolic description of antagonism between the Romans as the dominant power and the Christians as people who are powerless to oppose them. The author here *creates* the notion of conflict by using the dragon imagery which represents chaos and which the Hebrew Bible claims that Yahweh has subdued (see Isa. 51.9; Ps. 74.14). It is not necessary to suppose that this passage was provoked by the specific experience of persecution. It more obviously inculcates a world-view that expresses the inevitability of conflict between Rome and the Christians (in a situation where this may not have been obvious) and sets the participants in a particular light. John presents Rome in demonized terms as a way of telling the readers the attitude that he wants them to adopt towards the existing order.

The woman bears a male child (12.5). This child is expected to 'rule all the nations with a rod of iron' (cf. Ps. 2.9). This anticipates Christ's future rule over the nations which John thinks will be demonstrated on his return from heaven (see esp. 19.11-21; 20.4). The notion of 'shepherding', which means 'destroy', contrasts with the use of that term in 7.17 where Christ was said to 'shepherd' his flock. Readers remember the earlier passage. This 'shepherding' of the chosen ones means the subjection of their adversaries. 12.5b says that the child is snatched up to the throne of God (cf. 3.21). This expresses divine protection of him. Not even Rome can prevent the final triumph of the Messiah and his people. Readers may think of the ascension of Jesus which earlier Christian literature (e.g. Rom. 8.34) associates with the throne of God, but John is thinking here of ascension immediately after birth and does not draw directly on that tradition.

The woman flees into the wilderness where her place is prepared by God (12.6). There she is nourished for 1,260 days (cf. 11.9; Dan. 12.11). John thinks here of Israel's wilderness sojourn. The passage describes a retreat which illustrates the need for distance from prevalent forms of behaviour (cf. *Asc. Isa.* 4.13).

War in Heaven

12.7 describes the outbreak of war in heaven. Michael and his angels fight with the dragon. The dragon is cast down from heaven. Although he cannot prevail against the forces of Michael, there is nevertheless the suggestion, as in Daniel 10–12, that the contest is a hard-fought one in which the dragon provides credible opposition. In 12.9 the dragon and his angels are thrown down to earth. This explains the additional title 'the deceiver of the whole world' that he is given in this verse. The dragon is given a medley of other titles which leave his identity in no doubt: 'the great dragon...that ancient serpent, who is called the Devil and Satan, the deceiver of the whole world'.

The dragon's fall is paralleled in the Gospel tradition in Lk. 10.18 where Jesus says that he sees Satan fall like lightning from heaven. The tradition features also in *Ascension of Isaiah* 4 where Beliar descends from the firmament to appear as the emperor Nero. The fact that the dragon—which symbolizes Rome—is cast down from heaven in Revelation 12 is a way of limiting Rome's authority and thus of presenting a different view of their Rome-dominated society to the readers. They are told that heavenly warriors have already vanquished the dragon and that his presence on earth results from this prior defeat. It is thereby carefully controlled, despite Rome's seeming power. This mythology is an apocalyptic anticipation of the destruction of God's enemies and the beginning of Christ's reign which will be described at the end of the Apocalypse.

Satan enjoys a rake's progress in Jewish and Christian literature. The verb *śṭn* in the Hebrew Bible means 'to accuse', 'to be an adversary' and perhaps even 'to slander'. Satan is the heavenly accuser of the righteous in Job 1–2 and Zech. 3.1. He features relatively often in Jewish post-biblical literature (e.g. *Jub.* 23.29; *T. Mos.* 10.1). In rabbinic sources, Satan is mainly presented impersonally as the evil inclination that infects humanity; but he appears in a personal sense in the story of God's testing of Abraham (*b. Sanh.* 89b). He is described in the New Testament variously as 'the enemy' (Mt. 13.39), 'the evil one' (Mt. 13.38), 'the adversary' (1 Pet. 5.8) and 'the father of lies' (Jn 8.44). Revelation 12 must be set within this tradition. John defines and limits Satan's authority by describing his ejection from heaven. This presents Rome in demonized terms. The Apocalypse will later describe Satan's demise in the lake of fire and sulphur (20.10).

In 12.10 a heavenly voice (no doubt an angel's voice) celebrates God's victory over Satan. As earlier, it sings that salvation and power, the kingdom of God and authority of Christ have come, for the 'accuser of our comrades' has been thrown down. This voice gives the meaning of the visual symbolism in 12.7-9. It reminds readers, in the wake of that passage, of the demonic status of their social world. This is opposed to the view that many of them hold at present. The chorus anticipates the establishment of the new order where existing power structures and social relations will be overturned. This passage has the rhetorical function of persuading Christians to join in the battle by rejecting Satan in what is held to be his domain as they avoid all forms of compromise with Asian urban society.

12.11 states that the Christians have conquered Satan 'by the blood of the Lamb' and by 'the word of their testimony'. The first phrase makes the death of Jesus a victory over evil forces (cf. 5.5; Col. 2.15). The 'testimony' mentioned in this passage is not so much oral as behavioural. The statement that the martyrs 'did not cling to life even in the face of death' calls to mind what was said about the witnesses in ch. 11 and reinforces its meaning through repetition. 12.12 concludes this celebration of Satan's defeat by setting woes against the earth and the sea now that the devil has come down to them, 'because he knows that his time is short!' Spatial and temporal categories are fused together here to make Satan's ejection from heaven a sign of his future destruction. The chorus pronounces authoritative truth because they know that Satan has already been defeated in heaven.

The Woman and the Dragon Again

12.13-17 resumes the story of the woman and the dragon. The dragon pursues the mother of the child (12.13) but the woman is given the wings of an eagle to fly into the wilderness where she is shielded from the dragon (12.14). This story reinforces the point that the people of God inevitably conflict with the representatives of the pagan order. Readers should *expect* this to happen. The serpent pours water from his mouth to sweep the woman away (12.15). But the earth swallows the water that comes from the dragon (12.16; cf. Exod. 15.12; Num. 16.30). When the dragon realizes that his moves are futile, he gets angry and makes war on the woman's children (12.17). These children are called 'those who keep the commandments of God and hold the testimony of Jesus'. This means that they are people who adopt John's recommended behaviour. The phrase is a symbolic commentary on the opposition John thinks that Christians should expect to experience, and which the martyrdom theme in the Apocalypse illustrates. The chapter closes with the dragon standing on the seashore (12.18). This provides the link with the story of the beast that follows in ch. 13. The alternative reading 'and *I* stood' (which is found in some manuscripts) was introduced into the tradition to provide a firmer link with what follows.

Revelation 13

Chapter 13 is a notorious and difficult section of the Apocalypse. Hard on the heels of ch. 12, it portrays the Roman administration in demonic terms as a beast that comes up from the sea (13.1) and blasphemes God (13.6). Several remarks must be made before we read this material. First of all, there is no reason to suppose that the symbolism of this chapter (which looms large in the debate about the orientation of New Testament theology) should be taken any more or less literally than other parts of the Apocalypse. John brings into being a further rebirth of images whereby a variety of material is used to express antipathy to the existing order on the grounds that it is inimical to Christianity. This is the principal point of the passage. Secondly, the presentation of the readers' social situation has not changed perceptibly from the earlier chapters. We should not expect to find a new attitude in ch. 13. We do not find one there. The striking imagery reinforces what has been said already. This is that readers must avoid full integration with their social world which is symbolized under the image of the blasphemous Roman Empire. Chapter 13 carries forward John's intention of creating a crisis by presenting the Roman government in critical terms.

Revelation 13 and Romans 13

The major exegetical problem that Revelation 13 raises is that it has been thought to contradict what Paul says about the Christian attitude to the existing order in Romans 13: 'Let every person be subject to the governing authorities; for there is no authority except from God, and those authorities that exist have been instituted by God' (Rom. 13.1). With this compare the words, 'The beast was given a mouth uttering haughty and blasphemous words, and it was allowed to exercise authority for forty-two months' (Rev. 13.5). It seems on the face of it that John advocates an attitude to the Roman Empire that removes Paul's eirenic tone. Caution, however, must be exercised against the over-hasty conclusion that Romans 13 and Revelation 13 necessarily contradict each other in this matter. First of all, we have seen that Revelation was probably not addressed to the situation of a Domitianic persecution. This means that it would be wrong to interpret the material in a literal way as the rejection of Roman sovereignty by a beleaguered church that is taking its stand against totalitarian demands. The language is a rhetorical denunciation of the existing order and not a specific condemnation of Roman imperialism as such. It reflects the seer's malaise at his churches' conformity to their environment. John deliberately uses language that creates awareness of a crisis to advocate greater social distance among the readers.

Nor is the response that John advocates militaristic or one that necessitates action of anything other than a segregationist kind. In the logic of Revelation's eschatology, the way to defeat the beast is to accept the fact of its tyranny and to recognize that this will be of limited duration. Readers are encouraged to stand their distance from social accommodation and to see the existing order in a hostile way. Revelation 13 does *not* mean that readers must set aside what Paul says in Rom. 13.1, for Christians continued to be members of Graeco-Roman cities and they nowhere adopted the model of absolute sectarianism that is represented by the Qumran community (still less the militarism of the Zealots). Revelation uses virulent imagery to encourage a non-violent response among the readers in which their Christian 'sealing' becomes obvious through their conscientious non-participation in certain events.

Having said this, Revelation 13 certainly constitutes 'ideological resistance' to the fact of Roman domination. Not even Paul told the Roman Christians to like and admire the Roman overlords! Bauckham sees Revelation as one of the most effective pieces of political resistance literature from the period of the early empire (*Climax of Prophecy*, p. 338). There were many reasons why Roman domination was disliked by people of Jewish descent. Taxation and misunderstanding were merely two of them. It is remarkable that, in Revelation 13, we find the fiercest possible criticism of the existing order combined with the utterly passive belief that God alone will effect change. The anti-Roman language reflects John's more rigorous stance on the issue of social integration compared with Paul's. John encourages his readers to see the surrounding world as hostile, not friendly, and to keep a wary distance from it.

The apparent dissonance between Revelation 13 and Romans 13 is thus not so striking when Revelation's social situation and the purpose of its rhetoric are given appropriate consideration. The Apocalypse looks forward to the kingdom of Christ, as does Paul in Rom. 8.18-25. John presents the future kingdom as the standard by which the present life must be judged. It is important to observe that *not even if* Revelation was written in 69 CE can it be said that John encourages open resistance to Rome in the wake of the Neronian persecution. In reading this chapter, we must distinguish between the form of the symbolism and the social setting to which it is addressed. (I add, by way of a note to this section, that not all scholars are convinced that Paul himself was the author of Rom. 13.1-7, but this is not an issue that need concern us here).

The First Beast

Chapter 13 begins by describing a beast that comes up from the sea
(13.1). It will be followed in 13.11 by a second beast. These two beasts
continue the work of the dragon in their assault on the followers of
Jesus.

This first beast partially resembles the dragon. The description is less
precise than 12.3: 'on its horns were ten diadems, and on its head were
blasphemous names' (13.1). This possibly implies that the beast has ten
horns, but this information is not made clear. This beast is a hybrid that
resembles a leopard but it has feet like a bear and a mouth like a lion
(13.2). This description combines different elements from the four
beasts of Daniel 7. The dragon invests the beast with his power, throne
and authority (13.2b). This means that the beast exercises the dragon's
authority. The symbols may have changed but the presentation of the
Roman social world remains the same.

It is clear that this first beast is a symbol of Rome. The heads evidently
denote a sequence of emperors. Their identity is disputed, not least
because of the interpretative difficulties posed by 17.9-11 (see the Introduction). It appears from 13.3 that one of the beast's heads has a mortal
wound. This wound, however, is healed and the whole earth follows
the beast with wonder. The wounded head is generally taken to signify a
particular emperor: some think Caligula, who recovered from a serious
illness (see Suetonius, *Calig.* 14), but Nero is the more likely candidate.
The belief arose soon after Nero's death that he would return, either
from hiding in the East or from beyond the grave. This mythology was
still current in the early second century as we know from *Sib. Or.* 5.101-
104 (which comes from the reign of Hadrian) and from *Asc. Isa.* 4.1-4.
John preserves a form of this mythology in 13.3. It allows him to present
the pagan world in demonic terms by alluding to the supernatural power
of the Roman emperor.

John's reworking of imagery continues in 13.4. People worship the
dragon and the beast that bears its authority. They say: 'Who is like the
beast, and who can fight against it?' This question is a mocking parody
of the statement of Yahweh's uniqueness in Exod. 15.11 ('Who is like
you, O Lord, among the gods?'). It reminds readers of what they know
already, that God alone has the sovereignty and that the dragon is a
mere pretender. The statement that people *worship* the beast is strong
rhetoric indeed. It reinforces the fear of idolatry that undergirds the
Apocalypse as we saw in discussion of 2.14, 20. John presents the
Roman world in antithetical terms. He intimates that friendship with the
world means the service of God-opposing powers.

The beast is given a mouth to utter 'haughty and blasphemous words'
(13.5). This it does for 42 months. That recalls the behaviour of

Antiochus Epiphanes in Dan. 11.36 (cf. Dan. 7.8, 25; 2 Thess. 2.4). The passive 'was given' is deliberately vague. It might identify the dragon as the source of authority but it more likely refers to God so that the 'divine passive' is used. This would agree with the insistence of the whole Apocalypse that God determines all human events—even those that apparently work against his own people. The irony is that the beast does not recognize that God permits his every move. The figure of 42 months is another variant on the 'three-and-a-half times' that has featured several times already in the Apocalypse.

The beast blasphemes God, his name, his dwelling, and those in heaven (i.e. the angels, 13.6). There is a parallel for this blasphemy of the angels in Jude 8-10 which shows that the idea was a familiar one in early Christian apocalyptic. The thought is that the beast blasphemes every possible aspect of the heavenly world. No higher criticism can be made. This is *blasphemy*. John tells his readers how to regard a world order where the dragon and his beast are potent forces.

The beast is allowed to make war on the saints and conquer them (13.7). Its authority extends to 'every tribe and people and language and nation'. 12.7-9 has set the matrix in which this statement should be read. Readers know that the final sovereignty is God's and that the beast discharges power that he has been granted only temporarily. 13.7 develops the myth of Satan's fall by explaining that he harries *only* the people of God ('the saints'). Discipleship to Jesus is the crucial factor in determining how one fares in respect of the beast. The dualism once again tells readers to see their environment in hostile terms.

This polarized approach continues in 13.8. The Christians stand out because, unlike other people, they refuse to worship the beast. John says this is because their names have been written in the Lamb's book of life (cf. 3.5; 7.5-8). The predestinarian implications of this statement present Christians as necessarily distant from the aspirations of urban society. 13.9 contains a maxim, drawn from the sayings of Jesus, that the person with an ear should hear. Earlier in this book I called this 'the refrain' of the letters to the seven churches (chs. 2–3). This maxim introduces a proverb whose form varies across the manuscripts (13.10). The form given by the NRSV says that the captive will be taken captive and the person who uses the sword will be slain by the sword. This agrees with the words of Jesus in Mt. 26.52 and warns against the temptation to defend oneself with force. This form of words reminds the readers of the need for a peaceful co-existence with the present order while the eschatological age is born. Some scholars think that another reading, found in the fifth-century CE Codex Alexandrinus, is the more original. This softens the saying into a comment on the inevitability of persecution: 'If any man is to be killed with a sword, he is to be killed with a sword.' The agreement with the words of Jesus is the critical factor in deciding between these readings. One should probably argue that the majority text has the edge here for this reason.

The Second Beast

13.11 describes how a second beast emerges from the earth. This beast has two horns like a lamb but speaks like a dragon. Its lamb-like appearance makes it antitypical of Christ. There are parallels in this with the figure of 'Antichrist' in 1 Jn 2.18 in terms of the appearance of an eschatological opponent in the Christian scheme of the last things. The beast's true character is given by his speech. This links it firmly with the first beast and the dragon of ch. 12.

This second beast holds the authority of the first beast (13.12). It makes the earth and its inhabitants worship the first beast (cf. 13.4). The beast works great signs and makes fire come down from heaven (13.13). False miracles are a sign of the eschatological opponent in other Christian literature (see Mt. 24.24; 2 Thess. 2.9; *Asc. Isa.* 4). Calling down fire from heaven is attributed to the biblical Elijah (1 Kgs 18.38). This beast, however, is a *false* prophet (cf. Deut. 13.1) who acts in imitation (clearly, in *deliberate* imitation) of the Messiah. Its miracles deceive people into making an image of the first beast (13.14; cf. *Asc. Isa.* 4.11). This is not necessarily a reference to the imperial cult, for there is no statement that the beast forces people to sacrifice on behalf of the emperor which the Christians found offensive. The statement is symbolic and it criticizes the way that Rome held sway over the civilized world. It probably also criticizes the way that some emperors (Domitian included) were regarded as divine, albeit for the most part posthumously, but we should beware of confusing John's rhetoric with the actual situation addressed. The image of worshipping the beast, as before, invites the readers to consider where they stand in their social world and how they should react to it.

The effect of this beast's activity, according to 13.14, is that the 'inhabitants of the earth' are deceived and told to make an image for the first beast. This is in deliberate contravention of the Ten Commandments. Exodus 20.4 stipulates that 'you shall not make for yourself an idol, whether in the form of anything that is in heaven above, or that is on the earth beneath, or that is in the water under the earth'. That the beast should make such an image is a cause of great offence. The contrast is between a pagan religion, symbolized by an image, and a Christianity that proclaims the invisible God and the Lordship of Jesus. John allows no reconciliation between the two forms of religion. Those who follow Jesus must see all pagan religion as idolatrous.

13.15 states that the second beast gives breath to the image of the first beast. It speaks and causes those who will not worship its image to be killed. This illustrates in brief compass the impossibility of any compromise. Here, the critical action comes from the two beasts. John explains in parody why his readers cannot continue with the policy of social integration which some of them have adopted. The image of martyrdom illustrates the ultimate consequences of such behaviour. There is doubtless an echo here of the Neronian persecution (64 CE). This verse reveals awareness of a tradition of martyrdom that must have taken several decades to create (cf. *Asc. Isa.* 4.3). 3.15 recalls the events of 64 CE to draw readers back to an exemplary tradition that, it is implied, their present behaviour has begun to set aside.

The second beast furthermore causes its subjects to be branded on their right hands and foreheads (13.16). Branding was common in the ancient world. The branding of the slave and the practice of religious tattooing provide the closest analogies to this passage. This branding cleverly parodies the sealing of the tribes which the seer has seen already (7.5-8). It differs from the sealing in that the branding is required by a human agent but the sealing by the command of God. No one can bear two marks. John asks his readers which mark they prefer.

13.17 states that no one can buy or sell without the mark of the beast. This is a further call for those without the mark—that is, for Christians— to abstain from beneficial contact with pagan society. John hints in ch. 18 that trading relations with Rome were a source of concern in this respect. 13.17 reflects Rome's ability to direct the ancient economy through its great resources. It encourages readers who were merchants to consider whether they should be engaging in trading relations with Rome at all. The implication at any rate is that those who buy and sell bear the mark of the beast and that this is opposed to the sealing of God's elect. But we have no way of telling what concrete forms of action the Apocalypse produced among its readers. We can only note the different possibilities.

The number of the beast is given as the cipher '666'. This is said to be 'the number of a person' (13.18). Greek and Hebrew letters had a designated numerical value in antiquity (a practice called 'gematria'). The question of who this figure identifies is much discussed in the commentaries. The most common solution is that it stands for Nero when the Greek term *Nerōn Kaisar* is transliterated into Hebrew. This view is not without problems, for it requires a defective spelling of 'Caesar' and there are manuscript variants at this point. The variant '616' which is found in some of the manuscripts evidently derives from the calculation 'Nero Caesar' when the words are given in their Latin form. Nero's name is not mentioned by the earliest commentators on Rev. 13.18. The identification with Nero seems likely but it is not finally proven. Perhaps the figure is deliberately allusive, like the reference to the 'great city' in 11.8, which can bear more than one interpretation. If Nero is the correct identification, the fact that he is introduced under a cipher means that John is not so much interested in the historical Nero as in a mythological figure whose name created revulsion in Christian circles. The likely reference of the figure summarizes the chapter's essential terror and shows the mistrust with which John regards Rome and all its glory.

Revelation 14

Chapter 14 purposefully contrasts with ch. 13. The portrait of the Lamb and his elect on Mount Zion is set against the domination of the dragon and the two beasts. This chapter contains a collection of material that reinforces John's warning of judgment for those who do not keep to strict ethical standards. John promises that those who do what he asks will pass through the judgment and enjoy the Messiah's kingdom. He sets the experience of living in the Roman social world in its true light as the Lamb contrasts with the mythical creatures (14.1).

The Lamb and the Virgins

14.1-5 is a vision of God's elect as they stand with the Lamb on Mount Zion (cf. *4 Ezra* 2.42-47). The 144,000 bear his name and the name of his Father on their foreheads in contrast to the mark of the beast which is displayed by other people. This vision embodies a series of contrasts. The elect stand on Zion; the beasts come from the sea (13.1) and from the earth (13.11). Zion towers over them. This shows that those who follow the Lamb cannot be thwarted by the beasts. Some commentators worry that only the martyrs are designated by this passage (as by ch. 7), but it would be wrong to confuse this symbolic vision with John's actual eschatological expectations. This (apparently limited) figure is symbolic of all Christians inasmuch as they represent the true Israel of God. The fact that only adult male warriors are mentioned here again does not exclude women and children from the kingdom any more than does ch. 7 (see below).

In 14.2 John hears a loud voice from heaven. This sounds like many waters and like thunder, even like a harp (cf. Ezek. 1.24). It emerges from 14.3 that it is the new song that is sung by the redeemed. The text of this song is probably given by 15.3 (which is called 'the song of Moses... and the Lamb'). It represents the human contribution to the heavenly liturgy. The reference calls to mind Phil. 2.9-11 where representatives of the *whole* created order—not just the angels—worship the heavenly Jesus. There are parallels for humans joining the heavenly chorus also in the Qumran literature (e.g. 1QH 3.21-22). It is said here that *only* the Christian redeemed can learn the words of this song.

This song is a 'new song'. Its 'newness' calls to mind Hebrew Bible passages such as Ps. 96.1 but the adjective has a Christian connotation. The song is 'new' because it celebrates the sacrifice of Jesus (cf. 2 Cor. 5.17) which the Christians believed had effected a 'new covenant' (cf.

1 Cor. 11.25). A few years later Pliny would tell Trajan that the Christians rose early on a particular day of the week to sing a 'hymn to Christ as a God' (*Ep.* 10.96). This was the religious activity for which they were known in the ancient world.

The company of the redeemed are described under further images (14.4-5). They are said not to have defiled themselves with women and to be virgins; to follow the Lamb wherever he goes; and to have been redeemed from humankind as first-fruits for God and the Lamb. No lie is found in their mouth. The warrior imagery is prominent here (as in ch. 7). The first thing that is said about these warriors is that they are virgins. Some commentators—perfectly correctly—observe that unchastity is a regular biblical metaphor for religious infidelity (cf. 2.14, 20). The force of the allusion, however, is the fact that in the Hebrew Bible warriors must abstain from sexual relations to be in a state of purity for battle (see Deut. 23.9-14; 1 Sam. 21.5; cf. Lev. 15.18). The same rule is found at Qumran (see 1QM 7.1-7: 'No toddling child or woman is to enter their camps from the moment they leave Jerusalem to go to war until they return...All of them are to be men...unimpaired in spirit and flesh... Any man who is not yet cleansed from a bodily discharge on the day of battle is not to go down with them; for holy angels march with their hosts'). These 144,000 of Revelation 14 are men on active service. Their virginity indicates the importance of their mission. That is why they follow the Lamb wherever he goes and boldly enter the fray. They are about to undertake the eschatological battle. Their status as the 'first-fruits' (cf. 1 Cor. 15.20) means that the whole Christian body is included in the promise of salvation.

This interpretation of the passage means that it would be wrong to conclude that this passage encourages celibacy in view of the imminent end. That view was held by some Christians (e.g. Paul in 1 Cor. 7.8; Marcion and Origen), but the Apocalypse offers no support for it. In any event, the reference is to virgins and not to celibates. The fact that the Christian army are called virgins shows the symbolic nature of the reference. Their virginity means that they have not entered into defiling or compromising relationships. This striking icon shows the readers the defiling nature of their own condition and urges them to abstain from what they are doing (cf. 2 Cor. 11.2). It is far from clear (as with 1QM) how the material applies to readers' everyday lives, and by no means certain that any direct connection is intended. It would be wrong to take this passage out of context and to see celibacy as part of the desired lifestyle that John imposes on his churches.

14.5 continues the image of purity by saying that these people tell no lies. This looks back to Zeph. 3.13 which demands truthfulness of the remnant of Israel. These Christian redeemed are said to be without blemish (NRSV 'blameless'). This is an allusion to their priestly state (cf. Rev. 1.6; 5.10; 20.6). It has a Hebrew Bible background (see Lev. 21.17-

23). There is a further parallel in the passage from 1QM which says that the eschatological warriors must be 'unimpaired in spirit and flesh'. Battle-ready purity is the theme of John's symbolism. It has profound ethical implications for the readers.

The Angels and their Message

In 14.6 John sees an angel flying in heaven. This angel carries an 'eternal gospel' to proclaim to people on earth—to 'every nation and tribe and language and people'. The phrase 'eternal gospel' occurs only here in the New Testament, but the adjective 'eternal' is often used, especially in the Pauline and Johannine literature (e.g. in Jn 3.16 as a description of eschatological life). 'Eternal' means that Christ's people will enjoy his rule without restriction of time. The eschatological benefits are expected to be permanent ones. This prophecy is fulfilled at the end of the Apocalypse with the recreation of heaven and earth (21.1). The noun 'gospel' probably designates a particular message (see 14.7) and not 'the Christian gospel' in a generic sense. That the 'eternal gospel' is carried by an angel demonstrates the divine origin of this message.

The contents of the eternal gospel are disclosed by 14.7. The gospel proclaims the triumph of God over all opposition: 'Fear God and give him glory, for the hour of his judgement has come; and worship him who made heaven and earth, the sea and the springs of water.' This verse is a prophecy of impending judgment. It looks forward initially to the outpouring of divine wrath that is described in ch. 16, and beyond it to the description of the fall of Babylon in ch. 18. 14.7 is an apocalyptic announcement of this judgment in heaven that anticipates its exercise on earth.

In 14.8 another angel announces the fall of 'Babylon the great'. 'Babylon' is a symbol for Rome (cf. Isa. 21.9). The book of Daniel has influenced this passage. Daniel 4 describes the humiliation by God of the Babylonian king Belshazzar. Revelation 14.8 anticipates what will happen to another Babylon that refuses to display Belshazzar's humility in repentance. Rome is said to have made 'all the nations drink of the wine of the wrath of her fornication' (cf. Jer. 51.7). This links the eternal gospel of 14.7 specifically with the fall of Babylon in ch. 18.

14.9-10 pronounces the fate of those who bear the mark of the beast. A third angel states that these people will drink the wine of God's wrath. It will be poured unmixed into the cup of his anger; sinners will be tormented with fire and sulphur before the angels and the Lamb. 'Drinking the cup' is a biblical metaphor that symbolizes either domination (as in Jer. 51.7) or sorrow (as in Mk 14.36). Here it symbolizes both as the non-Christian world is made to recognize the power of the Christian God. God's wrath will be poured 'unmixed' to show its full force. Fire and sulphur is the Hebrew Bible's method of punishment by obliteration (see Gen. 19.24; Ps. 11.6; Ezek. 38.22; cf. Lk. 17.29). Later in the Apocalypse, Death and Hades are cast into the lake of fire and sulphur as their final place of punishment (19.14). 14.9-10 has important parallels with the Synoptic eschatology where the angels are expected to witness the destruction of the ungodly by fire in the presence of the Son of Man (see esp. Mt. 13.41-42; 25.31, 41; cf. also *1 En.* 48.9).

14.11 pronounces the everlasting character of this destruction. John says that the smoke of their torment will rise for ever and that they will have no rest. This contrasts with the rising incense that symbolized the prayers of the saints in ch. 8. The incense floats upwards in heaven; the smoke of destruction merely covers the earth. The statement that 'there is no rest day and night for those who worship the beast' is a significant one in early Christian eschatology. Several texts present 'rest' as the eschatological reward of the righteous (see 2 Thess. 1.7; Heb. 4-5; *Asc. Isa.* 4.15). These texts understand 'rest' as an earthly blessing that will result from the return of Jesus from heaven. The statement that those who worship the beast will lack 'rest' means that they will be excluded from the eschatological benefits. This explains the weighty language about punishment that is used throughout this chapter. One should beware of interpreting early Christian references to eschatological 'rest' as promising freedom from *specific kinds* of oppression. The term denotes eschatological emancipation in a general sense. It is founded on the notion of 'rest' that occurs in Ps. 95.11, with its background in Exod. 33.14. It cannot be taken as evidence that the Christians were suffering from Roman persecution.

14.12 gives this material an ethical application: 'Here is a call for the endurance of the saints, those who keep the commandments of God and hold fast to the faith of Jesus' (cf. 12.10). The vision of the Lamb and his elect jars with the earlier vision of the beasts. It gains its meaning from the angelic announcement of judgment for the ungodly. As throughout the Apocalypse, John implies that people fall into one or the other category. Those who do not stand on Mount Zion—which depends on the behaviour required by 14.4—will suffer as explained in 14.9-11. In the light of 14.12, we can see a potentially sinister meaning in the figure of 144,000 (14.3). This limitation of numbers (despite the statement about 'first-fruits' in 14.4b) implies that some may distance themselves from Christ's kingdom through their behaviour. That is a theme also of the Gospel tradition (see Lk. 13.22-30). 14.12 warns people not to let this happen and to persevere in their ethical separation because only this kind of behaviour will yield the eschatological benefits.

A Collection of Eschatological Visions

In 14.13 the seer hears a voice—presumably the voice of an angel—that pronounces on the blessed state of the dead: 'Write this: Blessed are the dead who from now on die in the Lord'. The Spirit (who is distinguished from this voice) adds that the dead rest from their labours and that their deeds follow them (14.14).

Death was a problem that increasingly troubled first-century churches as the return of Jesus proved further delayed (see 1 Thess. 4.14; 1 Cor. 15; 2 Cor. 5). The words 'from now on' on the face of it suggest that only those who die after the writing of the Apocalypse will be blessed, but this can hardly be the meaning of the verse. John offers assurance that *all* the dead will find 'rest'. The 'from now on' looks back to the sacrifice of Jesus which is the decisive moment in Revelation's eschatology. The succeeding verses give the meaning of this passage. We read there of the judgment over which the Son of Man presides. This blessedness is thus the emancipation of the elect which depends on the removal of the ungodly from God's kingdom.

The next vision describes the judgment (14.14-20). John sees a white cloud on which is seated 'one like the Son of Man'. He wears a golden crown and holds a sharp sickle. The Son of Man is here presented as the eschatological judge, as he is in the Gospels (cf. Mt. 13.41). His crown denotes authority and presents him as a regal figure, clearly as the Messiah. His sickle is for 'reaping', which means judgment. There is a close correspondence between this passage and the parable of the tares in Mt. 13.24-43 where the Son of Man sends out his angels to remove sin and the perpetrators of sin from the kingdom. It is clear that the direction of the Son of Man's movement in 14.14 is again from heaven to earth. This is a vision of the return of Jesus and of the judgment that his earthly appearance inaugurates.

In 14.15 an angel calls to Christ and tells him to begin the reaping because the harvest is ripe. This command clearly comes from God. It is mediated by the angel. Some commentators think that *Christ* sends out the angel who here reports back to him. Whatever the exegesis of this passage, Christ himself is said to reap the earth (14.16). There is no doubt that he is the agent of destruction and the angel merely a mediator.

In 14.17 another angel appears. In 14.18 yet another angel, one who has the power over fire, comes from the altar and tells the angel of 14.17 to reap the clusters of vine from the earth. Perhaps John has the 'vine of Sodom' of Deut. 32.2 in mind at this point because it is clear that these vines are destined for destruction. The vine is reaped by the angel after Christ has removed his elect. If readers think instinctively of the vine as a symbol of Israel, John effects a startling transition that stops them in their tracks.

This vintage is not for wine. It is thrown into 'the great wine press of the wrath of God' which is trodden outside the city (14.19-20). Blood flows from the winepress in copious quantities. This is a violent image of destruction. The background to it is Isa. 63.6 ('I trampled down peoples in my anger... I poured out their lifeblood on the earth'). There is an interesting parallel in the Targumic version of Gen. 49.11 where it is said that the Messiah will redden the mountains with the blood of the slain and resemble one who treads a winepress. That the judgment takes place 'outside the city' has a symbolic meaning. Jesus died outside Jerusalem (Heb. 13.12), as did Stephen (Acts 7.56). Executions were done there to avoid the ritual impurity that was associated with death near the holy place. John promises that God will punish the non-Christian world in a similar way to avoid the defilement that would otherwise be caused to his holy people.

Revelation 15

Chapter 15 falls into two halves. 15.1-4 describes the singing of the song of Moses in heaven. 15.5-8 describes how the angels prepare to cast the bowls of divine wrath onto the earth. This will be done in ch. 16. On my reading, 15.2-4 celebrates the end of the third woe which was announced as early as 11.14.

The Third Woe

At the beginning of ch. 15 John sees another portent. Seven angels bear seven plagues. These are called the last plagues that bring the wrath of God to an end (15.1). This information tells the reader that the Apocalypse is beginning to move towards its climax.

In 15.2 John sees a crystal sea (evidently because he is back in heaven; cf. 4.6). This is mingled with fire (a traditional accoutrement of the theophany; cf. Exod. 24.17 and Ezek. 1.27). Those who have 'conquered' the beast stand beside the sea and hold harps in their hands. They are portrayed as members of the heavenly chorus. 15.3-4 preserves the song that they sing. It is a hymn of two stanzas, both of four lines. The first stanza includes synonymous parallelism in which the second two lines repeat the thought of the first two lines. The second stanza is introduced by a rhetorical question ('Lord, who will not fear and glorify your name?'). This is followed by three reasons why people should fear God. Interestingly, this hymn has no christological content. This makes it less than likely that it represents the actual liturgy of John's churches. We are dealing with an imaginative composition that is shaped to suit the needs of the Apocalypse at this point.

The hymn is introduced by the statement that it is 'the song of Moses...and the song of the Lamb' (15.3). This links it with Exod. 15.1-8 where Moses and the Israelites sing a song to celebrate their safe delivery from Egypt. The description of the hymn as 'the song of the Lamb' is problematic given the lack of christological content. Perhaps the author means that the hymn is one that the Lamb himself sings. That would alleviate the problem of the change from subjective to objective genitive if the song concerns the triumph of the Lamb ('which Moses sang...about the Lamb') In this case, John may even see the Lamb as the leader of the heavenly chorus. That was an angelic function in Judaism (cf. *Asc. Isa.* 9.1), so that we would then have further evidence of an angelomorphic Christology in the Apocalypse. There is also perhaps the hint that Christ was active in the events of the Exodus, for which there is a parallel in 1 Cor. 10.4 (cf. Justin, *Dial.* 61, 128).

The song is placed in this position because it gives the meaning of the plagues that follow. The heavenly chorus gives an authoritative commentary on the impending visions of judgment. What follows in the Apocalypse demonstrates the justice and insuperability of the God who towers above the pagan deities and the society that venerates them. The hymn draws extensively on the language of the Hebrew Bible and it shows that John has meditated deeply on the Bible. Among the passages that have been identified as sources for the hymn are Exodus 15; Deut. 32.4; Ps. 11.2; 86.9; 98.2; 139.14; 144.17; Amos 4.13; and Mal. 1.11. The statement that all the nations will worship God offers a radically different assessment, which has roots in apocalyptic and eschatology, of the way that society viewed the Christians. Christians were often held in suspicion because the nature of their religious practices was not fully known. John says that, in the future, this position will be reversed and that the Christians will be justified when all others perish in the judgment. This information is disclosed in the form of an apocalyptic vision.

The statement that 'your judgements have been revealed' (15.4b) provides the cue for John to reveal the judgments of God. This he does in the second half of ch. 15. To begin the dénouement of the Apocalypse, John describes the 'temple of the tent of witness in heaven' being opened (15.5). This passage looks back to the similar words in 11.19 ('Then God's temple in heaven was opened...'). The correspondence is deliberate and suggests that John is making a special point in this context. This is that the third woe, which was presaged by the liturgical material in 11.15-18 and introduced by 11.19, has been completed with the liturgical celebration of 15.3-4. The correspondence between 11.19 and 15.5 lets the reader make this deduction from the Apocalypse, although John does not say explicitly that the third woe has been completed.

Out Come the Angels

The completion of the third woe sets the scene for the pouring of the bowls of wrath with which God's anger will be finished. Out of the temple come seven angels bearing the plagues (15.6). These angels are robed in linen and they wear golden girdles. The phrase 'tent of witness', which is used in Numbers (17.7; 18.2), calls to mind the wilderness sojourn that followed the Exodus from Egypt. It links these eschatological plagues with the Egyptian plagues (but only seven plagues are mentioned here in line with John's prevalent symbolism).

One of the creatures gives the angels the seven bowls of wrath (15.7). This emphasizes the divine origin of the impending misfortune. Readers are left in no doubt that this is God's final punishment of the earth. To heighten the air of solemnity, the temple is filled with smoke from 'the glory of God and his power', and entry is barred until the plagues have ended (15.8). (The background to this verse is the Hebrew theophanic tradition, especially perhaps Isa. 6.1-4 [cf. 1 Kgs 22.19] which says that the temple 'filled with smoke', evidently from the incense). The smoke symbolizes the presence of God and especially his arising for judgment. The barring of entry into the temple shows that an important event is under way. We read the details of the plagues in ch. 16.

Revelation 16

John now sees the plagues poured from the bowls by the angels. A voice commands the angels to pour the bowls onto the earth. The owner of the voice is not identified. It might be God's, but it could equally be an angel's or Christ's. There is no doubt, however, that the command to pour comes with the authority of God. God is the source of the plagues which are caused by and represent his wrath.

The outpouring of God's wrath begins. The *first angel* pours his bowl onto the earth (16.2). Those with the mark of the beast break out in sores like the Egyptians of Exod. 9.9-11. Where once the mark provided security, now it yields the most unpleasant effects. There is an implied reminiscence of the sealing (ch. 7) which protects the servants of God from the sores (again in perpetuation of the Exodus tradition).

The *second angel* pours his bowl onto the sea (16.3). The sea turns to blood and all the fish die. This statement recalls Exod. 7.20-21. The phrase 'like the blood of a corpse' shows the horrid effect of this plague. The *third angel* pours his bowl into the rivers and fountains (16.4). They all turn to blood. This metamorphosis recalls Ps. 78.44. The implication is that people have no good water to drink. The supernatural disaster produces unpleasant effects in the human world (cf. 8.11).

The pouring of the third bowl is followed by a liturgical interlude (16.5-7). The 'angel of the waters' sings that the Holy One is just in his judgment (cf. 15.3-4). This judgment is just because its victims have shed the blood of saints and prophets and so must be given blood to drink (16.6). From the altar—where the martyrs are (6.9)—comes the reply that God is certainly just and true in his judgments (16.7). There is a sense in which the determinism of 13.9-10 (the proverb about the inevitability of persecution) is turned here against those who are responsible for the persecution. The people who shed the blood of saints and prophets are made to drink their blood. There is possibly a distant echo of the tradition recorded in Mt. 23.34-35 that the blood of the righteous in Israel will be requited on the eschatological generation (and cf. Rev. 18.24 in this context).

The *fourth angel* pours his bowl on the sun (16.8). The sun scorches people. Despite their torment, they foolishly fail to recognize the true significance of the plagues. Instead of repenting and acknowledging God 'who had authority over these plagues', they blaspheme his name (16.9). Readers can only ponder the folly of those who act in this way. The *fifth angel* pours his bowl onto the throne of the beast. Its kingdom is plunged into darkness (16.10). People gnaw their tongues in pain.

This imposition of darkness recalls Exod. 10.21-29 (the ninth Egyptian plague). The notion of the world as a kingdom of darkness is a special Johannine theme (see Jn 3.19; 12.46). Perhaps there is also a hint of the tradition that lies behind Mt. 8.12; 25.30 and that speaks about the 'utter darkness' that is reserved for the ungodly. But still people 'cursed the God of heaven...and they did not repent of their deeds' (16.11).

The *sixth angel* pours his bowl on the river Euphrates (16.12). Its water dries up 'to prepare the way for the kings from the east'. This passage recalls 9.13-19 where the angels bound at the Euphrates are loosed to destroy a third of humankind. It is probably significant that the Euphrates separated the Roman Empire from the Parthians who are the best candidates for the 'kings from the east' in this reference. As with Jeremiah's 'foe from the north' (Jer. 1.14 *et al.*), the precise identity of the opponents is not made specific to sustain the note of uncertainty. One form of the *Nero redivivus* myth held that the emperor was in hiding in the East, so that mythological as well as historical opponents must be considered in this allusion. The verse calls to mind the manner in which the Israelites left Egypt (see Exod. 14.21), when the Red Sea parted to permit their safe passage.

Another Interlude

16.13-16 is another interlude before the outpouring of the seventh bowl. This interlude heightens the dramatic effect of the chapter. In 16.13, three foul spirits like frogs come from the mouths of the dragon, the beast and the false prophet. It is difficult to relate this material to the description of the sixth bowl (and even to decide whether a formal connection is warranted). 16.15 in particular seems ill suited to its context. Charles (characteristically) wonders whether the text is disturbed at this point (*Critical and Exegetical Commentary*, I, p. 49). But the material must be interpreted in its present form. The dragon has been introduced in ch. 12. The 'false prophet' is presumably the second beast of 13.11-17. John's entourage of mythical creatures reappears as a prelude to their final destruction. In this context, their deceitful character is heavily emphasized. The spirit that comes from their mouths is called a 'foul spirit', which means a 'lying spirit'. One thinks here of the 'spirit of falsehood' that features in the Qumran literature (see 1QS 3.13–4.1). As in the Gospels, evil spirits are connected with the opponents of Jesus and his followers. There are further parallels with 1 Jn 4.3 which speaks of 'the spirit of the antichrist'.

These foul spirits assemble the forces of the nations for the final conflict (16.14). The spirits are called 'demonic' and are said to perform 'signs'. In the language of early Christian eschatology, this means that they presage the end (cf. Mt. 24.24; *Asc. Isa.* 4.4-11). The notion that 'the kings of the whole world' join the conflict comes from Ps. 2.2 (cf.

Acts 4.26); 'the great day of God the Almighty' from Zeph. 1.14 (cf. Jude 6). 16.14 preserves the general apocalyptic notion, found in the book of Daniel (chs. 10–12), of a great world conflict, but gives it a specifically Christian orientation in the belief that these hostile powers will perish before the kingdom of Christ (cf. 1 Cor. 15.24). There is perhaps the sense, given that the spirits are the principal actors, that the 'kings' are morally neutral agents in the drama and inspired by supernatural opponents.

16.15a repeats the saying about the thief in the night (which has several New Testament parallels) from 3.3. This saying derives in one form from Jesus (Mt. 24.43). It was reinforced by its repetition on the lips of Christian prophets (like John himself). The frequent occurrence of this saying in the New Testament literature reflects the problem that the delayed return of Jesus was felt to cause for Christian eschatology. John offers reassurance that Christ will come but he leaves the timescale of this intervention tactfully imprecise. A non-specific prophecy of the *parousia* holds its currency much more easily than a precise and specific one.

A second prophecy is appended to this saying (16.15b). John adds a macarism which praises the person who keeps awake and does not let his nudity be exposed. This too has parallels in the preaching of Jesus, notably the parable of the wise and foolish virgins (Mt. 25.1-13). The point of that parable is that not even substantial delay means that the bridegroom will never come. John reflects the characteristic Jewish horror of nudity at this point. As opposed to Paul in 2 Corinthians 5, who uses nudity as a symbol for death, John calls his readers to a state of eschatological alertness. He says that those who claim to be Christians must stay alert or else they will face the judgment.

16.16 predicts that the kings of the world will assemble at the place called Harmagedon in Hebrew. Harmagedon means 'mountain of Megiddo'. Megiddo was well known as a battlefield in the ancient Near East (see, e.g., Judg. 4–5). Commentators who accept this etymology are puzzled by the knowledge that Megiddo is a plain and not a mountain; but, as throughout the Apocalypse, symbolism is more important to John than topographical accuracy. The alternative etymologies proposed for Harmagedon are all unconvincing. This reference to Megiddo may have been suggested by Judg. 5.19-20 (cf. Wis. 5.17) which says that the stars fought there for Israel. John perhaps understands the stars as angels and takes the reference to imply a conflict in which heavenly forces become involved (cf. Dan. 10–12).

The Seventh Bowl

After this interlude, the *seventh angel* pours his bowl into the air (16.17). A voice comes from the throne with the words, 'It is done!'

This means that the final judgment of God has been undertaken (cf. Jn 19.30). Suddenly there is lightning, thunder and an earthquake such as has never been seen before (16.18; cf. 4.5; 8.5; 11.19). The 'great city' splits into three parts (16.19). The other cities and nations fall. John says that God 'remembers' Babylon and makes her drain the cup of his wrath (16.19).

The 'great city' and 'Babylon' are both names for Rome (cf. 11.8). Some have disputed this identification, but John expects that every city will fall. Under those circumstances, it is natural for Rome to head the list. The fall of Rome is described in more detail in the next two chapters of the Apocalypse. The notion that God 'remembers' is used in the Hebrew Bible both of his mercy for Israel (Gen. 9.15; Lev. 26.45) and of his punishment of sinners (Ps. 137.7; Hos. 7.2; 8.13). The word here carries the second and more sinister sense. The reference to the cup repeats the image of 14.10 ('they will also drink the wine of God's wrath') and shows that this prediction is fulfilled in the seer's concluding visions.

The islands and mountains disappear (16.20). There is a similar description in *1 En.* 1.6 ('mountains and high places will fall down and be frightened'). This (much earlier) reference shows the apocalyptic ambience from which this passage is constructed. Hailstones drop from heaven (16.21). Each weighs a hundredweight (cf. Josh. 10.11; Ezek. 38.22). But, once again, humankind curses God in a further demonstration of its folly (16.21b).

Revelation 17

Chapter 17 continues the description of the final judgment. John turns his attention specifically to Rome. He portrays the Roman Empire under the image of the whore and the beast in terms that recall the language of ch. 13. This chapter further demonizes Rome, and encourages its readers to stand their distance from the conventions of Asian urban life.

One of the angels of the bowls tells John that he will see the judgment of the 'great whore' who is 'seated on many waters' (17.1). The whore stands for Rome in John's apocalyptic symbolism. The term has the implied meaning that life under Rome means obeisance to pagan gods. The angel continues that the 'kings of the earth' have committed 'fornication' with her and that people have become drunk with the wine of her fornication (17.2). In my discussion of the letters I showed that 'fornication' means social accommodation (e.g. 2.14, 20) in a context where the eating of meat sacrificed to idols is mentioned. John again uses the Jewish horror of unchastity to encourage social distinctiveness among his urban readers.

In 17.3 the angel carries the seer in the spirit into the wilderness. There, John sees a woman seated on another scarlet beast full of blasphemous names and with seven heads and ten horns. The promise of 17.1 is here fulfilled. There is a tradition in both the Hebrew Bible (1 Kgs 19) and Christian literature (Mt. 4; *Asc. Isa.* 2.7-11) that apocalyptic experience takes place in the desert. Perhaps solitude contributed to the experience of revelation. We are evidently to think of John as once again on earth and transported by the spirit in a mysterious journey similar to that described by Ezekiel (Ezek. 11.1). This beast recalls the two creatures of ch. 13, especially the first beast with its ten horns and seven heads (13.1). The scarlet colour emphasizes the woman's status as a whore. The seven heads symbolize the seven hills of Rome. 17.9 will say that they stand for seven emperors.

The whore is clothed in purple and scarlet and covered with jewels (17.4). She holds a golden cup full of 'abominations and the impurities of her fornication'. Purple was a royal colour (see Dan. 5.7) and scarlet splendid, despite its pejorative overtones. Revelation reserves the colour white and the plainness of linen for the faithful servants of God (e.g. 3.3; 19.8; cf. Ezek. 9.3; Dan. 10.5). The woman's gaudy appearance contrasts with the earlier description of the martyrs (see 3.4-5, 18; 4.4; 6.11). This makes for an important subversion of images. The splendours of life under Rome, symbolized by loud colours, are presented as a false glory in view of the purity that John demands. This point is also made by the reference to the cup. Its colour may be golden but it contains only abominations (cf. 17.2). What is superficially attractive has been poisoned by corruption.

The whore has a mysterious name on her forehead (17.5). Evidence from Seneca (*Controv.* 1.2) and Juvenal (*Sat.* 6.123) shows that this was the practice of Roman courtesans. John picks up this tradition to criticize Roman domination. The adjective 'mysterious', which has sometimes (but incorrectly) been taken as part of the inscription (as by the AV), gives the meaning of 'the name' and shows that it has a cryptic meaning (cf. 2 Thess. 2.7). John proceeds to disclose this meaning: 'Babylon the great, mother of whores and of earth's abominations.' This revelation of the whore's name contrasts with John's refusal to disclose the hidden name of God (3.12). John thereby distinguishes between true Christian apocalypticism (with its heavenly origin) and its demonic and inferior imitation.

17.6 introduces a yet more grotesque image. This idolatrous woman is said to be drunk with the blood of the saints and the martyrs of Jesus. The Neronian Persecution (64 CE) remained an enduring Christian memory as we know from *Asc. Isa.* 4.3, *1 Clem.* 5.4 and Ignatius, *Rom.* 4.3. The author presents Rome as gorging herself on Christian blood in a striking reminiscence of that event. It is not necessary to suppose that Revelation addresses a *current* situation of persecution to explain this imagery. The language is primarily symbolic but it recalls earlier events. It involves a further development of the 'drinking blood' theme from 16.6 which makes the point that Rome will be punished for her arrogant behaviour. The image is a vivid one which rightly engages all readers of the Apocalypse.

The angel promises to tell John the 'mystery' of the woman and the beast (17.7). Frustratingly for modern commentators, John is more concerned to show that the forces of God will overcome the powers of evil than to identify this beast in detail. We do not know whether a more explicit identification had already featured in John's teaching before his writing of the Apocalypse, but this is perhaps not unlikely.

John says that the beast 'was, and is not, and is about to ascend from the bottomless pit and go to destruction' (17.8). The first part of this statement is modelled on the earlier descriptions of God (1.4; 4.8) and Christ (1.18; 2.8). It presents the beast as their demonic and inferior counterpart who has no permanent existence. The 'was' alludes to his earlier activity—probably to the Neronian persecution, but also more generally to the whole history of Roman domination. John says that the beast currently 'is not'. This alludes to his imminent unleashing on earth: 'he is to ascend from the bottomless pit'. That reflects the Christian eschatological belief, found earlier in the Apocalypse, that a powerful opponent will appear immediately before the kingdom of Christ (cf. 2 Thess. 2.3-8). The 'pit' is the dwelling-place of Abaddon/Apollyon which was mentioned in 9.11 (cf. 11.7). 20.3 presents it as the dragon's place of intermediate confinement.

The beast's appearance is said to amaze 'the inhabitants of the earth' (17.8). This is due to the fact that 'those whose names have not been written in the book of life from the foundation of the world' (cf. 3.5) fail to recognize its demonic character. They are completely taken in by the beast. John reminds his readers that they have been enlightened about the beast's place in the eschatological scheme and that their knowledge will help secure their place in the Messiah's kingdom (provided that they remain faithful to the ethical teaching John gives them in the Apocalypse).

The Interpretation of the Vision

John now turns to the question of the beast's identification (17.9-14). As in 13.18, he says that 'a mind that has wisdom' is needed. This indicates that John will continue to use symbolism but that his imagery permits a historical interpretation. Readers must decipher the interpretation from their own knowledge. No doubt first-century readers would have been less puzzled by the symbolism than are readers today (but it is not certain that *everything* was clear to them).

John gives the beast's 'seven heads' two related interpretations (7.9). He identifies them both as the seven hills of Rome ('seven mountains on which the woman is seated'; cf. Virgil, *Aen.* 6.782) and as 'seven kings', that is, seven Roman emperors (17.9). 17.10-11 discusses the identity of the emperors in question. The seer says that 'five have fallen, one is living, and the other has not yet come'. When this emperor comes, he will reign for 'only a little while' (17.10). In 17.11 the beast of 17.8 is identified as an eighth king 'who belongs to the seven' and 'goes to destruction'.

It is impossible to be certain about the identity of these emperors despite the apparent simplicity of the allusion, as the different interpretations that have been proposed for this passage show all too clearly. The problem is to know where the list begins and whether all the reigning emperors are included in it. Robinson (who dates Revelation in 69 CE) begins his interpretation with Augustus and includes the so-called 'soldier emperors' (Galba, Otho and Vitellius) in the list (*Redating*, pp. 221-53). This makes the reigning emperor Galba and 'the one yet to come', Otho. Yet 17.9-11 can also be read to accord with the date attested by Irenaeus if the list begins with Caligula and the reigns of Galba, Otho and Vitellius are omitted as too short to be considered significant. Domitian would then be the reigning emperor and Nerva the 'one yet to come' (he acceded in 96 CE). Care must be taken to acknowledge the ambiguity of 17.10-11 in discussion of the date of the Apocalypse.

The language is primarily symbolic and mythological and it does not necessarily offer a full historical precision.

17.12 interprets the ten horns. These are said to be ten kings who have not yet received a kingdom. John says that they will receive authority for one hour together with the beast. These horns are evidently foreign kings whom most commentators identify with the Parthians. Again, the force is mythological and not literal: the horns are eschatological symbols and not actual monarchs known to the author. They will reign for only a short time and be 'united in yielding their power and authority to the beast', whose authority remains as yet unchallenged (17.13).

Because the kings are united with the beast, they are opposed to the Lamb (17.14). John allows for no 'middle position'. He says that they will make war on the Lamb but that the Lamb will conquer them because he is 'Lord of lords and King of kings'. These Jewish titles for God present Christ as a divine being (for their background see Deut. 10.17; *1 En.* 9.4). The Lamb will conquer the beast just as God conquers his enemies in Hebrew Bible mythology (e.g. Ps. 74.13-14). That will be the final victory over the forces of evil. John adds that 'those with him are called and chosen and faithful' in echo of his earlier symbolic description of the Christians (cf. 14.4).

The interpretation continues in 17.15. The waters on which the whore is seated (17.1) are said to be 'peoples and multitudes and nations and languages'. This obvious hyperbole includes the whole social order in the seer's condemnation and shows that the Apocalypse is not set against Rome's world domination in any limited sense. John, like Jesus before him, is not interested *only* in the removal of Roman sovereignty. His goal is the advent of Christ's kingdom and the recreation of the existing order (chs. 20–22). John here criticizes Rome because Rome is responsible for the arrangement of things as they are. She sits on the waters. The waters flow round her. The whole picture, not just the centrepiece, receives John's forthright condemnation.

17.16 introduces a sinister note into the vision. The horns and the beast turn against the woman, strip her naked and leave her desolate. They devour her flesh and burn her up with fire. The language derives from Ezek. 16.37-41 and 23.25-29 which describes the fate of adulterous Israel at the hands of foreign lovers. There is an echo also of the fate of Antiochus Epiphanes in Dan. 11.40-45 who is expected to perish after the opposition of his subject kings. In Rev. 17.16, the *beast* joins with the kings in attacking the whore. This reworks the imagery of ch. 13 to imply that the Roman Empire is suffering from demonic opposition, and apparently from internal conflict. 17.17 adds that God has put it into the hearts of the kings to give their kingdom to the beast 'until the words of God shall be fulfilled'.

17.18 formally identifies the woman as 'the great city that rules over the kings of the earth'. This statement brings the chapter to its climax and removes any lingering doubt about its meaning. The force of the statement is not merely to identify the 'great city' as Rome but to indicate both the universal nature of Rome's tyranny and the punishment that this will bring. The judgment begins with Rome because Rome rules the Mediterranean world.

Revelation 18

Chapter 18 describes the fall of Babylon (Rome). This is the final act of destruction. It precedes the Messiah's return from heaven in 19.11. This chapter voices a powerful economic critique of the Roman Empire. It explains the consequences of Rome's fall for those who enjoy trading relations with the city.

The Fall of Babylon

In 18.1 an angel appears from heaven. He is said to possess great authority. The earth shines with his splendour. This angel's high status signifies the importance of his revelation. It concerns the fate of Babylon: 'Fallen, fallen, is Babylon the Great!' (18.2; cf. Isa. 21.9). He adds that Babylon has become the dwelling-place of demons and the haunt of every foul spirit, bird and beast (cf. the LXX text of Isa. 13.21; Jer. 50.39; and Zeph. 2.14). This passage utilizes a medley of biblical passages to describe the fall of Rome which John regards as the greatest disaster so far. It is an obvious reversal in fortune which subverts the perception of reality that readers hold at present.

18.3 repeats the image of the 'wine of the wrath of her fornication' (cf. 17.4). John adds that the merchants of the earth have grown rich from 'the power of her luxury'. This draws attention to the economic aspect of John's criticism which stands to the fore in this chapter. John criticizes trading relations with Rome because they let the merchants benefit from the existing order which John holds demonic. Such relations provided the opportunity for the kind of compromise that John criticizes in his letters. As previously, there is the implied suggestion that those who engage in such activities must consider their position carefully.

Another heavenly voice speaks in 18.4. It tells 'my people' to come out from Babylon and to take no part in her sins, for fear that they may share her plagues. The voice does not necessarily belong to God (it could be an angel's) but the words are certainly God's, as the vocative shows. The nearest Hebrew Bible analogy is Jer. 51.45 where the prophet tells people to leave Babylon before the city's destruction. John the Apocalyptist's command to leave this latter-day Babylon has a symbolic sense which advises readers to maintain high social boundaries.

18.5 states that Babylon's sins are heaped as high as heaven (cf. Jer. 51.9) and that God has remembered her iniquities (cf. 16.19). 'Remembering' means 'punished'. Judgment follows sin in the Christian understanding (cf. Rom. 2.16). 18.6 presents God's judgment on Babylon in the form of the divine imperative. Render to Babylon as she has rendered to others and repay her double for her deeds! Mix a double draft for her in the cup that she has mixed! (cf. Isa. 40.2; Jer. 17.18). Babylon will be punished because she has 'glorified herself and lived luxuriously' (18.7). She will be given a similar torment and grief. Babylon thinks that she is a queen and not a widow who has seen grief (cf. Isa. 47.7-8). Her plagues will come in a single day. The city will be tormented with pestilence, mourning and famine. It will be burned all in one go—'for mighty is the Lord God who judges her' (18.8). Rome had not often been defeated in battle—but John says she will not be able to withstand the divine onslaught that is soon to be unleashed against her.

The kings of the earth who have committed fornication with Babylon stand far off to mourn her destruction (18.9-10). They lament that her destruction has come in one brief hour. Such weeping is not without self-interest, however generous it seems. The fall of Babylon means that those who benefit from her custom will be deprived of their income from trade.

The Merchants are Bankrupt

Bauckham has shown the economic importance of trading relations with Rome for the different provinces of the empire (*Climax of Prophecy*, pp. 338-83). 18.12-13 is a list of merchandise that will not be sold when Babylon falls. The piling up of information is characteristic of the apocalypse genre. It shows the breadth of knowledge to which the different writers aspire. Ezekiel 27 supplies the idea of a list of merchandise but John fills out the details himself (and arranges it in different categories). Bauckham notes this is the longest extant list of Roman imports in the literature of the early empire (*Climax of Prophecy*, p. 350). The merchandise is typical of the new-found wealth of Roman families in the late first century CE.

Gold is an obvious luxury. It was used by wealthy Romans (see Tacitus, *Ann.* 3.53; Pliny, *Nat. Hist.* 33.39-40). Silver was also prized by the wealthy. Precious stones were criticized by Pliny who thought them an unhealthy passion (*Nat. Hist.* 37.2). Pliny saw pearls in much the same light (*Nat. Hist.* 9.105). Linen was beginning to replace wool as a raw material for clothing in Rome. It no doubt had different degrees of fineness. Purple, silk and scarlet were expensive too (cf. *Nat. Hist.* 9.127). Thyine or citrus wood was imported from Africa and used to make tables. Even in the first century, Pliny complained that the fashion for ivory was threatening the survival of the elephant (*Nat. Hist.* 8.7). Other woods that the Romans used included maple, cedar and cypresses. Iron had a variety of applications, not least the manufacture of arms. Marble was popular in Rome; Augustus boasted that he found Rome brick and left it marble (Suetonius, *Aug.* 28.3).

Cinnamon (18.13) was valued for a variety of purposes. Spice came from India. Incense was used for religious ceremonies and for fragrancing a room. 'Ointment' includes myrrh and was expensive. Frankincense was used at funerals. Wine was profitable to produce, more so apparently than corn, hence Domitian's edict that the provinces must halve their viticulture. Oil was imported from Spain and Africa. 'Fine flour' is distinguished from ordinary flour; the best came from North Africa (see Pliny, *Nat. Hist.* 18.89). Wheat was needed in large quantities and was imported. Cattle were imported from Greece and Italy (according to Strabo 6.2.7; 7.7.5, 12); Strabo mentions the importation of rams for breeding as well (3.2.6). Horses were brought from Spain and Cappadocia; chariots from Gaul. Slaves come last in the list (lit. 'bodies and souls of men'—the 'and' is epexegetic). Many slaves came from Asia Minor; skilled or beautiful slaves could be considered extravagances (see Tacitus, *Ann.* 3.53).

This list of merchandise shows the kind of goods from which 'the merchants of the earth' were making money from the Romans. This explains their lamentation in 18.11, 15-17 which is spoken from the perspective of those who were used to profitable trading relations with Rome. This passage is not a distant and academic interest in other people's fall in profits. It has an important social and economic function in the Apocalypse. John includes this material because, in all probability, some of his readers were doing very well from their trade with Rome, either as producers or exporters and possibly as both. The seven churches would probably have included some who made their living in this way. The passage warns reasonably prosperous and complacent readers to stand their distance from the influence of the Roman system which is represented in the Apocalypse under the symbols of the whore and the beast. John does not indicate in precise terms *how* he wants readers to do this, but Thompson's model of 'high social boundaries' applies across a number of practical situations—not least in the banquets and trade associations that were an important part of commercial life in the Asian cities (see *Book of Revelation*). The imagery encourages readers to make their own deductions about their lifestyle from it. John's criticism of trading relations may have been a very painful message for some of his readers.

18.14 summarizes this reversal of fortunes in a dirge. The fruits and dainties which brought pleasure have gone and they will never be replaced. 18.15-17a continues the description of the mourning of the merchants. Some of the extravagances that were mentioned in 18.12-13 are repeated here to make the point that the disaster is a substantial one.

In 18.17 the 'shipmasters and seafarers, sailors and all whose trade is on the sea' join the ranks of the mourners. These people earned their living from taking the produce from the provinces to Rome. Their living vanishes, too. 18.18 records the dirge of the seafarers: 'What city was like the great city?' (cf. Ezek. 27.32). In 18.19, these people cast dust on their heads. John here offers an important historical commentary on the position that Rome enjoyed in the first-century world: 'All who had ships at sea grew rich by her wealth!' Bauckham's study (*Climax of Prophecy*, pp. 338-83) shows that this is not hyperbole but contains a considerable truth. The effect of the divine judgment is well described in the stark conclusion of this passage: 'For in one hour she has been laid waste' (18.19). This is a sharp reminder of the complete transformation that John expects God's judgment to effect.

Heavenly Rejoicing

18.20 changes the tone from mourning to rejoicing. It is an isolated oracle which tells the 'saints, apostles and prophets' to rejoice over Babylon's judgment. 'Saints' designates human beings as well as angels in Jewish and Christian literature (cf. Rom. 1.7; 15.26; 1 Cor. 6.1). Human beings are obviously meant here. 'Prophets' means Christian prophets and not their Hebrew Bible counterparts (cf. 1 Cor. 12.28; Eph. 2.20). This call for rejoicing has a special piquancy if some of John's readers were profiting from trade with Rome. We remember that the function of the heavenly chorus is to give the true meaning of earthly events. In 18.21, the fall of Babylon is depicted in further symbolic terms as an angel picks up a stone like a millstone and casts it into the sea. The millstone, being a large stone, plummets to the bottom. This is the force of the allusion. The fall of Rome is a mighty catastrophe. The following verses show the consequences of this fall in a further list of revealed information.

18.22-23 is a list of things that will no longer be seen or heard when Rome falls. The list begins with harps and minstrels, flutes and trumpets. Harps are played in the Apocalypse by the elders (5.8) and conquerors (15.2); trumpets by the angels (chs. 8-9). The playing of heavenly instruments contrasts with the silence that is now imposed on Rome (cf. 8.1). The city's silence is a sign of mourning if not of total destruction. Babylon will also lose her artisans and corn-grinders, her light and her weddings (cf. Jer. 25.10). John says that this is because she has deceived the nations with her sorcery (18.23). The heavenly chorus has good reason to celebrate because Rome's fall prepares the way for the coming kingdom of Christ (19.11; cf. 11.15).

18.24 sets the seal on this chapter. It gives in summary the reason for Babylon's fall: 'And in you was found the blood of prophets and of saints, and of all who have been slaughtered on earth'. This statement answers the question of the martyrs that was raised in 6.10: 'How long will it be before you judge and avenge our blood on the inhabitants of the earth?' Chapter 18 offers an apocalyptic demonstration that this anticipated vengeance has now been achieved. 18.24 comments powerfully on the inevitability of divine retribution. This is an important theme of the Apocalypse which is repeated here as John begins to look towards the return of Christ from heaven.

Revelation 19

The scene is now set for the introduction of the Messiah's kingdom. The description of Babylon's fall is followed by a victory cry in heaven (19.1-8). 19.9-10 is a brief interlude in which an angel refuses John's worship. 19.11-21 marks the watershed of the Apocalypse. It describes how Christ returns from heaven to commence his judgment on earth.

The Victory Cry

At the beginning of ch. 19 the heavenly chorus celebrates God's judgment of the whore of Babylon and his avenging of the blood of the saints (19.1-2; cf. Deut. 32.43). This passage picks up themes that have become familiar in the Apocalypse and asserts with vigour that God's justice cannot be thwarted. The chorus adds that the smoke of Babylon's destruction will rise for ever and ever (19.3). This demonstrates the severity of the punishment which, like the new creation, has no end.

In 19.4 the elders and creatures prostrate themselves before God and cry, 'Amen! Hallelujah!' (cf. 5.6-10). In 19.5 a voice comes from the throne. It calls on the servants of God to praise him (cf. Ps. 113.1). Since the voice comes from the throne, it can hardly belong to an angel. 3.21 (and probably also 5.6) locates the Lamb on the throne of God. He must be the speaker here. If so, the Lamb again appears as the leader of the heavenly chorus (cf. 15.3). This is further evidence for an angelomorphic Christology in the Apocalypse.

In 19.6, the heavenly multitude responds to the voice from the throne. These are the vast numbers of people mentioned in 7.9 and 15.2-3. They cry, 'Hallelujah! For the Lord our God the Almighty reigns.' The chorus continues that the marriage of the Lamb has arrived and that his bride is prepared for the wedding (19.7). There is a fusion of imagery here (as so often in the Apocalypse). The notion of the eschatological feast ('the messianic banquet') is familiar in the New Testament, especially the tradition of the sayings of Jesus (see, e.g., Mt. 8.11). It has its origins in Jewish eschatology (see, e.g., 1QS 6.2-5). It is here combined with the notion of the wedding which is also familiar from the Gospels (Mt. 22.1-14; 25.1-13) and from the Hebrew Bible. Hosea 2.19 speaks of an 'everlasting betrothal' between God and Israel. In Revelation, the thought is that the betrothal is past and that the wedding day has arrived. In this case, the bride must be the church. Christ comes from heaven to join her. The wedding symbolizes the eschatological climax that will be described in the last part of the Apocalypse. There is no hint here, as in the parable of the wedding feast (Mt. 22.1-10), that those who are invited to the feast spurn the invitation. But there is indeed the admonition that only the worthy will experience the blessings of the end time.

19.8 states that the bride is arrayed in fine linen. This linen recalls the dress of the 24 elders in 4.4 and the promise made to the righteous in 3.4. It is interpreted at the end of this verse as 'the righteous deeds of the saints'. Here we have a further call for ethical action. John constructs a scenario in which Christ returns from heaven to claim his bride. It is implied that the bride must be in a pure condition for the wedding. The linen dress symbolizes this state of purity. As before, the Christian eschatological hope is made the basis of John's ethical appeal. John tells his readers that *only* the pure belong in the church. Those who want to share Christ's kingdom must adopt the behaviour that John recommends. The fine linen *is* the righteous deeds of the saints (19.8). Those who do not do 'righteous deeds' do not wear the linen, nor will they share the eschatological destiny that it represents.

We must not underestimate the realism with which the first-century Christians hoped for the return of Christ and for the establishment of his kingdom as an earthly entity. Whether or not John expects a banquet in the literal sense, he clearly does anticipate the return of Christ from heaven quite literally. John is at one with all of first-century Christianity in this. That his language is symbolic does not obscure the realism of his future hope, which takes the distinction between heaven and earth seriously. 20.4 will describe the earthly rule of Christ as the preparation for the re-creation of heaven and earth in 21.1.

Do not Worship an Angel!

19.9 pronounces another formula of blessing (macarism). The angel says, 'Blessed are those who are invited to the marriage supper of the Lamb.' In 19.10, John falls at his feet to worship this angel but he is told not to do so because the angel is a 'fellow-servant' who holds with him 'the testimony of Jesus'. It is difficult to decide whether this genitive is subjective or objective (and neither need really be excluded). To this is added the command to 'worship God' and the statement that 'the testimony of Jesus is the spirit of prophecy'. Here again it is difficult to know whether the genitive is subjective or objective. The saying appears to mean that the true prophet will proclaim what Jesus tells him to proclaim. This perhaps gives the edge to the subjective genitive at this point ('the testimony which comes from Jesus'). That would tie in with the overall theme of the Apocalypse which is that John must proclaim Christ's message to the churches. The implication is that a false prophet, like the Jezebel mentioned in 2.20, has not genuinely been commissioned by Christ.

19.10 stands in a wider tradition which surfaces in other apocalypses and where an angel tells the seer to worship the divine being(s) alone (cf. *Asc. Isa.* 7.21-22; *Apoc. Zeph.* 6.11-15). The background to this tradition is the Hebrew habit of prostration before the angelophany (see, e.g., Dan. 10.8-9), to which is here added the offering of worship which originally did not belong to that tradition. It is not necessary to suppose that this tradition developed because some Christian (or even Jewish) circles worshipped the angels as a supplement or alternative to the worship of God. There is a little evidence that angels were venerated in Judaism (see Stuckenbruck, *Angel Veneration*, pp. 200-203), but this was never done to the exclusion of the worship of God. The Apocalypse gives no sign at all that angelolatry was widespread in John's churches. 19.10 is more than anything a rhetorical device that draws attention to the divinity of the Messiah who will come from heaven to establish the new order. This device turns the spotlight on Christ who now enters the action through his return to earth.

The Return of Christ

19.11 marks the watershed of the Apocalypse. John sees heaven opened (an apocalyptic event in itself) and a white horse on which Christ is seated. Christ himself is not named initially. It is said that 'its rider is called Faithful and True, and in righteousness he judges and makes war'. It is, however, obvious to whom this description refers. White is the symbolic colour of righteousness in the Apocalypse. It is attributed both to the conquerors (3.4) and to the elders (4.4). It is not surprising to find it here attributed to Christ. The picture is of the skies opening to let Christ undertake his final journey from heaven to earth. This passage shares the Gospels' hope for the return of the Son of Man (e.g. Mt. 13.41; 26.64) but the language is distinctive to the Apocalypse, particularly the use of militaristic symbolism. It has something in common with Jewish eschatology (cf. 1QM; *2 Bar.* 72; *Pss. Sol.* 17.23-27). Christ returns to earth to carry out the judgment and introduce his kingdom (20.4). This will be the prelude to the recreated order (21.1).

19.12 recalls some earlier passages from the Apocalypse. The first half of the verse recalls 1.12-16 in its statement that Christ has 'eyes like a flame of fire'. On his head are many diadems. This description purposefully contrasts with the hydra-like appearance of the beast in chs. 13 and 17. It illustrates in symbolic form the belief that Christ is 'Lord of lords and King of kings' (17.14). The reference to Christ's mysterious name recalls 3.12 and the promise that mystical knowledge will be disclosed in the eschatological age (cf. 14.1; 17.5). This section of the Apocalypse (19.13, 16) reveals Christ's mysterious name under the principle that what belongs to the end time can be revealed in a description of the end time. That is why the Apocalypse closes with the command, which disagrees with other apocalypses (and indeed with 10.4b), that the words of the prophecy must *not* be sealed because 'the time is near' (22.10). The knowledge disclosed in the Apocalypse is authoritative knowledge because it has been gained through revelation. The rationale of the Apocalypse is that this can now be revealed because the eschato-logical age is impending.

As earlier, the white colour is referred to the fact that Christ's garment is dipped in blood (19.13; cf. 7.14). This clash of imagery refers to the sacrifice of Jesus from which the Christology of the Apocalypse takes its cue (cf. 5.6; 14.19-20; and the Palestinian Targum to Gen. 49.11). That the returning Messiah wears bloodstained robes confirms that his victory has been won. It shows the price of that victory. Christ's return to earth is the end of a contest whose outcome has never been in doubt in the apocalypse.

The first of Christ's mystical names is 'The Word of God' (19.13). This was a familiar title in early Christology (see Jn 1.1-18; cf. Heb. 4.12). This passage has a background in earlier Jewish literature, especially the description of Wisdom in Wis. 19.15-16 where the Word of God is said to be a warrior who leaps down from heaven. John's Gospel is relevant too. Where Jn 1.1-18 describes the enfleshment of the Word of God, John the Apocalyptist describes his second appearance on earth. Revela-tion's language is further reminiscent of the Hebrew Bible theophanies (e.g. Zech. 14.5) where God himself appears on earth for judgment.

The heavenly Christ is followed by the angel hosts (cf. Mt. 13.41), as God is attended by angels in the Hebrew theophanies (19.14; e.g. Zech. 14.5; *1 En.* 1.9). The angels' white linen dress indicates their heavenly origin and implies their ethical purity. The distinctive feature of this passage is that the angels, like Christ, are seated on white horses. From the mouth of Christ proceeds a sharp sword with which he will strike down the nations (19.15; cf. Isa. 11.14). John holds in common with Heb. 4.12 the belief that the word of God has an irresistible power. The Apocalypse has much to say about the power of demonic opponents. John says here that Christ will vanquish all opposition at a single stroke. The swiftness of his victory contrasts with the protracted opposition to the Christians before the eschatological age was born.

Christ will now 'rule' the nations with a rod of iron (19.15). The Greek word 'to rule'—*poimainein*—was used in 7.17 to describe Christ's tender care for his redeemed. 19.15 deliberately recalls that pas-sage and says that Christ's care involves the subjection of those who oppress the people of God. The implied note of vengeance in this passage derives from Ps. 2.9. The last phrase of 19.15 ('he will tread the wine press of the fury of the wrath of God the Almighty') recalls the imagery of 14.19-20.

19.16 discloses more mysterious names of Christ. On his robe and thigh are inscribed the words, 'King of Kings and Lord of Lords'.

1 Timothy 6.15 shows this title was not invented by John but that it circulated more widely. Its source is the divine acclamation 'Lord of lords' in Deut. 10.17 (cf. Ps. 136.3) and the epithet 'King of kings' of Ezek. 26.7 and elsewhere. The attribution of this title to Christ is another example of the transference of titles for God to Jesus in early Christianity (cf. Phil. 2.9-11 in this context). This mystical name, although purportedly revealed to the readers, is not in fact new to them for it has been mentioned already in 17.14.

In 19.17 an angel announces the 'great supper of God'. This is a variation on the wedding feast of 19.7 which we have seen to denote the eschatological banquet. This angel is said to be 'standing in the sun'. That is probably a symbolic declaration that the kingdom of darkness has been brought to an end (cf. 9.2). Righteous figures are often connected with the sun in Revelation (see, e.g., 1.16; 7.2; 10.1; 12.1).

This angel calls to the birds of heaven and tells them to eat the flesh of the vanquished (19.18). 19.18 mentions several different groups of vanquished. The impression is that all of these have perished in the eschatological battle and that, because of their deeds, they will not enjoy the kingdom of Christ. There are echoes here of the procession to the caves in 6.15-16 where people try in vain to hide from the wrath of the Lamb. Chapter 19 confirms that this procession is futile and that no one (of whatever rank) can shelter from the wrath of the Lamb which is now quite visibly displayed.

These people will perish in the final battle. 19.19 describes this event which was anticipated in 16.16 (but the name, Harmagedon, is not mentioned here). The beast and the kings of the earth (the imagery comes from ch. 17) gather to make war on the heavenly army. The beast is captured along with the false prophet (19.20). Both are cast into the lake of fire and sulphur (2.20b). The combination of these punitive elements denotes the severity of their punishment.

The armies of the beast are destroyed in the wake of their leaders (19.21). They are killed by the sword from the mouth of Christ. The birds gorge themselves on their flesh. It becomes clear from 20.12-15 that this is merely an intermediate punishment. It precedes the general resurrection and the 'second death' that are mentioned in the next chapter.

Revelation 20

Chapter 20 describes what happens on Christ's return. John mentions Satan's imprisonment (20.1-3) and Christ's rule on earth with the martyrs (20.4-6). This is followed by the further activity of Satan (20.17) and the general resurrection and judgment (20.11-15). All of this is preliminary to the re-creation of heaven and earth which are described in ch. 21.

Satan's Imprisonment

In 20.1-3 John sees an angel descend from heaven with the key of the 'bottomless pit' and a 'great chain'. This pit is the abyss which was mentioned in 9.2 and which was said to be opened in that verse. Now the angel seizes the dragon, binds him and throws him into the pit (cf. *1 En.* 88.1) in preparation for his final punishment. Chapter 20 makes it clear that this abyss is a 'holding-place' and not the place of final perdition. At the end of the thousand-year period 'he must be let out for a little while' (20.3). This prediction is fulfilled in 20.7-10 when Satan reappears to receive his final destruction.

John carefully distinguishes the punishment of the dragon (20.1-3) from that of the beast and the false prophet in 19.20. The thought is that the dragon, or Satan, as the instigator of the opposition and the source of the beast's authority (13.4), has not yet been vanquished (as these others have been). He has more work to do. This is why his final punishment is postponed until 20.10. The eschatology of the Apocalypse has some distinctive features when compared with the other New Testament documents. We shall note these as our reading of the final chapters proceeds.

Satan is initially said to be bound in the pit for the period of a 'thousand years' (20.2). This figure derives from Ps. 90.4 ('For a thousand years in your sight are like yesterday when it is past, or like a watch in the night'). The same figure appears in later Christian eschatological calculation through the influence of the book of Revelation. Its use here is related to the belief that the saints will reign undisturbed on earth with Christ for a thousand years before the general resurrection (20.4).

In 20.3 the pit is locked and sealed to prevent Satan's escape. This means that, despite his seeming power, Satan is subjected to the authority of God. The coming of Christ's kingdom means that there is no place for the kingdom of Satan. As in the parable of the strong person (Mt. 12.29), which John conceivably knew, the coming of the stronger

person restrains the strength of even the strong one. Satan's imprisonment is a provisional declaration that his rule is over (cf. 12.7-9). His
tyranny will finally be eradicated in the middle of this chapter.

Christ's Kingdom on Earth

20.4 is one of the most familiar but also controversial passages in the
whole Apocalypse. The opening words ('Then I saw thrones') recall the
theophany of Dan. 7.9 as if John deliberately recollects the moment
when judgment is given for 'the people of the saints of the Most High'
(Dan. 7.27) in the heavenly court. John says that 'those seated on them
were given authority to judge'. The judges' identity is not disclosed. It is
possible that they are angels but more likely that they are 'the Twelve'
who are said in Mt. 19.28 and parallels to assist the Son of Man in his
judgment. The thought is that the eschatological age has the character
of a theocracy in which God's rule is discharged by Christ who is assisted
by the Twelve as the heads of the tribes of Israel.

20.4 says that those who 'had been beheaded for their testimony to
Jesus and for the word of God' and who 'had not worshipped the beast
or its image and had not received its mark' come to life and reign
with Christ for a thousand years. The reference to beheading (a Roman
method of execution) makes these people martyrs. We have seen that
martyrs feature prominently as symbols for the righteous in the Apocalypse. There is no attempt to specify their number as there is in 7.4. Nor
are they distinguished from the greater multitude of Christians as they
are in 7.9. In John's symbolism, these martyrs are probably the entirety
of the Christian dead who are distinguished from the rest of the dead
(i.e. the non-Christian dead) in 20.5. The thought is that *only* those who
do what John requires will share the first resurrection.

20.6 supports this broader understanding of 20.4: 'Blessed and holy
are those who share in the first resurrection. Over these the second
death has no power, but they will be priests of God and of Christ, and
they will reign with him for a thousand years.' Here it is said that those
who share the first resurrection are the 'priests of God and of Christ'.
This means the whole company of faithful Christians. Their participation
in the first resurrection is made, as it were, the guarantee that 'the second death' will not harm them. To interpret 20.4 as applying to the martyrs *alone* is by implication to exclude non-martyred Christians from the
eschatological benefits. This seems an unlikely interpretation, and it mis-
takes the nature of John's symbolism by confusing his imagery with
reality.

This hope for the earthly reign of the saints contrasts with other New
Testament literature in detail but not in fact in the overall orientation of
its eschatology. Unique here are the specification of the 'thousand years'
as the duration of the earthly reign of Christ and the suggestion that

there will be two resurrections. The notion of more than one resurrection probably derived from the eschatology of Dan. 12.1-2 which appears to describe a selective resurrection in which 'many' of the dead will arise to receive appropriate reward or punishment. The notion of a temporary messianic kingdom features in *4 Ezra* 7.28-29 and *2 Bar.* 40.3, both of which were written around the same time as Revelation. One wonders whether John was influenced at this point by apocalyptic traditions that were circulating in the later first century CE. It would be wrong to call Rev. 20.4 a 'temporary' messianic kingdom in the sense that Christ's rule is destined to be replaced by something else within the existing order. It is, however, true to say that 20.4 is merely an intermediate stage and not the goal of Revelation's eschatology, which is the recreation of heaven and earth in ch. 21.

The distinction between the first and the second resurrections must be seen in this light. The notion of the first resurrection reflects the long-established Jewish belief that the martyrs will be vindicated by God. The distinction between the two resurrections highlights the importance of this vindication as John presents it. The second resurrection means that the ungodly will be punished when the vindication of the martyrs has begun. The Apocalypse thus retains belief in universal resurrection but distinguishes different phases within it in order to make judgment a prominent feature. The resurrection of the ungodly permits their judgment and eternal punishment in the lake of fire (20.15). John's scheme ensures that the godly are rewarded and the ungodly justly punished.

Satan is Released

20.7-8 describes what happens when the thousand-year period of 20.4 ends. Satan will be released from his prison and emerge to deceive the nations 'at the four corners of the earth, Gog and Magog'. He will gather them for battle (20.8). This passage is probably to be linked with the reference to Harmagedon in 16.16 and the unnamed battle of 19.19. We now find the absolutely final conflict in which the forces of evil are destroyed for ever. Gog and Magog are symbols for the world as it stands opposed to God (cf. Ezek. 38.2, 9). 20.7-8 is a dramatic and pictorial representation of the stance that readers must take against the delights of the world in their various communities. This is a battle in which the forces of God will prove victorious, John tells his readers.

20.9-10 describes the downfall of the enemy forces. The nations march from all over the earth and 'surround the camp of the saints and the beloved city' (cf. *4 Ezra* 13.1-12; Hab. 1.6). This image derives from Ps. 34.7 where the angel of God encamps around those who fear God and delivers them. John applies this Hebrew background to the forces of Satan. Fire comes down from heaven and consumes them (20.9b), as in the story of Elijah where fire from heaven consumes the enemy soldiers (see 2 Kgs 1.10-12; cf. Lk. 9.51-54). In 20.10 the devil is thrown into the lake of fire and sulphur as his place of final punishment. He joins the beast and the false prophet (19.20) to experience everlasting torment.

Resurrection and Judgment

After this punishment, a white throne is erected (sc. on earth, 20.11). Earth and heaven flee from the presence of its holy occupant. The scene is reminiscent of that described in the *Similitudes of Enoch* (*1 En.* 62) where the Son of Man dispenses judgment against the ungodly from his position on the throne of God. The 'white' colour in this passage reflects the holiness of God. The 'one who sat' on the throne is God, less obviously Christ (although cf. 2 Cor. 5.10). The notion of heaven and earth fleeing from the divine presence once again recalls the futile passage to the mountain caves described in Rev. 6.15. Wicked people can find no shelter from the wrath of the Lamb.

In 20.12, the dead stand before the throne and the books are opened. This passage mentions two different kinds of books. The first is the heavenly ledger which records all human deeds. This is familiar from other apocalypses (e.g. *Asc. Isa.* 9). The Lamb's book of life is a special feature of the New Testament Apocalypse. It contains the names of the redeemed alone. This reinforces the ethical dualism and signifies that salvation is for the righteous alone. It is said by Rev. 3.5 that names can be deleted from the Lamb's book as well as inserted in it so that there is no necessary predeterminism of salvation. The reference to the book of life says as much about ethics as it does about eschatology.

In 20.13 the sea gives up its dead, as do Death and Hades. All are judged according to their deeds. In 20.14 Death and Hades are thrown into the lake of fire (cf. 20.10). This is 'the second death' of which John speaks. As in Paul's understanding of eschatology (1 Cor. 15.26), death is the last enemy to be destroyed. All whose names are not written in the book of life are thrown into the lake of fire (20.15). This is the place of ultimate perdition which permits of no escape. The second death brings eternal damnation from which the beneficiaries of the first resurrection are happily delivered.

Revelation 21

Chapter 21 explains what happens after the enemies of God have been destroyed. The chapter anticipates the recreation of heaven and earth (21.2) and the descent of the heavenly Jerusalem (21.2). This is the final goal of John's eschatology.

Eschatological Re-creation

The Messiah is now on earth and presiding over his kingdom. The victory has been won and the ungodly judged and destroyed. John turns his imagination to the renewal of the created order. The existing creation—heaven and earth—vanishes to be replaced by a new and perfect counterpart (21.1). There are parallels in this with what Paul says in Rom. 8.18-25. Paul speaks of the 'hope that the creation will itself be set free from its bondage to decay and will obtain the freedom of the glory of the children of God'. Revelation uses different language but the hope for the renewal of creation is strikingly similar in the two texts. This correspondence shows that it was a major item of hope in the context of early Christian eschatology.

The background to this eschatology is the Isaianic hope that the 'former things' will pass away (e.g. Isa. 65.17; 66.22). Isaiah mentions the specific hope for the recreation of heaven and earth on which John draws at this point. The hope for the renewal of all things is found in other Jewish apocalypses such as *1 En.* 45.4-5; *4 Ezra* 7.30-31; and *2 Bar.* 74.2-3. The real difference between the eschatology of Paul and that of the Apocalypse lies in the timing of the earthly kingdom (20.4). John separates this from the renewal of all things by the description of Satan's further activity (20.7-10). John's contact with Pauline eschatology shows that the Apocalypse stands nearer the mainstream of the New Testament than is sometimes imagined.

John does not say that the heavens and earth will be destroyed (although that may be implied), but merely that they will 'vanish'. The reason for this is that their perfect counterparts have now appeared. The language of apocalyptic is to the fore here. Like the new Jerusalem in 21.2, the new heaven and earth appear as pre-existent realities that are revealed from heaven by the will of God. The one significant feature of this new creation is that it has no sea (21.2). Probably this is because the sea is regarded as the domain of chaos in the Hebrew Bible (see, e.g., Isa. 27.1) which the kingdom of Christ has subdued. This does not detract from the fact that the gulf between heaven and earth is breached in this passage. John expects this removal of these boundaries to be a feature of the eschatological age.

In 21.2 the new Jerusalem descends from heaven, prepared like a bride for her husband. The idea that the true Jerusalem is a heavenly reality is found in Jewish (e.g. *4 Ezra* 7.26) and other Christian literature (e.g. Gal. 4.26; Heb. 12.22). The notion of the heavenly city as a bride reworks the imagery of the wedding feast (19.9) and it provides an alternative to the view that the *church* is the bride of Christ which features in ch. 19. It is utterly characteristic of John to reshape his imagery in this way. John says that the eschatological age will yield a closer union between heaven and earth in which the heavenly realities become accessible to people who have previously known of them only through apocalyptic revelation.

A voice from the throne pronounces on this blessed state of affairs: 'The home of God is among mortals' (21.3). This statement makes the last point precisely. God, whose dwelling-place is heaven, has become an accessible deity because the barrier between earth and heaven has been removed. God now dwells with his people. This passage is similar once again to Paul's comment that in the eschatological age 'God will be all in all' (1 Cor. 15.28). The fact that John uses symbolic language makes it inappropriate to ask whether he is guilty of anthropomorphism (i.e. of describing God in human terms) at this point. The passage directly echoes the Holiness Code of Lev. 26.11-12 and its promise that 'I will make my dwelling in your midst, and I shall not abhor you'. For all this, the hope for God's immediate presence appears to be a realistic one. The context of Leviticus 26 makes it clear that this promise is reserved for those who keep the commandments of God (see Lev. 26.3, 14). John's imagery thus contains a scarcely veiled admonition in the suggestion that only those who are obedient will experience the presence of God. The reader knows that the disobedient have already been cast into the lake of fire (21.15), and draws an appropriate conclusion from that information.

The description of the future blessing continues in a medley of promises (21.4). God will wipe away every tear from people's eyes. Death will be no more (cf. 1 Cor. 15.26). Crying and pain will disappear. This is because the 'first things' have passed away (cf. Isa. 35.10). There can be no more direct statement that the eschatological age has fully arrived than this description of the new creation.

The one seated on the throne (i.e. God himself) says, 'I am making all things new' (21.5). He commands John to write down what he hears, adding that 'these words are trustworthy and true'. The command to write is a familiar instruction in the Apocalypse (cf., e.g., 1.11). The message that John is to write is announced in 21.6, 'It is done!' (cf. Jn 19.30). This refers to the new creation and to the provision of eschatological benefits which are described in the rest of the chapter. The voice repeats the statement, 'I am the Alpha and the Omega', from 1.8 (21.6). This means that the God who created the world will bring it to perfection. Creation and eschatology are part of a homogeneous process in the Apocalypse. This is related to belief in the uniqueness of the Jewish God by which John sets much store. To this is added the statement that God will give the thirsty water from the spring of the water of life (Isa. 55.1). As is appropriate to the last times, scriptural prophecy is now shown as being fulfilled.

21.7 repeats the promise that those who 'conquer' will inherit these benefits. This sets the seal on the Apocalypse and repeats its basic theme. 'Conquering' means 'persevering till the end'. This promise is set in the future tense to provide a warning to the readers. John says that (only) those who persevere will know the intimate presence of God. Repetition emphasizes the ethical aspect of the message and shows that John is not writing an eschatological treatise alone. He is using (his version of) the Christian eschatological tradition to call his readers to a separate form of life, so that eschatology undergirds the ethical appeal.

21.8 states the other side of this picture by reasserting the warning of judgment for the ungodly. There follows a list of ungodly. Those mentioned here are types. There is really only one distinction, between those who do and those who do not follow what John says. The different groups all have relevance for the situation John addresses. 'The cowardly' head the list because they lack the courage or motivation to stand out against the attractions of Asian urban life. 'The faithless' abandon their principles by acting in this way. The rest of the list criticizes such people in the familiar language of the Pentateuch (sorcerers, idolaters, liars and the like). It introduces an ethical dualism which reinforces the urgency of the challenge: *only* those who obey the message will escape the lake of sulphur that awaits the ungodly and that is here again called 'the second death' (cf. 20.6, 14).

The New Jerusalem

In 21.9 one of the seven plague-angels tells John that he will see the bride, the wife of the Lamb. In 21.10 the angel carries John in the spirit to a high mountain where he sees 'the holy city Jerusalem coming down out of heaven from God'. The seer has *already* seen this in 21.2, but the logic is that of an apocalyptic vision and not of an ordered narrative. The repetition sets the new Jerusalem at the centre stage of John's eschatology. It draws attention to the purity of the revealed city. This suits the ethical argument since it reflects the sense of separateness that John requires of his readers. The fact that John finds no problem with repetition shows his manner of working in the Apocalypse. Repetition and variation are important stylistic devices. They reinforce its essentially simple message.

The second half of ch. 21 is devoted to a description of the new Jerusalem. The holy city is said to possess the glory of God and the radiance of a translucent crystal (21.11). It has a high wall with 12 gates (21.12). These gates are inscribed with the names of the tribes of Israel. This description is modelled on the later chapters of Ezekiel where the prophet describes the temple and the new Jerusalem in considerable detail (Ezek. 40–48). It calls to mind Paul's statement that 'the Jerusalem above' is the mother of the Christians (Gal. 4.26), and the expectation of the author of Hebrews that Christians are journeying towards a city that has yet to be revealed from heaven (Heb. 12.22). This hope for the new Jerusalem was central to Christian eschatology, as these passages show. It implies a view among the Christians that they were the true Israelites to whom the biblical promises would be granted.

In 21.14, the wall of the city is given 12 foundations, on which are written the names of the 12 apostles. The apostles are presented as the foundation-stones on which subsequent building has occurred (cf. Eph. 2.20). It is difficult to accept that this passage was written in the 60s when many of the apostles were still alive. It better suits a situation in the 90s, the date for which I argued in the Introduction. The interpreting angel holds a golden measuring-rod to measure the city (21.15; cf. Ezek. 40-41). There is an obvious parallel with the measuring of the temple in 11.1-2, but with the difference that the earthly sanctuary has now been replaced by its true and heavenly counterpart. Gold symbolizes heavenly artefacts in the Apocalypse (cf. 4.4; 5.8; 9.13). This measuring-rod is golden because it is used to assess the heavenly Jerusalem that has now appeared on earth.

The nature and dimensions of the city are described in some detail (21.15-21). Jerusalem apparently has a cubic shape. Commentators often compare this with the shape of the inner sanctuary in 1 Kgs 6.20. This is a plausible background given John's interest in priestly matters in the Apocalypse. The city's dimensions are given as 12,000 stadia (i.e. fifteen hundred miles, 21.16). There is an obvious link with the 144,000 of ch. 7 which allows for 12,000 warriors from each of the 12 tribes. In 21.17, the wall of the city is said to measure 144,000 cubits. 21.18 adds that the wall is built of jasper and that the city resembles gold, clear as glass. Perhaps this indicates a jasper inlay and not a wall built completely of jasper, but in any event the reference links this passage with the description of the throne of God in 4.3. The jasper colour shows that the whole city embodies God's presence. This is the theme of the entire chapter given that John anticipates the removal of the barrier between heaven and earth in the eschatological age.

The foundations of the city are adorned with jewels (21.19-20). Twelve different jewels are mentioned. The number is clearly symbolic. The model for this passage is the description of the High Priest's breastplate in Exod. 28.17-20 (but John's list displays several differences from that passage). The overall impression is that no imaginable expense has been spared in the construction of this city. As an example of this, the gates of the city are said to be 12 whole pearls (21.21). There is an interesting parallel in *b. Sanh.* 100a and *b. B. Bat.* 75a which state that God will set pearls and other gems in the gateways of Jerusalem. The Apocalypse quite conceivably reflects early rabbinic tradition at this point. John says also that the streets of the city are pure gold, transparent as glass (21.21). This repeats the image of 21.18 and applies to the streets what was said there about the walls of the city. The implied link with ch. 4 reinforces the point that the whole city embodies God's presence.

In 21.22—most unusually—the holy city is said to have no temple. This is a striking departure, not just from Ezekiel, but also from the earlier chapters of the ·Apocalypse which describe a heavenly altar, the central feature of a temple (6.9). The implication is that the temple as a symbol of the divine presence vanishes now that the divine presence itself has been revealed from heaven and is embodied in the city. This rebirth of images has the logic once again of the apocalyptic vision. The temple is now said to be the Lord God Almighty and the Lamb (and not a lesser building). The city similarly has no need of sun and moon, for the glory of God is its light and its lamp is the Lamb (21.23; cf. Isa. 60.1, 'Arise, shine; for your light has come, and the glory of the Lord has risen upon you'; Isa. 60.19-20, 'the Lord will be your everlasting light, and your God will be your glory').

21.24 adds that the nations will walk by this light and that kings will bring their glory into it. This too is Isaianic in origin; Isa. 60.1-3 anticipates that the nations will come to Jerusalem in the last days. Isaiah's thought that Israel is the light of the nations is here taken up most effectively by the Apocalypse. 21.24 describes the eschatological pilgrimage of the Gentiles to Jerusalem in fulfilment of Hebrew prophecy. Chapter 21 closes with the promise that the gates of the city will never shut and darkness never fall (21.25). Darkness symbolizes evil powers that have already been destroyed in John's scheme of eschatology. By contrast, the glory and honour of the nations will pour into Jerusalem (21.26). This repeats the thought of the Gentile pilgrimage from 21.24 and echoes the thought of Isa. 60.5 ('the wealth of nations shall come to you'). It is essential to John's eschatological symbolism that the Gentiles will be included in Israel in the last days. This is what Paul also believed (Rom. 11.26). The point is that those who engage in pagan practices will be subordinated to the God of Israel whose will the Apocalypse claims to disclose in John's strict ethical message.

Revelation 22

Chapter 22 brings the Apocalypse to its full conclusion. The chapter falls into two parts. 22.1-5 completes John's vision of the eschatological climax. 22.6-21 is an epilogue. It consists of a collection of oracles and sayings that makes the work complete.

In 22.1-2, the angel shows John the water of life. This is bright as crystal and it flows from the throne through the streets of the city. This image alludes to the story of creation in Genesis 1–3 and perhaps also to Ezekiel's description of the sacred river (Ezek. 47.1-12). On either side of the river stands the tree of life which produces its fruit each month. The leaves of this tree are for the healing of the nations (22.2). The statement that the tree provides 12 different fruits draws on the numerical speculation which pervades the Apocalypse and to which the 12 foundation jewels (21.19-20), the numbers of the sealed (7.5-8) and the dimensions of the city (21.16) are related. This makes it a thoroughly Christian tree in John's symbolic logic.

John's vision completes what is lacking in the Genesis story of creation. According to Genesis, Adam and Eve's crime was to eat from the tree of the knowledge of good and evil. This resulted in their expulsion from the Garden of Eden. Their banishment prevented access to the tree of life that offered the prospect of immortality. Now, John declares, the tree of life is freely offered even to the nations—the Gentiles—who are healed by its leaves. What was inaccessible in the primaeval age has become accessible in the eschatological age, just as God and the Lamb are now accessible beings. In this sense, it seems, the end is almost better than the beginning and it completes what was lacking even in the early chapters of Genesis.

Nothing accursed (i.e. forbidden by the Law) is found in the new Jerusalem (22.3-4). The throne of God and the Lamb is there (22.3; cf. 3.21; 5.6). The servants of God see God's face as they worship (22.4). In apocalyptic Judaism the vision of the face of God is reserved for certain angels alone (cf. Tob. 3.16-17). It is specifically denied to Moses in the context of the Sinai theophany (see Exod. 22.20b)—and even to John earlier in the Apocalypse (ch. 4). John now says that the servants of God enjoy the same vision of God as the angels. The knowledge enjoyed by heavenly beings is shared between people on earth because the barrier between heaven and earth has been breached. 22.4 says further that the name of God will be written on people's foreheads. This calls to mind the sealing of the saints (ch. 7) and the reference to the mystical names in 3.12 whose force we saw to be both mystical and eschatological.

Where the beast had branded his followers (13.16), the servants of Jesus declare their true identity with the opponents removed from the scene.

22.5 repeats the promise that night will be no more. John says that the Lord God will be the light of his people and that 'they will reign forever and ever'. This passage indicates that the new order will be without limitation of duration. This is related to the view that death has been destroyed which is expressed in 20.14. It also reflects the provision of fruit from the tree of life which is made available in 22.2. This means that it is possible to detect a clear eschatological scheme in Revelation. This involves the *parousia* (19.11), the establishment of Christ's kingdom (20.4) and the recreation of heaven and earth (21.2). This is by no means different to what Paul believes (Rom. 8.18-25), but John sets it in the context of his unique apocalyptic imagination.

Epilogue

22.6 introduces the collection of sayings that conclude the Apocalypse. John insists on the trustworthiness of his text by mentioning once more the divine origin of the revelation (22.6). John makes a direct link with Hebrew prophecy at this point. He states that the Apocalypse comes from 'the God of the spirits of the prophets'. Behind this statement stands the conviction that God does nothing without revealing it to his servants, the prophets, which Amos had articulated (Amos 3.7). The statement that this prophecy concerns 'what must soon take place' (22.6) is John's own. It lends force to the Apocalypse by the assertion, grounded in primitive Christian eschatology, that judgment will soon overtake those who ignore it. But those who heed the words of the promise will enter the kingdom of Christ and reign there for ever and ever.

22.7 has the form of a first-person address by the heavenly Christ. It amplifies 22.6 by promising that Jesus is coming 'soon' (cf. 22.20). The first-person form indicates the divine origin of this promise and thus confirms its authenticity. To this is added a macarism that advocates careful adherence to the prophecy (22.7b).

22.8-9 is similar in tone to 19.9-10. John says that he falls down to worship the angel but that the angel rebukes him, saying that he is merely a fellow-servant with John and that God alone should be worshipped. This passage anticipates a *possible* situation where an angel might be venerated and counters it with an *actual* command to worship God alone. This literary device diverts attention from a preoccupation with the agent of revelation and towards the divine beings who are the source and content of the revelation.

22.10 tells the seer not to seal up the words of the prophecy 'for the time is near'. This contrasts, no doubt purposefully, with the command given Daniel in Dan. 12.4 where he is told to seal up his oracles. It also contrasts with the command to 'seal up' what the seven thunders disclosed in 10.4. The implication of 22.10 is that the revelation need not be sealed because its fulfilment is nigh. This bold declaration of eschatological proximity does much to explain the absence of pseudonymity in the Apocalypse. John assures readers that what he promises will soon come to pass. This encourages them to be vigilant about their social separation.

22.11 is an odd proverb which tells people—both evil and righteous—to persist in their behaviour. The meaning is that there is no time to change because the end is near. There is a faint echo here of prophetic rhetoric such as Jer. 13.23 ('Can Ethiopians change their skin or leopards their spots?'). Early Christian literature (including the Apocalypse) does allow people opportunity for repentance before the return of Christ (see, e.g., 1 Thess. 4–5). 22.11 is rhetorical mockery which encourages and does not prohibit repentance.

22.12 repeats the promise about Christ's imminent coming. John combines this with the theme of retribution which is familiar from other New Testament literature (see esp. 2 Thess. 1.7-8). 22.13 repeats the Alpha and Omega from 1.8 and 21.6. Here, the title is applied to Christ and not to God. 22.14 describes the character of those who enter the new Jerusalem. These are said to be those who have washed their robes (sc. in the blood of the Lamb, 7.14). In ch. 7 it is made clear that this means faithful Christians, who are consequently in a state of purity. 22.14 contains further veiled ethical exhortation and warns people not to miss out on the eschatological benefits by ignoring the words of John's prophecy. 22.15 by contrast describes life outside the city. It looks back to 14.20 and 21.8 and the description of those who perish in the wrath of God. The implication is that *only* the righteous will enter the new Jerusalem and that everyone else will be punished. Here, the message of the Apocalypse is summarized to bring the text to conclusion.

22.16 makes Jesus send the angel of revelation to the churches. The titles 'the root', the 'descendant of David' and 'the bright morning star' (cf. 2.28; 5.5) all have messianic connotations. 22.17 is a poetic passage that makes the Spirit and the bride say 'Come'. The bride here is the church, the idea being that the Holy Spirit operates in the church in the period before the return of Christ. This verse offers the water of life to those who will receive it. This develops the prophetic invitation of Isa. 55.1 ('Ho, everyone who thirsts, come to the waters') with reference to John's own imagery of the water of life (22.1; with parallels in the Fourth Gospel, Jn 4.14; 7.38).

22.18-19 warns readers not to augment or subtract from the words of the prophecy. The model for this is Deut. 4.2. The similar statement the *Letter of Aristeas* 310-11 shows that John employs a common formula at this point. John says that those who ignore the words of the prophecy will lose their share in the tree of life and the holy city. 22.20 reinforces the urgency of this ethical appeal with a further eschatological assertion couched in the first-person form. Jesus—'the one who testifies to these things'—says unambiguously, 'Surely, I am coming soon'. This gives the ethical appeal an urgency through the promised nearness of the eschatological climax. 22.21 concludes the Apocalypse with a benediction. This reflects the (partially) epistolary form of the text (cf. 1 Cor. 16.23) and reinforces the impression of eschatological urgency to which its ethics are constantly related.

Conclusion

So far, I have offered a chapter-by-chapter reading of the Apocalypse and tried to find the meaning of the different parts of the text. I said in the Introduction that I would do this before I considered the structure of the Apocalypse. I do not intend to suggest by this that structure is an unimportant issue. Indeed, my readers will have observed that in places I have commented on structural matters already. This is inevitable in the reading of any text. I now want to consider this matter more formally and examine the way in which the Apocalypse is put together. I shall make some observations on the way in which this issue affects our interpretation of the text.

The Structure of the Apocalypse

In examining the structure of the Apocalypse, we must take seriously what the text itself says about the occasion of its first delivery. 1.3 states in the introductory macarism, 'Blessed is the one who *reads aloud* the words of the prophecy...' This makes it clear that the Apocalypse was composed for oral delivery. Despite its heavy visual symbolism, the Apocalypse depends for its initial effect on an aural response. The act of hearing stimulates the reader to consider the meaning of the different symbols employed in the text. Although we encounter the Apocalypse in the form of a written text, it is important to remember that this was not so for the very first readers. Not all of them could read and write. They could, however, listen to the unfolding visions and make a creative mental engagement with them.

The orality of the Apocalypse means we should expect the text to have relatively clear divisions: divisions that are clear to the ear and do not need minute textual study to disclose them. Indeed, under the assumption that hearing is different from reading, we might even say that we should expect *different kinds* of divisions in John's work from a text that was originally designed for reading. And again, although most texts in the ancient world were declaimed rather than 'published' in the modern sense, John's Apocalypse has a logic peculiar to its genre which must be distinguished from the logic of a Gospel or letter—and further from an epic like the *Iliad* or the *Aeneid*. The orality of the Apocalypse explains the division of the material that we find there (including the ambiguity of the third woe, where 15.5-6 is a much clearer aural marker than a literary one).

It is, however, worth observing, when this point is conceded, that Revelation also has some quite intricate features that are not obvious on the first hearing of the text. Bauckham notes as an example the seven macarisms of the Apocalypse which have no structural significance (*Climax of Prophecy*, p. 29). It is likely that these and similar features would have become fully obvious only after the initial reading of the Apocalypse. This shows that the Apocalypse is very far from a hasty and disposable composition. Its full intricacy becomes evident only on further and repeated study. This intricacy suggests that the text was not designed to be read merely once but that John's intention was for it to be read on a number of occasions so that its full impact could register in the minds of the audience.

So to the major divisions of the Apocalypse. These for the most part are relatively clear. 1.1-3 is a prologue that introduces the Apocalypse and explains the nature and grounds of the revelation. 1.4-20 (the salutation) greets the churches and amplifies this information. John describes his experience of revelation on Patmos (1.9-11) and his vision of the heavenly Christ (1.12-20). Chapter 1 gives the strong impression that the Apocalypse is conceived as a letter to the churches, whatever similarities it displays with the genres of prophecy and apocalypse. This impression is reinforced in chs. 2-3 where the churches are directly addressed by Christ in the form of the letters.

This identification of prologue, salutation, and epistolary introduction is matched by the observation that 22.6-20 has the nature of a conclusion or epilogue. John's vision of the new Jerusalem ends in 22.5 with the statement that the Christian redeemed 'will reign forever and ever'. There is a discernible shift in tone at this point. It is obvious that 22.6 begins the conclusion of the Apocalypse because its language is similar to 1.1. This deliberate repetition, combined with the seemingly 'resolved' nature of 22.5, shows that the revelation has drawn to a close and that John begins his 'signing off'. The concluding formula of grace, with its parallels in the New Testament letters (e.g. 1 Thess. 5.28), means that the letter format is retained at the end of the text. This is the major structural framework into which the apocalypse and John's prophetic convictions are inserted.

Chapters 4 and 5 belong together. They describe John's vision of the heavenly court and authenticate the material that follows in the Apocalypse. If the vision of the heavenly Christ (ch. 1) authenticates the letters to the churches (chs. 2-3), the vision of God and the Lamb (chs. 4-5) authenticates the rest of the text. The unfolding sequence of visions is carefully introduced in this way.

The body of the Apocalypse must be seen as a coherent whole despite the (sometimes awkward) problems of transition that it raises. It is clear that John has incorporated more than one cycle of material in his text. The Apocalypse unfolds in a sequence of explosions, not unlike a fireworks display. This loose unity must be acknowledged as a stylistic feature that guides any talk of 'structure' in the text.

The reference to the scroll in ch. 5 is important structurally. It comes as the first item of revealed knowledge after John's vision of the heavenly court. The scroll tells the readers they will see the unmasking of eschatological secrets through heavenly revelation. Indeed, it seems that part of the purpose of the theophany is to introduce this scroll and to present the Lamb as alone worthy to open it on the grounds of his victory (5.5). John's vision of the scroll (5.1) leads naturally to the contents of ch. 6 where the opening of its six seals (and the disasters they reveal) is explained.

Within ch. 6 we saw that juxtaposition of imagery is an important compositional feature. The four horsemen signify death (6.1-8). The fifth seal, by contrast, reveals the martyrs beneath the heavenly altar (6.9-11). This juxtaposition contrasts the punishment of the pagan world and its supporters with the victory-through-conflict of the faithful people of God. It demonstrates in visionary form, at the beginning of the Apocalypse, the themes John wants his readers to hear and which have already been presented to them in the form of the letters.

The rhetorical question in 6.17—'for the great day of their wrath has come, and who is able to stand it?'—makes for a pause for breath on a natural caesura. This is followed by the important interlude of ch. 7. The status of ch. 7 as an interlude is confirmed in 7.2 where John says that he sees another angel who bears the seal of the living God. This reference to a *different* seal reminds the reader that the seventh seal of the original scroll has yet to be opened and that there will be a delay before this happens. This delay is confirmed also by the command to the four angels to wait until the servants of God have been sealed on their foreheads (7.3). This delay is a textual indication to readers to watch what happens next in the Apocalypse. It tells them that significant information is about to be disclosed.

The sealing of the servants of God explains in visionary form that these people will be spared the disasters that are described in the rest of the Apocalypse. There is an important link with the portrait of the martyrs in 6.9, for the greater multitude of 7.9 is said to be robed in white. White is the symbol of righteousness in the Apocalypse. John tells his readers, in the form of this interlude, that destruction is impending and that ethical strictness is the only way to avoid it. They can hardly ignore the fact that 'sealing' has an ethical meaning in the Apocalypse. The interlude reinforces this message for them.

8.1 resumes with the statement that the Lamb opens the seventh seal. This produces seven angels with seven trumpets. John's artistry is obvious again. The opening of the seventh seal is followed by silence in heaven (8.1) and the further interlude of 8.3-5 (the incense and the fire) which John introduces for dramatic effect. Finally, the first six angels blow their trumpets (8.6 onwards). These trumpets herald plagues. The description of these plagues becomes longer as the list progresses through ch. 9.

Intertwined with these trumpets are the three woes that attend the last three blasts. The 'woes' are an important feature of the Apocalypse. Although they do not necessarily provide *structural* markers, they do add a contrapuntal note to the text by showing that what happens there is permitted by the will of the triune God. Although 'three' is not a number of constant symbolic significance in the Apocalypse (thus Bauckham, *Climax of Prophecy*, p. 32), it is surely significant that three such woes are described. This seems related to John's emerging view of the Trinity. The first woe is the appearance of the locusts in 9.1-11. I have interpreted the second woe as everything that happens between 9.13 and 11.14, and the third as the entire contents of 11.15 to 15.4. These woes almost intrude into the division of material. They interrupt the sequence of sevens in a way that makes the reader ask why they are inserted. Their presence draws attention to God's role in the destruction. The fact that the woes are by implication accomplished in 15.4 does have the structural point of showing that John's thought is beginning to move towards the eschatological climax at this point.

With this comment to hand, the structure of chs. 11–15 is relatively clear. There is the sense that something remains unfinished at the end of ch. 9. The seventh angel has yet to blow his trumpet. He will not do so until 11.15. The shows indicates that something of importance will again be disclosed. There follows the reference to the second scroll which John is told to eat in ch. 10. John's eating of this scroll is followed immediately by the statement, set at a significant point in the Apocalypse, that he 'must prophesy again about many peoples and nations and languages and kings' (10.11). One can hardly ignore the implication of this statement that what follows will disclose the content of John's prophecy against these different bodies. This directs attention to the material set between the command to prophesy (10.11) and the blowing of the seventh trumpet in 11.15. That is the story of the two witnesses.

It is far from accidental that the theme of witness is foregrounded in this way. John is calling the church to a vigorous witness. Here, he contrasts the destiny of the faithful witnesses with the opposition and fate of the pagan world. This is the message of the Apocalypse in microcosm. The two witnesses maintain an unimpeachable testimony until the time of demonic opposition. Their witness, death and resurrection results in an earthquake in which seven thousand die (11.13). In contrast to the plagues, this promotes belief among those who experience it.

The function of this section, set within the context of the second woe, is to emphasize the value of faithful witness to Jesus and its eschatological reward. Only a rigid distinction from the pagan world, John argues, will lead to this destiny. That the 'second woe' contains material about judgment *and* vindication reinforces the distinction between righteous and sinners and shows that the outlook of the Apocalypse is by no means universally pessimistic. There is a sense in which this description of the *woe* reinforces the message of salvation for the righteous through the force of the dualism. The structure of this section thereby coheres with the ethical appeal John imparts.

The onward transition from 11.14 is carefully handled. The seventh trumpet is blown after the statement that 'the second woe has passed' (11.14). Characteristically, a surprise follows. Instead of the third woe, the heavenly chorus announce that 'the kingdom of the world has become the kingdom of our Lord and of his Messiah'. (11.15). This leads to the apocalyptic announcement of 11.19 ('Then God's temple in heaven was opened, and the ark of his covenant was seen within his temple; and there were flashes of lightning, rumblings, peals of thunder, an earthquake, and heavy hail'). This passage brings the reader to chs. 12-14, whose precise function in the Apocalypse has long puzzled interpreters.

It is evident that 15.5 provides a retrospective link back to 11.19 with its further reference to the angels and the temple. This observation gives the intervening material a self-contained quality and provides justification, on the basis of 14.4, for the view that it is associated with the third woe. I have argued that 15.5 has a prominent aural quality which cannot fail to make an impression when the text is declamed. This means that chs. 12-14 must be understood cumulatively as the third woe. This material contrasts Roman dominance (ch. 13) with the vision of the Lamb and his elect on Mount Zion (ch. 14). It insists that the dragon cannot destroy the woman, however hard he tries (ch. 12). The contrast implies that Roman influence is ephemeral, although it is undoubtedly prominent at the time of writing. The cry of the heavenly chorus in 15.3-4 picks up the chorus of 11.15-18 and gives the meaning of the intervening material. This is that 'the nations raged, but your wrath has come, and the time for judging the dead' (11.18) and that 'all nations will come and worship before you, for your judgments have been revealed'. Chapters 12-14—the third woe—celebrate the downfall of the enemy forces following their futile attempt to discredit the servants of God.

15.5 is prospective as well as retrospective. 15.5-8 brings the reader to the final outpouring of God's wrath which is described in ch. 16 and leads to 'the judgment of the great whore who is seated on many waters' (17.1). Chapter 17, unambiguously albeit allusively, identifies the whore as Rome prior to her destruction. The city's fall is announced at the beginning of ch. 18. The bulk of ch. 18 laments the city's destruction by various interested parties. This is followed in the first half of ch. 19 by the celebration of the heavenly chorus (19.1-8), which relates the fall of Babylon to the marriage of the Lamb and the bride (19.7).

A new section of the Apocalypse begins in 19.11. This is introduced by the phrase 'Then I saw heaven opened' (cf. 4.1). John now describes

Christ's return to earth (19.11-21). 19.11–22.5 is another self-contained section which describes the Messiah's earthly kingdom and the recreation of heaven and earth. This deliberately contrasts with the earlier material. At the end of the Apocalypse, John describes the rewards of the righteous following the final destruction of the ungodly. Chapters 19 and 20 narrate the final judgment. 21.1–22.5 explains what takes place thereafter. 22.6-21 brings the text to its close and authenticates the contents of the Apocalypse.

The Significance of Seven

This short survey has shown that the number seven is an important structural marker in the Apocalypse. Seven churches are mentioned in chs. 2–3. Seven seals are described in chs. 5–8. 12.1-14.20 narrates seven visions (including the infamous ch. 13). This is followed (in 15.1–16.21) by the seven bowls of divine wrath which lead to the fall of Babylon (16.19-21). The Apocalypse also mentions seven thunders (10.3-4) and seven kings. One can hardly ignore the symbolic significance of this figure that appears so often in Revelation.

The number seven probably relates to Jewish speculation about the days of the week. Seven were the days of creation according to the book of Genesis (ch. 1) and seven acquired added significance in Christian eschatological speculation. *Barnabas* (late first/early second century CE) understands the present age as lasting seven thousand years (including the pre-Christian period and the messianic kingdom) on the grounds that one day is as a thousand years in God's sight (*Barn.* 15.3-8; cf. Ps. 90.4). Its author thinks the seventh millennium the sabbath and that the eighth millennium will be the beginning of a new world. Revelation also expects the eschatological age to begin after a sequence of seven events has been completed. The constant repetition of this figure in the Apocalypse reinforces this point. This is part of the periodization of history familiar in apocalyptic literature. The author uses the concept of the week to emphasize that certain difficulties must be endured before the transformation of the existing order, and to insist that the hope for transformation is a viable one.

The apocalyptic tradition determines John's view that some of these difficulties have been overcome already (cf. Dan. 10-12). Revelation 12.14 says that the woman flies into the wilderness to be nourished for 'a time and times and half a time'. This enigmatic figure amounts to 'three and a half', that is, half a week of seven days, the figure that Daniel mentions in Dan. 12.7. This is bound up with the psychology of assurance and with John's ethical appeal. The Apocalypse is, however, ambiguous about when Jesus will return, as is all New Testament literature (see, e.g., Mk 13.32). This time is said to be 'soon' (22.20); but the symbolism of the Apocalypse, including the apparent precision of

17.9-14, leaves no scope for those who would fix the times and seasons exactly.

Bauckham observes that the precise way in which the three series of sevens are linked to each other varies in the Apocalypse (*Climax of Prophecy*, pp. 8-18). The seven seal-openings are linked to the seven trumpets by the technique of overlapping or interweaving. In the case of the seven trumpets and seven bowls, the seventh trumpet (11.15-19) is separated from the appearance of the seven angels with the bowls (15.1) by chs. 12–14, so that the sequence of bowls is clearly marked as a development of the seventh trumpet. The three series of judgments are distinguished from the letters to the churches by means of structural markers. A difference between the letters and the judgments is the observation that the letters have a 3 + 4 structure but the judgments a 4 + 3 structure.

The existence of the '4 and 3' structure encourages readers to discern a sense of order in the text. The seven seals form a paradigm for the seven trumpets. When it comes to the seven bowls (ch. 16), the reader knows that these will be presented in a 4 + 3 sequence. Here, however, there is no intercalation as in the earlier sequences. This, perhaps surprising variation, draws attention to the finality of the end as the bowls are poured onto the earth without interruption to introduce the eschatological climax.

The Problem of the Author

We must now consider the problem of John the author's identity and interests. This is a question that I addressed only summarily in the Introduction. I want to probe this matter further because there is in fact quite a bit more we can say by looking at the way he has written his Apocalypse.

Every text has an 'actual author'. The 'actual author' is the person who puts pen to paper and leaves a text in its finished form (or *originally* finished form). We may or may not know the identity of a text's 'actual author'. In the case of Revelation, we know that this was a John (1.9). This John was apparently a well-known prophet on the Asian Christian scene. But we do not know *which* John he was, or very much else about him. Even the reason for his presence on Patmos is obscure. In this book I have tried to discern traces of this John's contact with Johannine Christianity. But these traces are never 'exclusively Johannine' in the sense of 'unmediated by the author's own unique process of reflection'. This John was a scriptural thinker of outstanding ability who reshaped his images to produce a dazzling display of new symbolism. That visionary capacity of the Apocalypse gives the text its power. We can at least say that this John was an exceptional figure in his use of the Hebrew Bible and his reshaping of early Christian traditions. For this reason alone (and there are many others) the Apocalypse deserves its place in the New Testament canon, despite its sometimes bizarre qualities.

Our restricted knowledge of John is a sobering reminder that we cannot get back to the 'actual author', still less to the *intentions* of the actual author, from a simple reading of the Apocalypse (however tempting it may be to conclude otherwise). This has an important, and no doubt an obvious, implication for the nature of the reading process. It would be wrong to approach a text expecting to discover the full intentions of the author (and only these) from our encounter with it. We may, indeed, discover something of what the author wants to communicate. That depends on our skill and interests as readers. This is because readers construct the meaning of the text through their engagement with it. Reading is a complex process that depends to a large degree on the way we habitually respond and on our disposition at the time of reading. The latter changes with different moods and circumstances. For this reason, inevitably, I find Revelation a different text now from when I first seriously encountered it 20 years ago. Something will be wrong if I do not find different meanings in it 20 years from now. This is an inevitable and healthy part of the reading process.

One further thing must be said about John's status as the 'actual author' of Revelation. What little we know about the human mind shows that our interpretation must allow as much for his unconscious as for his conscious imagination in the construction of the Apocalypse. The unconscious is the repository of our total life experiences. These include the influences and assumptions that were imparted to us at a formative age, and on which we have subsequently drawn; and everything else that has happened since infancy. Not even John was consciously aware of all the influences that operated on him and attended the rebirth of imagery in his Apocalypse. Unconscious influences are, if anything, more interesting than conscious influences because they show what the author's mind is really like beyond his conscious communication. The concept of 'authorial intentionality' is thus exploded, not just by the nature of the reading process, but also by what we know about the art of writing and the hidden cycle of experiences that lies behind it.

The portrait of John that we reconstruct from Revelation is a portrait of what has come to be called 'the implied author' (see Booth, *Rhetoric of Fiction*, pp. 73-74; and Iser, *Implied Reader*). The 'implied author' is the impression of the author that the reader gains from reading a text. This of course depends both on the self-portrait that the actual author chooses to reveal there and also on the process of discernment that the reader brings to the text. This is by definition a complex process. The author will not be aware of all the nuances potentially imparted by the text to a reader. The reader may even find meanings with which the actual author would disagree. The implied author is a construct that emerges in the mind of the reader in the act of reading. The implied author varies from text to text and, conceivably, from one part of a text to another.

John's 'implied author' in the Apocalypse has approximately the following qualities. His primary face is of a person commissioned by Christ to write to the churches. The letter form is very marked in Revelation with its salutation (1.4-5) and formal conclusion (22.21). This is confirmed by chs. 2–3 where John does indeed write letters to the churches. That John writes letters at the dictation of a divine being is what the Apocalypse says the author is doing. This point must be given serious evaluation when investigating the implied author in the Apocalypse.

Other facets can be added to this portrait. In terms of his literary exemplars, John self-consciously follows the Hebrew apocalyptic and prophetic traditions. Apocalyptic was to some extent the child of prophecy (although prophecy was not its only parent). John is conscious of drawing on *both* traditions. We should therefore examine both in turn.

The apocalyptic tradition in Judaism dates from the third century BCE with the appearance of the earliest sections of *1 Enoch*. It is right to say that parts of the Hebrew Bible—notably, the later chapters of Zechariah—anticipate such material, but we should not speak formally of 'apocalyptic (literature)' any earlier than the sources allow us to do so. The writing of Daniel in the Antiochian Crisis (c. 165 BCE) marked a crucial moment in the development of Jewish apocalyptic. Daniel was addressed to a situation of crisis in Judaism. It prescribes an eschatological remedy for that situation. With Daniel, eschatology became an indelible feature of the apocalyptic tradition. Himmelfarb distinguishes two *different kinds* of apocalypse genre in the history of Jewish literature (*Tours of Hell*, pp. 61-62). She claims these are typified by Daniel and by the early chapters of *1 Enoch* respectively. These two different types concentrate (a) on the end of human history and (b) on the more general contours of the heavenly world that are revealed to the seer in the course of a mystical ascension. Himmelfarb thinks that these two genres were fused together in the first century CE. Nearer the mark, perhaps, is the distinction made by Collins and others in 1979 between a Type 1 apocalypse, with no otherworldly journey, and a Type 2 apocalypse where an other-worldly journey is a central feature. This distinction is important for defining the wider phenomenon of apocalypticism, which is the world-view that emerges from the apocalypses and is found even in texts that are not apocalypses. Any interpretation of apocalypticism must be broad enough to accommodate this interest in eschatology, but also the wider interest in other information which the literature displays.

John's use of the apocalyptic tradition lets him present his ethical perspective as a heavenly mystery and claim that this has been revealed to him in the form of an authoritative disclosure. We saw in the Introduction that it is impossible to assess John's claim to revelation beyond observing the possibility of an underlying mystical experience. The most obvious benefit of the implied author's use of apocalyptic categories is the authority that stems from his claim to revelation. John says he has seen the heavenly Christ and that Christ commissioned him to write to the churches. This means, on the rhetorical level, that the Apocalypse embodies a claim to authority which cannot be countered by human speech. This is surely part of the reason why John adopts this convention in writing. His implied author is an authoritative creature who speaks at the divine behest and tells the churches heavenly secrets with authority.

A further feature of the apocalypse genre is the way it tends to polarize opinions and protagonists through the use of mythological categories. This is obvious in Revelation. John's symbolism divides humankind into two different camps. We find this initially in the letters to the churches. The churches are assessed according to how they respond to John's position on social accommodation. Where John feels that improvement is needed, he uses the names of well-known sinners: the Balaamites (2.14), for instance, and 'that woman Jezebel' (2.20). The Nicolaitans of 2.6, 15 doubtless also fall into this category.

In the body of the Apocalypse there is a striking polarization between those who are sealed by God (7.5-8) and those who bear the mark of the beast (13.16-17). These are all-embracing and mutually exclusive categories. A person is either one thing or the other. One cannot be both. The refusal to acknowledge 'middle ground' allows John carefully to emphasize the behaviour he requires. It is implied that those who will not demonstrate the purity represented by the sealing are gravitating towards the kingdom of the beast, symbolized by its mark. Behaviour is the criterion by which people will be judged and destroyed if necessary. The warning of judgment is a rhetorical device that encourages people to live out John's vision of ethics. Ethics are heavily foregrounded in this way.

We must also see John's claim to write prophecy (1.3) as embodying a claim to authority. The early Common Era witnessed a debate about the possibility of contemporary revelation. A passage from the rabbinic literature articulates the view that, with the death of Malachi, 'the Holy Spirit ceased in Israel' (*t. Soṭ.* 13.3). This statement is often compared with a passage from 1 Maccabees which states that, when Judas and his band had torn down Antiochus's defiling altar, 'they stored the stones in a convenient place on the temple hill until a prophet should come to tell what to do with them' (1 Macc. 4.46). It is certainly true that the turn of the eras witnessed the growing awareness that there was no new revelation in Israel (hence the moves towards the canonization of the Hebrew Bible), but the view that prophecy was regarded as *ceasing* at this time needs careful exposition. Apocalyptic must be seen as a parallel, if formally distinct, mode of revelation that resembled the prophetic literature in its claim for visionary access to the divine presence. Apocalyptic breathes the confidence of authority which stems from that revelation. Secondly, Wis. 14.28 clearly knows the activity of prophets, albeit false prophets, so that prophets were clearly sufficiently prominent at the time to attract critical attention. Prophets featured also in the Pauline churches (1 Cor. 12.28). This evidence certainly qualifies the bald statement that prophecy ceased in Israel with the death of Malachi. It suggests that there was a reluctance to acknowledge new revelation but with significant exceptions.

John's use of the term 'prophecy' shows that he sees his work by analogy with the Hebrew prophets. This conviction also requires careful statement. John does not think that his work replaces the prophets, or even enjoys a status identical with the prophets. The fact that he often cites or paraphrases the prophets shows that he regards their work as possessed of irreplaceable authority. But there is nevertheless a considerable claim to authority in John's statement that he writes 'prophecy' (1.3) and in his interpretation of the prophetic writings. This process of interpretation, found throughout the Apocalypse, implies that John discloses the authentic meaning of what the prophets said. This is evident, for instance, in his use of the 'water' motif. Two passages in Revelation show that Isa. 55.1 ('Ho, everyone who thirsts, come to the waters') features prominently among the sources of this motif. These are 7.17 ('he will guide them to springs of the water of life') and 21.6 ('to the thirsty I will give water as a gift from the spring of the water of life'). In these two references John takes up Isaiah's theme of the provision of water and makes *Christ* the source by whom the commodity is provided. John gives the impression that he provides the true meaning of Isaiah's prophecy. This interpretation is related to his eschatological view that the kingdom of Christ will soon appear. A similar christological and eschatological understanding of Scripture is found also in Paul (1 Cor. 10.4; cf. 1 Cor. 10.11). The implied claim to authority in both writers is a striking one.

This aspect of John's role as implied author should also be compared with the self-understanding of the Teacher of Righteousness in the Qumran community: 'And God told Habakkuk to write down that which would happen to the final generation, but he did not make known to him when time would come to an end' (1QpHab 6). This statement shows the rationale of Bible reading among the Essenes. It recognizes the primacy of the biblical text but asserts that there is more to the meaning of the text than was disclosed by the original author. The *Habakkuk Commentary* states that the Teacher of Righteousness knows the timing of the end and thus the actual meaning of the prophecy. The Teacher thereby accepts the authority of the Bible but has the ability to disclose its authoritative interpretation which was denied to the original writer.

John's Apocalypse bespeaks a similar understanding of authority, albeit with a different method of interpretation and an insistence on apocalyptic revelation. John does not adopt the *pesher*-style of the Qumran biblical commentary where the meaning of each part of the text is explained. John rather reworks the prophetic imagery to provide a new and coherent whole (what Farrer called 'the rebirth of images' [*Rebirth*]). This is the unambiguous declaration that John's work has divinely mandated authority. We should remember that the prophets held authority in early Christian churches second only in rank to the apostles (1 Cor. 12.28) but that the number of the prophets, and the respect in which they were held, was declining as Christianity moved beyond the apostolic age (see *Asc. Isa.* 3.21-31, which was written perhaps 20 years later than Revelation). John's claim to prophetic authority has a striking air for these reasons. The Apocalypse as prophecy declares the living words of God himself—the words of the one 'who is and who was and who is to come' (1.4). As with John's use of the apocalypse genre, this is bound up with the need to gain authority for what Revelation says.

All of this means that the implied author in Revelation is an authoritative figure who is commissioned by Christ to disclose revealed mysteries to the seven Asian churches in the form of the letters. John's claim to be a prophet and his use of the apocalypse genre convey this air of authority. Both make the implied author a significant figure, well known as such to the churches, who gives his readers a warning about their Christian authenticity. They must either heed his words, seeing the pagan world as demonic and not welcoming, or they will face the judgment under which that world stands. John creates the awareness of a crisis to impart this perspective to his readers, in what was for them essentially a non-crisis situation.

One further question remains about John as the 'actual author' of Revelation. How much of the text did he write? There has been a difference in opinion as to whether John is essentially an author, composing his text from a variety of traditions, or an editor who fused together several earlier writings to create this Apocalypse. This dispute is germane to the apocalyptic tradition as a whole. Within the gamut of Christian literature, comparison might helpfully be made with the *Ascension of Isaiah* which R.H. Charles said in 1900 was composed of three earlier documents but which the most recent scholarship now sees as a literary unity (see the review of Charles in Pesce, 'Presupposti', pp. 13-76). How one regards an apocalypse, so it seems, is at least to some extent a reflection of scholarly trends and interests. This difference of opinion reflects the complexity of both texts which contain awkward transitions and occasional inconsistencies.

A powerful argument for Revelation's literary unity is the existence of John's 'special language', which features throughout the Apocalypse, and the brilliant way in which John treats the Hebrew Bible. It would be extraordinary to find more than one person who did both these things in the history of early Christianity given the uniqueness of John's method and mind. John's reworking of imagery is a consistent feature of the Apocalypse. This suggests that the work was written as a whole and that its occasional awkwardness was introduced by John himself. The view I have taken in this book is that John wrote the Apocalypse using a variety of traditions but without substantially incorporating earlier documents. In doing so, he has written a remarkable text.

The 'Message' of the Apocalypse

I have suggested that, despite the internal complexities of the text, the 'message' that John's Apocalypse brings its readers is a relatively simple one. It concerns John's request for people to be wary of full engagement with Asian urban life because John thinks that this brings dangers to people whose religious ideology requires a fundamental holiness, or separation, in the face of pagan religion and praxis. I have held the readers' 'actual situation' disclosed by the two references to meat-eating in 2.14, 20 which John sees as a significant religious issue. In this, John adopts a more rigorous position than Paul had done, and he forbids Christians to participate in this activity. He gives as the reason for this prohibition the word 'fornication' (2.14, 20), which I have understood in metaphorical terms, in line with its Hebrew Bible background, to designate flirtation with pagan religion and standards.

This situation is met by the dualism of the Apocalypse. John emphasizes his desired position to draw his readers' attention to it. He does this by painting the pagan world in demonic colours as wilfully opposed to God. Both the Roman administration and those who benefit from it are demonized in this way. This effectively reminds readers that, as Christians, they must have nothing to do with a world order that stands in opposition to God.

This desired response explains John's choice of the apocalypse genre. John could presumably have written a pastoral missive, as did Paul, or sent messengers to the churches to bring them oracles in person. He did neither of these things but sent the churches his Apocalypse. We have seen that the Apocalypse encourages perception of a crisis to recall its readers to a particular pattern of behaviour.

The constant warnings of judgment are linked to this symbolism. Especially in the letters, John tells people they must not presume on their Christian position and that only a committed response will bring them through to the kingdom of Christ. The recollection of biblical sinners (with its parallels in Jude) is an important element in John's rhetorical strategy. 2.14 is an example of this: 'You have some there [i.e. Perga-mum] who hold to the teaching of Balaam, who taught Balak to put a stumbling block before the people of Israel, so that they would eat food sacrificed to idols and practise fornication.' John does not so much expound the nature of the situation as offer a symbolic commentary on it. The Balaamite reference is John's evaluation of what was happening. His condemnation of full social integration is made with reference to the Hebrew Bible.

Reading the Apocalypse, as we have done, draws the reader to John's vision of the recreated order with which his text concludes. This is not done to provide a systematic description of Christian eschatology for its own sake, but to draw attention to John's foregrounded link between ethics and eschatology. At the end of the Apocalypse, 22.19 warns of the consequences of diluting John's message of judgment. Readers are thereby encouraged to do what the Apocalypse says and to let the often bizarre symbolism impact on them and challenge their perception of reality as the pagan social world with all its glory is destroyed before their eyes.

This is the message John wants his readers to hear. His apocalypse presents them with a dualistic world-view and a starkness of choice which leaves little doubt about how they should act. In response to the letters, they must leave the sinful collaborators and stand their distance from the pagan world. In so doing, they will enjoy the first resurrection and pass through the kingdom of Christ to the recreated order which is the goal of John's eschatology.

Themes of the Apocalypse

At the end of this book, I want to examine some of the themes of the text and set them in broader perspective. This furthers the task of 'making sense of the text' which has been my principal aim in this book. It will also, I hope, link Revelation more firmly with the other New Testament texts than has sometimes been done in the past. The demon-stration of such continuity is an important part of Apocalypse studies. It works from the principle of separating genre and ideas which I have invoked already.

Cosmology

One cannot read any apocalypse without considering the question of cosmology. 'Cosmology' is the understanding of the relation between heaven and earth which pertains in a particular text. By virtue of its genre, an apocalypse claims to disclose the realities of heaven to people with their more limited perspective on earth. This involves a distinction between heaven as the repository of authoritative knowledge and earth as the place of earnest but more limited enquiry. Between the two is set a gulf—often symbolized by the sky—which signifies the divide that the unaided mind cannot breach. The essence of an apocalypse is that there is an *apokalypsis*, or revelatory unveiling of heavenly secrets. Without the claim to revelation, there is no apocalypse.

The manner of revelation varies across the Jewish apocalypses, but the conviction of contact with heavenly beings is a consistent theme of them all. They often describe a heavenly journey in which the seer ascends through a variety of heavens towards the throne of God. In my exegesis of Revelation 4–5, I observed that the vision of God's throne and courtroom is frequently presented as the first or most important aspect of the heavenly mysteries in apocalyptic literature. There are at least two reasons why this is so.

The first reason is that the vision of the heavenly world is, perfectly properly, a vision of God himself. One can hardly imagine that a mystic would ascend to heaven and not learn something about the divine character. The fact that in some apocalypses (including Revelation) the seer does not see the form of God does not obscure the fact that the vision of God's throne—including the throne-creatures and angels (and Christ in Revelation)—is regarded as an ineffable mystery.

The second reason for the vision of God is that this authenticates the disclosure of secrets that follow in the text. God himself, as it were, permits the disclosure of the secrets of his dwelling-place. In the Jewish view of the world, God is the source of everything that exists. That the seer sees the throne of God legitimates his access to the lesser mysteries by the permission of the creator himself.

In those apocalypses that describe a heavenly ascension, the number of the heavens varies. The Hebrew Bible generally knows of only one heaven but the enigmatic phrase 'heaven of heavens', which occurs more than once (e.g. Deut. 10.14), inspired the Jewish mystical imagination. Thus, for instance, in the throne-vision of *1 Enoch* 14 the seer enters two heavenly palaces (evidently heavens) to approach the presence of God. The figure of 'seven' heavens features in many apocalypses (e.g. the original version of *2 Enoch*; the *Ascension of Isaiah*). The figure of seven heavens occurs in rabbinic literature too (*b. Hag.* 12b). Some apocalypses were reworked as they circulated to allow for even more heavens than this (e.g. *2 Enoch*). The effect of this multiform cosmology is to emphasize the esoteric nature of the revelation. This is in itself an authenticating device which distances God from the human world.

The book of Revelation agrees with the Hebrew Bible in mentioning only one heaven. This single-storied cosmology is in keeping with the majority of New Testament writings. Jesus described God as 'in heaven', not 'in the heavens' (Mt. 6.9). Not even the Fourth Gospel, for all its interest in the heavenly origins of Jesus, specifies more than one heaven. The one real exception is Paul in 2 Corinthians 12 who mentions three heavens. It is clear from Paul's context that this is an exceptional statement which depends on the fact that his apostolic qualifications have been denigrated in the Corinthian community. He responds to this by describing his own apocalyptic experience, as if in other circumstances he might have been much more reluctant to do so. 2 Corinthians 12 raises the question of whether the early Christians knew and assumed belief in more than one heaven but did not normally mention it in their literature. The rabbinic dispute about the issue, which is mentioned in *b. Hag.* 12b, shows that this was an uncertain question at the time. Christian reserve towards multiplying the number of heavens is perhaps to be explained with reference to their belief that Jesus had accomplished a full divine revelation. This created the belief that speculation about heavenly matters was unnecessary. We know that some Christian circles actually questioned the value of apocalyptic experience (see Jn 3.13). It may be (if the Apocalypse is connected with Johannine Christianity) that this dispute waged internally in Johannine circles.

John's sequence of 'sevens' shows that he almost certainly knew of the importance of this figure in apocalyptic literature. We must conclude that he incorporates a single-storied cosmology for a reason, and that it is not accidental. The cosmology appropriately preserves the distinction between heaven and earth (4.1) and insists on the revealed character of the Apocalypse. It guarantees the authenticity of John's message and functions as a powerful rhetorical tool in communicating his message to the readers. But it must also be considered in company with the restricted interest in angelology and other heavenly secrets when compared with the Jewish apocalypses. This suggests that John's interest in eschatology plays a part in the selection of cosmology, and that the device of otherworldly journeying (apart from John's ascension to heaven in 4.1) is not a significant feature of the New Testament Apocalypse.

Theology

Theology is a major concern of all early Christian literature, including the Apocalypse. It is equally a concern of the Jewish apocalypses. What we read about God in Revelation stands firmly in both traditions.

There is more than one kind of theological expression in Revelation. In the first place, John draws extensively on the visual symbolism that pervades the Apocalypse. This is obvious in ch. 4 when he enters the heavenly throne-room. We should include John's vision of the heavenly Christ (1.12-16) in this category. Another expression of theology is what I shall call 'affirmations of the divine character'. These are statements about what God is like: often liturgical statements with a biblical base. The most obvious example is the description of God as 'him who is and who was and who is to come' which is found in 1.4 and elsewhere.

These expressions of theology are mutually complementary within the shifting pattern of John's language and imagery. John's theology anticipates the final revelation of the eschatological age. The implication of the statement that the new Jerusalem has no temple is that God and the Lamb will become accessible deities (21.22). This will be the time when the vision of God—now the privilege of the seer alone—is granted to all the redeemed. At that time, descriptions of God will presumably become redundant, as will the apocalyptic vision. Since the Hebrew Bible calls the Torah a light and a lamp (Ps. 119.105), it can only be significant that 22.5 expects 'they need no light of lamp...for the Lord God will be their light'. The implication is that the written text, with all its problems of mediacy and mediation, will vanish before the reality that it signifies.

I have said something about the visual aspect of Revelation's theology already. Revelation 4 has an extensive background in the Jewish visionary tradition. Ezekiel 1.26-7 describes a vision of God which presents him as it were in human form and seated on his throne-chariot. Isaiah 6.1-4 describes an appearance of the deity to the seer on earth, as does 1 Kgs 22.19. *1 Enoch* 14 (third century BCE) marks a development in the Jewish mystical tradition when it makes the seer ascend to heaven to see the enthroned deity. Similar ascensions are found in the post-biblical apocalypses (e.g. the *Apocalypse of Abraham*). The further development of this tradition is reflected in the text called *Hebrew Enoch* or *3 Enoch* (fifth or sixth century CE) where the transformed Enoch is identified as the throne-angel Metatron and dethroned when a rabbi exclaims there are two powers in heaven (ch. 16).

John's vision of God is elaborated in an implicitly trinitarian direction. This is evident in the reference to the 'seven spirits of God' (4.5) and the description of the Lamb in ch. 5. One would not expect anything else in a Christian apocalypse. The language used to describe the Trinity is neither the formula of Mt. 28.19 nor the *homoousion* talk of later Christianity. It is doubtless significant that John does not refer to *the* Spirit of God in his opening theophany. This does not, however, obscure the fact that in Revelation 4-5 we find important early evidence for trinitarian theology set within the context of the developing Christian mystical tradition.

John's descriptions of God are the fruit of a long process of meditation on biblical themes which involves his subconscious imagination. At the heart of his meditation stands the Jewish conviction that God is the creator. This is evident in the threefold formula of 1.4 and also in the key passage, 4.11: 'You are worthy, our Lord and God, to receive glory and honour and power, for you created all things, and by your will they existed and were created.' Belief in God as the creator of the physical universe is a major theme of the Hebrew Bible (see, e.g., Gen. 1). John's statements about creation have several facets. First of all, John insists that the human world exists as an act of willed creation (4.11). That is to say, it is not the by-product of some primordial residue but the conscious formation of a universe by God. There is also the hint that God continues to will and sustain that which he created. This emerges in John's offer of eschatological salvation, and in the fact that the judgment of sinners has not yet been carried out. Thirdly, John insists that this God who creates and sustains is *the* God, the only God. This strong polemic stands against all the claims of pagan idolatry. John will only introduce his description of Christ as the second divine being, in ch. 5, once this monotheistic principle has been firmly articulated.

Sin and Salvation

The contribution that the Apocalypse makes to the development of Christian doctrine should not be underestimated. John by implication excludes the view that the universe is anything else than the unique creation of a sovereign God. It is axiomatic for John that God's being is an eternal one (see 10.6, the statement that the angel swore 'by him who lives forever and ever'). In this sense, the statement of 1.8 that God is the Alpha and the Omega and the one 'who is and who was and who is to come' has eschatological significance. John looks back to what God has done in the act of creation to provide a link with his hope for the new creation with which the Apocalypse ends. There is an inexorable link between creation, eschatology and ethics in Revelation. The new creation is presented as the perfect counterpart of the old creation which, it is implied, is a less than perfect entity.

This doctrine of the new creation poses a potential theological problem for readers of the Apocalypse. There is an assumption, at least in Pauline theology, that the unredeemed universe is troubled by sin. Paul relates this to the story of Adam in more than one passage (see, e.g., Rom. 5; 1 Cor. 15). But we look in vain for any references to Adam or for a developed doctrine of sin in the Apocalypse. Indeed, John's promise of the new creation is presented as a theological assumption—a matter of hope—and not as a theological argument as such. Yet it would be wrong to say that the Apocalypse lacks any justification of its eschatology. This justification is the assumption (more often than the explicit statement) that the hopes of the biblical writers will be fulfilled. In 21.5, John cites the words of Deutero-Isaiah, 'See, I am making all things new', to provide exegetical justification for his belief in the new creation. We come back to my earlier observation that John recognizes the authority of the Hebrew Bible while assuming that he can supply its true and authentic interpretation (and often without acknowledging his sources). The hope for the new creation is thus founded on biblical analogies.

Nor does the Apocalypse lack a realistic understanding of sin. An early passage says of the heavenly Christ, 'To him who loves us and freed us from our sins by his blood' (1.5). This shows that sin—a basic problem for all New Testament theology—is not neglected in the Apocalypse.

The letters to the churches have a clear understanding of 'sin'. John refers more than once to typical biblical sinners. He promises judgment for those who neglect his message. The ethical demand is clearly articulated in the Apocalypse. One might be inclined to say that it is articulated almost more clearly there than in any other New Testament text. John is helped by the dualistic world-view that derives from the apocalyptic tradition. Moreover, chs. 12-14 embody a mythological presentation of sin, if by 'sin' is meant a fundamental attitude of rebellion towards God. That John does not articulate a formal *doctrine* of sin is more a question of perspective than a fundamental theological difference from the other New Testament literature.

To this must be added the recognition that the God of the Apocalypse is a God of eschatological judgment. Time and again, John speaks of scourges, plagues and destruction. Although the language is symbolic, this does not obscure the fact that John expects a process of judgment in which the righteous will be rewarded and the ungodly punished. This is what the heavenly ledgers and the book of life signify (20.12). This perspective is firmly anchored in the Jewish and Christian eschatological tradition. There are obvious parallels in the *Similitudes of Enoch* (*1 En.* 37-71), the parables of Jesus (e.g. Mt. 13.40-42) and in 2 Thess. 1.7-9.

John's warning of judgment is related to his ethical appeal. The Apocalypse embodies a dualistic contrast between the kingdom of God and the kingdom of Satan. People belong either to one or the other, but never to both. This dualism is most obvious in the comment addressed to the church in Smyrna: 'I know the slander on the part of those who say that they are Jews and are not, but are a synagogue of Satan' (2.9). Those who are not true Jews—the people of God—are the synagogue of Satan, regardless of their religious profession. No middle ground is allowed. Part of John's message is to explain how the two different kingdoms *inevitably* conflict. John tells his readers that those who ignore him are allied to Satan. He warns that they will lose out on the eschatological benefits for this reason.

Christology

The Apocalypse enshrines a Christology that associates Christ with the throne of God. I observed the exegetical dispute in 5.6 as to where the Lamb stands in respect of the heavenly throne, but argued that this passage can be addressed through the evidence of 3.21 and 22.3. These two references associate the Lamb with the throne of God. It would be surprising if 5.6 does not have the same meaning. Such enthronement symbolism has a clear theological significance in the Apocalypse. It presents the Lamb analogously to God. The Lamb's divine status is signified also by the transference to him of divine titles (e.g. 'Alpha and Omega' in 22.13). The most striking indication, however, is the worship of the Lamb in the heavenly world. This is evidenced most obviously by 5.13, which is addressed 'to the one seated on the throne and *to the Lamb*' (italics added). This passage associates the Lamb with God over against the angels. His reception of worship makes the Lamb unquestionably a divine being.

This portrait of Christ has an important background in Jewish and Christian theology. I shall briefly consider the Jewish evidence. The term 'monotheism' is often employed to describe the nature of Jewish theology in the pre-Christian period. By this is meant the belief that there is only one true God and that he alone must be worshipped. The (admittedly rather scarce) evidence from post-biblical Judaism indicates that, although angels are sometimes venerated in several different ways, this is never conceived as a substitute for the worship of God (see Stuckenbruck, *Angel Veneration*, pp. 45-204). This consistent worship of the one God *alone* is the determining factor in Jewish religion.

The roots of the Jewish interest in angels lie deep in the Pentateuch. The strand of material that describes the 'Angel of the Lord' sometimes seems to confuse the Angel *with* the Lord in a way that permits an ambiguous interpretation. There is an example of this in Exod. 3.1-6 (the angelic manifestation to Moses at Horeb). Exodus 3.2 says of this experience that 'the angel of the Lord appeared to him in a flame of fire out of a bush'. The narrator continues: 'When the Lord saw that [Moses] had turned aside to see, God called to him out of the bush...' What began as an angelophany now appears as a theophany. The redactor's combination of sources doubtless explains this ambiguity, but the final form of text is striking nonetheless. It makes God address Moses when the narrator has said that an angel appears. This ambiguity allowed later exegetes to find described here the appearance of a second *divine* being who is introduced as an angel. Thus Philo referred the angelophany to the Logos (*Vit. Mos.* 1.66) and Justin Martyr to Christ (*Dial.* 59-60; *1 Apol.* 62-63).

In the post-biblical literature we find a burgeoning angelology. One strand of belief describes how an angel appears on earth as a man. Tobit 3.16-17 explains how God told Raphael to descend from heaven to perform two acts of healing on earth. The beginning of Tobit 5 finds Raphael on earth, apparently in human form. Of this angelophany the narrator says, 'Tobias...went out and found the angel Raphael standing in front of him; but he did not perceive that it was an angel of God' (5.4). This is because Raphael has assumed the form of a man. The ruse is sustained until ch. 12 where Raphael tells his astonished fellow-characters: 'I am Raphael, one of the seven angels who stand ready and enter before the glory of the Lord' (12.15). Raphael then vanishes at the moment when they perceive his true identity. This material bears a striking affinity to the notion of the divine Word who appears as Jesus which is found in the Prologue to the Fourth Gospel (Jn 1.1-18). Another form of this angelic influence is found in the second-century

Ascension of Isaiah where the heavenly Christ descends through the seven heavens disguised as an angel and appears on earth as Jesus by passing through Mary's womb.

A second strand of angelology holds that exceptional humans are transformed into exalted heavenly beings by means of ascension from earth. This is said about Moses in the second-century BCE poem called the *Exagoge* which was written in Egypt by a person called Ezekiel the Tragedian (see Jacobson, *Exagoge*). The *Exagoge* describes how Moses was installed by God on his throne and reigned there, evidently as a vice-gerent. This circumvents the problem of anthropomorphism by placing a transformed and visible human on the throne in place of the remote and now invisible deity. The *Similitudes of Enoch* also install a mediator, who is called both the Son of Man and the Elect One, on the throne of God where he dispenses judgment on God's behalf. This strand of angelology effectively ranks the transformed human above the angels in subjection to God. It is not difficult to see that it influenced emerging descriptions of Jesus, especially that strand of New Testament Christology which describes the heavenly enthronement of Jesus (e.g. 1 Pet. 3.18-22).

A third strand of angelology is the appearance of an exceptional angel who is described in language that recalls the theophany. This looks back in one sense to the Pentateuchal material we considered. It is found in Dan. 10.5-6: 'I looked up and saw a man clothed in linen, with a belt of gold from Uphaz around his waist. His body was like beryl, his face like lightning, his eyes like flaming torches, his arms and legs like the gleam of burnished bronze, and the sound of his words like the roar of a multitude.' This passage calls to mind several features of the appearance of God himself which is described in the opening chapter of the prophet Ezekiel (esp. Ezek. 1.26-27). The torches, the lightning, the beryl and the roar of the multitude all come from that passage. The effect of this language is to associate the angel in Dan. 10.5-6 with the visual appearance of God, as if to make him an exceptional angel who mediates revelation to the seer. Daniel 10.5-6 in turn is a resource for the description of the heavenly Christ in Rev. 1.12-16 in such a way as to indicate that angelic categories are important for John's Christology.

In this book, I have called the Christology of the Apocalypse an 'angelomorphic Christology'. I cited with approval Fletcher-Louis' description of this term:

> We propose the use of the term angelomorphic wherever there are signs that an individual or community possess specifically angelic characteristics or status, though for whom identity cannot be reduced to that of an angel. In this case we understand the word angel to be defined by the constellation of characteristics and motifs which commonly occur across a broad spread of Jewish texts from the second Temple and early rabbinic periods (*Luke–Acts*, pp. 14-15).

This definition allows for a connection between the human and the heavenly world and for a broader understanding of the term 'angel' than is suggested by the romantic conception of a heavenly being with wings and flaming eyes that emerges from the Gospels. An angelomorphic Christology recognizes that Christ has connections with both the human and the heavenly world (however the relation between them is expressed) and that he is not *merely* an angel but transcends the angels through his unique relation to God.

The origins of Christology lies in the experience of Jesus' disciples after the resurrection. All four Gospels (but not Paul) refer to the empty tomb of Jesus. The Gospels (except the original Mark) and Paul also describe visionary experience of Jesus either in connection with or after the discovery of the empty tomb. The appearance of the heavenly Christ to the disciples in this way convinced them that something unprecedented had happened in his death. This 'unprecedented something' was the belief that Jesus had come to share the glory of God and that he was now a divine being entitled to worship. Paul articulates this conviction in 1 Cor. 8.6: 'For us there is one God, the Father, from whom are all things and for whom we exist, and one Lord, Jesus Christ, through whom are all things and through whom we exist.' The earliest source that we have for the worship of Jesus is Phil. 2.10-11: 'At the name of Jesus every knee should bend, in heaven and on earth and under the earth, and every tongue should confess that Jesus Christ is Lord, to the glory of God the Father.'

This Pauline passage helps to explain the Christology of Revelation. Revelation always presents Christ as a divine being. In Rev. 5.13, for instance, we find worship addressed to God *and* the Lamb. We must acknowledge a subordinationist strand in Revelation's Christology. By this, I mean that John does not present the Lamb as God's equal *in every respect*. We saw that in 1.5 Jesus is *not* said to have eternal existence and that he is introduced as 'the firstborn of the dead'. In the description of the heavenly throne-room (chs. 4-5), the Lamb's position in heaven depends on the fact that God occupies the throne. This subordinationism agrees with other New Testament Christology. John 14.28 (roughly contemporary with the Apocalypse) makes Jesus say that the Father is greater than he. In 1 Cor. 15.24, Paul says that Christ will hand over the kingdom to the Father at the eschatological climax. To this Paul adds in 1 Cor. 15.28 that 'then the Son himself will also be subjected to the one who put all things in subjection under him, so that God may be all in all'. Revelation once again follows the wider path in this subordinationism. The technical definition of Christ as 'of the same substance' as the Father (the so-called *homoousion* formula) would not be formally adopted by Christianity until the Council of Nicaea in 325 CE.

Revelation is strongly influenced by an angelomorphic Christology. John's thought is deeply rooted in the Hebrew Bible. He turns naturally to Dan. 10.5-6 to resource his opening vision of Christ in 1.12-16. John echoes this language in 3.18; 19.12; and elsewhere. I have shown that he draws on a wider apocalyptic tradition that stems from Dan. 10.5-6 and reflects the widespread influence of that passage in the early Common Era. The unique feature of John's use of Daniel 10 in Rev. 1.12-16 can be shown by comparing Revelation with the use of the same passage in another apocalypse.

In ch. 11 of the *Apocalypse of Abraham*, the seer witnesses an angelophany similar in many respects to that described in this passage from Revelation:

> And I stood up and saw him who had taken my right hand and set me on my feet. The appearance of his body was like sapphire, and the aspect of his face was like chrysolite, and the hair of his head like snow. And a kidaris [was] on his head, its look like that of a rainbow, and the clothing of his garments [was] purple; and a golden staff [was] in his right hand (*Apoc. Abr.* 11.3).

Here, we find the appearance of another heavenly mediator whose description looks back to Daniel 10 and, through that passage, to Ezekiel 1. The difference from Revelation is that the mediator in the *Apocalypse of Abraham* is merely an angel. No attempt is made to claim divinity for him, still less to offer him worship. Revelation 1.12-16 is by contrast a vision of the heavenly Christ, and thus of a divine being who we know from 3.21 and ch. 5 to be associated with the throne of God, and who in 5.13 receives the worship of the whole creation in company with God himself. This is a significant difference from the Jewish apocalypse. It shows the new theological direction which the Christian movement took from the moment of its very beginning.

The use of angelomorphic categories in Revelation must to this extent be contrasted with the function of angelic and even angelomorphic motifs in the Judaism of the early Common Era. Revelation's Christology allows that Christ transcends the angels through his association with God. It is that early Christianity did not find it inappropriate to use material that derived from angelology to frame its descriptions of Christ in this way. Angelology would continue to be used in Christian circles for this purpose for many decades to come (see Knight, *Disciples of the Beloved One*, pp. 157-66).

Trinitarianism

It is often, and correctly, said that the Apocalypse offers a 'trinitarian' perspective that reflects the emerging Christian belief in three divine beings. Trinitarianism came to be defined in Christian theology as belief in the one God who subsists in three persons, each of whom is 'of the same substance' as the other. This more precise, and much later, formulation of belief is absent from the Apocalypse as it is from the other New

Testament literature. Nor are the three divine beings ever mentioned in Revelation in a formula akin to the baptismal charge of Mt. 28.19 where the Father, the Son and the Holy Spirit are mentioned together without discrimination of precedence between them. The Apocalypse presents a theology in which God and the Lamb are divine beings who receive worship but where the status of the Spirit is much less clearly defined. The author speaks of '*the* Spirit' as the agent of revelation (e.g. 1.10; 2.7; 4.2-3) but also of the '*seven* spirits' who stand before the throne of God (1.4; 3.1; 4.5; 5.6).

One wonders what to make of this ambiguous evidence. Revelation 1.4b-5 knows of a threefold divine source of grace and peace, even if the second member of the formula is said to be 'the seven spirits who are before his throne' (cf. 4.5). It is possible that John's language is deliberately archaic or else that it has been modified to accord with the sequence of 'sevens' which we have seen is an important structural device of the Apocalypse. John does speak elsewhere of *the* Spirit in the singular (e.g. 22.17) and we must presume that, if he had a connection with the Johannine school, he would have had a high understanding of the Spirit imparted to him in the course of his Christian formation.

The Spirit's role in the Apocalypse in many ways resembles that attributed to the Spirit of God by Ezekiel (Ezek. 2.2; 3.12; 11.1). This resemblance may be deliberate. The Spirit is said to be the moving force in Ezekiel's theophany (Ezek. 1.12, 20). We know from Rev. 1.12-16 that John drew on this passage in writing his Apocalypse. It would be natural for him to borrow the idea of the Spirit from there. John, however, never makes the Spirit receive worship. The ambiguity of his pneumatological language indicates the uncertainty that was felt about the Spirit's status at the time of writing. It is sobering to recollect that the question of the Spirit's full equality with the Father and the Son would occupy Christian theologians for centuries to come.

Eschatology

Finally, the eschatology of the Apocalypse. Eschatology undergirded the whole of the early Christian movement. Jesus proclaimed the imminent kingdom of God (Mk 1.15). He evidently anticipated a delay before the kingdom fully arrived, but probably not a substantial one (see Mk 9.1). After his death, the belief that Jesus is Lord (1 Cor. 8.6) led his followers to expect that the kingdom of God would be realized through his return from heaven when the eschatological judgment would take place on earth. The New Testament sources (including Revelation) are unanimous that the Messiah's kingdom is to be an earthly one. This view is found in 1 Corinthians 15 where Paul expects the acquisition of a body from heaven by people on earth to effect their transformation there. There is a further exposition of this idea in 2 Corinthians 5. The mature Paul continued to expect the earthly kingdom of Christ as we can see from

Phil. 3.20-21. This hope was not diminished by his belief that he himself might achieve the resurrection of life through martyrdom (Phil. 1.23), for in his theology resurrection was to precede the kingdom so that the dead would not be deprived of participation in the kingdom.

This hope for the earthly kingdom of Christ continued into the second century, and indeed beyond it. The author of the *Ascension of Isaiah* (c. 120 CE) expects the returning Christ (who is called 'the Beloved One' in this apocalypse) to preside over an earthly kingdom (4.15) before the righteous ascend to heavenly immortality (4.17). Justin Martyr (c. 150 CE) knows of Christians who were contemptuous of the hope for an earthly kingdom, but he himself supports it (*Dial.* 80). Book 5 of Irenaeus's *Adv. Haer.* (c. 185 CE) is specifically devoted to the question of eschatology. This part of Irenaeus's work anticipates a literal resurrection of the flesh and an earthly reign of the Messiah, despite the fact that Irenaeus also subscribes to the theory of recapitulation which posits a destiny for the human person beyond the present life. The hold that this belief in literal resurrection exercised on the church was only broken in the fifth century under the influence of Augustine's *City of God*, although it was challenged on a number of occasions before this.

The book of Revelation thus stands within an established tradition when its author anticipates the future reign of Christ on earth. The expression of this future hope derives from the language of Christian eschatology and not exclusively from the apocalypse genre. The author of Revelation, in company with the Synoptic Eschatological Discourse (Mk 13 and par.) and Paul in 2 Thessalonians 2, anticipates a sequence of problems before Jesus returns to establish his kingdom. The Apocalypse offers the most explicit description of the return of Christ and its effects in the New Testament literature. John states that the return of Christ will result in the final battle (19.11-21), his temporary reign with the saints (20.4), the final judgment (20.11-15) and the recreation of heaven and earth.

The distinctive feature of Revelation's eschatology is the evidence that ch. 20 offers for belief in more than one resurrection. The first resurrection is said to be that of the martyrs ('those who had been beheaded for their testimony to Jesus'); the second, of the rest of the dead (20.4-5). John states that the martyrs will reign on earth with Christ for a thousand years before the second resurrection (20.4). This distinction between the participants gives the idea of the two resurrections its meaning. The point is that, although the false beast and the prophet have been destroyed already (19.20), Satan's tyranny is not yet complete. He will be destroyed only after further conflict (20.7-10). In the logic of Revelation's symbolism (particularly ch. 7), we should assume that the martyrs of 20.4 are symbolic of the whole Christian body and not just part of it. The idea of the two resurrections comments on the power of Satan's tyranny but also on the inevitability of punishment for those who subscribe to it.

There is interesting rabbinic evidence for the concept of the 'second death' in *Targ. Isa.* 65.5-6 where the Targumist equates the 'second death' with Gehenna. As in Revelation, the thought is that it symbolizes the final punitive obliteration, after the resurrection, and is thus distinguished from the process of human death. John alone of the New Testament writers uses this concept. The Targumist provides Jewish corroboration for what he says.

It is important to recognize that the earthly reign of the saints (20.4) is an intermediate stage in John's eschatology and not its final goal. The final goal is the recreation of heaven and earth which is described in 21.1. The earthly reign of the saints, paralleled by the imprisonment and unleashing of Satan, is a variation on the theme of opposition to the righteous which features in other New Testament eschatology. The affinities of Revelation 21 with other New Testament eschatology should briefly be noted. The Gospels anticipate that the Son of Man's return from heaven will inaugurate a process of judgment. This is described in the parables, as for instance in the parable of the sheep and the goats (Mt. 25.31-46). Matthew 19.28 comments intriguingly on the aftermath of this event, '*At the renewal of all things*, when the Son of Man is seated on the throne of his glory, you who have followed me will also sit on twelve thrones, judging the twelve tribes of Israel' (italics added). On this view, the future will disclose a complete reordering of present reality in which a transformed Israel will emerge to be governed by the Messiah and his 12 disciples. Romans 8 contains important evidence too: 'The creation waits with eager longing for the revealing of the children of God...Creation itself will be set free from its bondage to decay and will obtain the freedom of the glory of the children of God (Rom. 8.19-21).

This material shows that Revelation 21–22 finds a place within the context of New Testament eschatology and cannot be considered an eccentricity when compared with that material. John's hope for a new creation matches the Gospels and Paul. To be sure, his symbolism is distinctive. John's vision of the new order finds no place for the sea (21.1). His description of the new Jerusalem in the second half of ch. 21 is highly symbolic. We should, however, look through the veneer of this symbolism to the realism of the hope that lies behind it. John's Apocalypse reminds readers of the impending new order to recall them to a particular pattern of life. This link between eschatology and ethics is an indelible feature of the Apocalypse.

Bibliography

Aune, D.E., *Prophecy in Early Christianity and the Ancient Mediterranean World* (Grand Rapids: Eerdmans, 1983).

Bauckham, R.J., *Jude and the Relatives of Jesus in the Early Church* (Edinburgh: T. & T. Clark, 1990).

—*The Climax of Prophecy: Studies on the Book of Revelation* (Edinburgh: T. & T. Clark, 1993).

—*The Theology of the Book of Revelation* (NTT; Cambridge: Cambridge University Press, 1993).

Bauer, W., *Orthodoxy and Heresy in Earliest Christianity* (ET; London: SCM Press, 1972).

Berger, P., *The Sacred Canopy* (Garden City, NY: Anchor Press, 1969).

—*A Rumor of Angels* (Garden City, NY: Anchor Press, 1970).

Booth, W., *The Rhetoric of Fiction* (Chicago: University of Chicago Press, 2nd edn, 1982).

Bruce, F.F., 'Revelation', in G.C.D. Howley (ed.), F.F. Bruce and H.L. Ellison (consulting eds.), *A New Testament Commentary: Based on the Revised Standard Version* (London: Pickering & Inglis, 1969), pp. 629-66.

Charles, R.H., *The Ascension of Isaiah* (London: A. & C. Black, 1900).

—*A Critical and Exegetical Commentary on the Revelation of St. John* (2 vols.; Edinburgh: T. & T. Clark, 1920).

Charlesworth, J.H., *The Old Testament Pseudepigrapha* (2 vols.; London: Darton, Longman & Todd, 1983-85).

Collins, A.Y., *Crisis and Catharsis: The Power of the Apocalypse* (Philadelphia: Westminster Press, 1984).

Collins, J.J. (ed.), 'Apocalypse: Morphology of a Genre', *Semeia* 14 (1979).

Collins, J.J., and J.H. Charlesworth (eds.), *Mysteries and Revelations: Apocalyptic Studies since the Uppsala Colloquium* (JSPSup, 9; Sheffield: Sheffield Academic Press, 1991).

Farrer, A.M., *A Rebirth of Images* (Westminster: Dacre Press, 1949).

Fletcher-Louis, C.H.T., *Luke-Acts: Angels, Christology and Soteriology* (WUNT, 94; Tübingen: Mohr Siebeck, 1997).

Garrow, A.J.P., *Revelation* (London: Routledge, 1997).

Hengel, M., *The Johannine Question* (London: SCM Press, 1989).

Hennecke, E., and W. Schneemelcher (eds.), *The New Testament Apocrypha* (ET; 2 vols.; London: SCM Press, 1963-64).

Hill, D., *New Testament Prophecy* (London: Marshall, Morgan & Scott, 1979).

Himmelfarb, M., *Tours of Hell: An Apocalyptic Form in Jewish and Christian Literature* (Philadelphia: Fortress Press, 1983).

Iser, W., *The Implied Reader* (Baltimore: The Johns Hopkins University Press, 1974).

Jacobson, H., *The Exagoge of Ezekiel* (Cambridge: Cambridge University Press, 1983).

Knight, J.M., *The Ascension of Isaiah* (GAP, 2; Sheffield: Sheffield Academic Press, 1995).

—*Disciples of the Beloved One: Studies in the Christology, Social Setting and Theological Context of the Ascension of Isaiah* (JSPSup, 18; Sheffield: Sheffield Academic Press, 1996).

Kümmel, W.G. *Introduction to the New Testament* (ET; London: SCM Press, rev. edn, 1973).

Longenecker, R.N., *The Christology of Early Jewish Christianity* (SBT, 17; London: SCM Press, 1970).

Mounce, R.J., *The Book of Revelation* (NICNT; Grand Rapids: Eerdmans, rev. edn, 1998).

Otto, R., *The Idea of the Holy: An Inquiry into the Non-Rational Factor in the Idea of the Divine and its Relation to the Rational* (ET; repr.; Oxford: Oxford University Press, 1981).

Pesce, M., 'Presupposti per l'utilazzione storica dell'Ascensione di Isaia: Formazione e tradizione del testo; genere letterario; cosmologia angelica', in M. Pesce (ed.), *Isaia, il Diletto e la Chiesa* (Brescia: Paideia, 1983), pp. 13-76.

Ramsay, W.M., *The Letters to the Seven Churches* (ed. Mark W. Wilson; Peabody, MA: Hendrickson, updated edn, 1994).

Robinson, J.A.T. *Redating the New Testament* (London: SPCK, 1976).

Rowland, C.C., 'The Vision of the Risen Christ in Rev. i,13ff.: The Debt of an Early Christology to an Aspect of Jewish Angelology', *JTS* 31 (1980), pp. 1-11.

—*The Open Heaven* (London: SPCK, 1982).

—*Revelation* (London: Epworth Press, 1993).

Russell, D.S., *The Method and Message of Jewish Apocalyptic* (London: SCM Press, 1964).

Scott, K., *The Imperial Cult under the Flavians* (repr.; New York: Arno Press, 1975).

Schüssler Fiorenza, E., *The Book of Revelation: Justice and Judgment* (Philadelphia: Fortress Press, 1985).

Stone, M.E., 'Lists of Revealed Things in the Apocalyptic Literature', in F.M. Cross, W.E. Lemke and P.D. Miller (eds.), *Magnalia Dei: The Mighty Acts of God* (Garden City, NY; Doubleday, 1976), pp. 414-52.

—'The Question of the Messiah in 4 Ezra', in J. Neusner *et al.* (eds.), *Judaisms and their Messiahs* (Cambridge: Cambridge University Press, 1987), pp. 209-25.

Stuckenbruck, L.L., *Angel Veneration and Christology: A Study in Early Judaism and in the Christology of the Apocalypse of John* (WUNT, 70; Tübingen: Mohr Siebeck, 1995).

Sweet, J.P.M., *Revelation* (Trinity Press International New Testament Commentaries; London: SCM Press; Philadelphia: Trinity Press International, 1990).

Swete, H.B., *The Apocalypse of St. John: The Greek Text with Introduction, Notes and Indices* (London: Macmillan, 1906).

Theissen, G., *The Social Setting of Pauline Christianity: Essays on Corinth* (ET; Edinburgh: T. & T. Clark, 1982).

Thompson, L.L., *The Book of Revelation: Apocalypse and Empire* (Oxford: Oxford University Press, 1990).

Vermes, G., *The Complete Dead Sea Scrolls in English* (London: Allen Lane, The Penguin Press, 1997).

Index of References

NEW TESTAMENT

Index of Authors